PRINCIPLES OF PRICING

Pricing drives three of the most important elements of firm success: revenue and profits, customer behavior, and firm image. This book provides an introduction to the basic principles for thinking clearly about pricing. Unlike other marketing books on pricing, the authors use a more analytic approach and relate ideas to the basic principles of microeconomics. Rakesh V. Vohra and Lakshman Krishnamurthi also cover three areas in greater depth and provide more insight than may be gleaned from existing books: 1) the use of auctions, 2) price discrimination, and 3) pricing in a competitive environment.

Rakesh V. Vohra is the John L. and Helen Kellogg Professor of Managerial Economics and Decision Sciences at the Kellogg School of Management, Northwestern University, where he is also Director of the Center for Mathematical Studies in Economics and Management Science. He previously taught at the Fisher School of Business, Ohio State University; MIT's Sloan School of Management; and the Wharton School, University of Pennsylvannia, and is the author of *Advanced Mathematical Economics* (2005) and *Mechanism Design: A Linear Programming Approach* (Econometric Society Monographs, Cambridge University Press, 2011). Professor Vohra received his doctorate in mathematics from the University of Maryland.

Lakshman Krishnamurthi is the Montgomery Ward Distinguished Professor of Marketing at the Kellogg School of Management, Northwestern University, where he has taught since 1980. He chaired the marketing department from 1993 to 2004 and has served as Academic Director of the Pricing Strategies and Tactics program since 1995. Professor Krishnamurthi is the recipient of the Paul Green and Donald Lehmann awards from the *Journal of Marketing Research*, the John D. C. Little award from *Marketing Science*, and numerous teaching awards at Kellogg. He earned his doctorate in marketing from Stanford University.

Principles of Pricing

An Analytical Approach

RAKESH V. VOHRA

Northwestern University

LAKSHMAN KRISHNAMURTHI

Northwestern University

CAMBRIDGE
UNIVERSITY PRESS

32 Avenue of the Americas, New York NY 10013-2473, USA

Cambridge University Press is part of the University of Cambridge.

It furthers the University's mission by disseminating knowledge in the pursuit of education, learning, and research at the highest international levels of excellence.

www.cambridge.org
Information on this title: www.cambridge.org/9781107010659

First published 2012
Reprinted with corrections 2013
Reprinted 2013

A catalog record for this publication is available from the British Library.

Library of Congress Cataloging in Publication data
Vohra, Rakesh V.
Principles of pricing : an analytical approach / Rakesh V. Vohra, Lakshman Krishnamurthi.
    p. cm. Includes bibliographical references and index.
ISBN 978-1-107-01065-9
1. Pricing. I. Krishnamurthi, Lakshman. II. Title.
HF5416.5.V64   2011
658.8′16–dc23   2011031550

ISBN 978-1-107-01065-9 Hardback

To Sangeeta, Sonya, and Akhil
Rakesh V. Vohra

To my father, who valued his son very highly
Lakshman Krishnamurthi

Contents

ONE

Introduction

Many businesses focus on driving volume or reducing costs, rather than increasing price, under the mistaken belief that they have greater control over volume and costs than price. Yet, a 1 percent increase in price (holding volume fixed) has a greater impact on operating profit than a 1 percent increase in volume or a 1 percent decrease in cost. By not seizing the initiative on price, businesses abrogate decisions about price to competitors, customers, and the channel. A careful analysis and understanding of those same actors could help them price in a more profitable manner – hence, this book, which is designed to communicate the fundamental principles of pricing.

There is a science to pricing rooted in economic theory. Under a set of assumptions about consumer and market behavior, we can derive prescriptive pricing rules. These rules provide guidelines and help in understanding how prices will and should change when the underlying environment changes. As nothing straight ever came from the crooked timber of humanity, there is also an art to pricing as well.[1] How products and services are positioned and communicated to consumers can affect their price perception. Even objectively identical products are able to command different prices.

The first step in formulating a pricing strategy is to understand the behavior of buyers. We start with the assumption that buyers are rational, suggesting that mad dogs and Englishmen are not the only ones who go out into the noonday sun. The assumption attracts criticism and deserves

---

[1] Macaulay's advice on the relationship between theory and practice applies: "he who has actually to build must bear in mind many things never noticed by D'Alembert and Euclid."

discussion. First, what precisely does it mean to be *rational*?[2] Second, why is it reasonable to assume that buyers are rational?

There are two aspects to the definition of rationality. First, buyers are *consistent* in their likes and dislikes *all the time*. For example, if on a given day one likes oranges, then one should, other things equal, consider five oranges to be at least as preferred as four oranges.[3] In other words, more of a good thing is better than, and certainly no worse than, less. If one prefers apples to oranges and oranges to cherries then, other things being equal, one should prefer apples to cherries. These kinds of restrictions do not eliminate the possibility that on hot days one prefers ice-cold beer to hot chocolate, and the reverse on cold days.[4] Note the qualifier, *other things equal*. Under identical conditions, separated in time, one's likes and dislikes are the same. The second aspect requires that when asked to choose from a set of things, outcomes or possibilities, one will chose that which one likes the most. Pride, shame, and guilt play no role in the definition of rationality.

Does this provide an accurate description of how buyers behave?[5] Not always, but it does not mean that the assumption is without merit. Buyers may not be rational all the time, but they are not (unless they are lunatics) irrational all the time either.[6] Further, even if buyers occasionally depart from rational behavior, these departures can take many different forms. The view we take here is that the rationality assumption is a useful and powerful starting point to understanding pricing strategy. The art of pricing enters when one leavens the conclusions based on rationality with both experience and an understanding of how the context of the purchase decision affects the buyer. These issues are discussed in greater detail in Chapter 2.

---

[2] The reader who thinks that rationality does not require a definition should ponder the following: I'll give you a million dollars to do something irrational.

[3] We assume that one can, at no cost, dispose of oranges if one chooses.

[4] Except in England, where warm beer is preferred in all weather.

[5] Amartya Sen offers this parable on life in a world of rational people: "Where is the railway station?," he asks me. "There," I say, pointing at the post office, "and would you please post this letter for me on the way?" "Yes," says he, determined to open the envelope and check whether it contains something valuable.

[6] It brings to mind an anecdote related by the economist Vilfredo Pareto about Gustav Schmoller. At a conference, Pareto presented a paper, only to be to interrupted repeatedly by Schmoller with the assertion, "There are no laws in economics!" The following day, Pareto spied Schmoller in the streets. Hiding his face and pretending to be a beggar (which Pareto could do, as he dressed badly), Pareto approached Schmoller. "Please, sir," Pareto inquired, "can you tell me where I can find a restaurant where you can eat for nothing?" According to Pareto, Schmoller replied, "My dear man, there are no such restaurants, but there is a place around the corner where you can have a good meal very cheaply." "Ah! So there *are* laws in economics!" replied Pareto.

Pricing is difficult because of uncertainty about how much the buyer will part with. It becomes important, then, to be able to estimate just how much a buyer will pay. In Chapter 3 we provide an overview of methods for doing just that and discuss the pros and cons of each.

In choosing a price, one must understand how one's buyers, as well as one's competitors, will react to it. To understand their reactions, it is useful to disentangle one from the other. For this reason we focus in Chapter 4 on how a monopolist should set prices. The monopoly case allows us to ignore the presence of competition and focus on how one's buyers react to one's price. In addition, the monopoly price sets an upper bound on the price one can charge, absent collusion. Would it not be helpful to know the best one can do?

The monopoly environment also allows one to compare and contrast the three ways in which prices are set:

1. **Haggling/negotiation**
   The oldest form of price setting and still going strong, even on the Internet.
2. **Posted price**
   The seller announces a price and waits for buyers willing to transact at that price. This is really a particular haggling strategy in which the seller makes a "take it or leave it" offer.
3. **Auctions**
   The seller has buyers compete among themselves to determine the price at which a transaction will be executed. Like a posted price, this should be viewed as a particular haggling strategy.

We discuss the pros and cons of these three methods for price setting in Chapter 5. An example of the kind of question we ask (and answer) is this: Which of the three price setting methods generates the highest revenue/profit?

A single price is never optimal as long as there is heterogeneity in valuations among consumers. How should one customize the price of the same product or service to different segments (otherwise known as price discrimination, but that sounds so pejorative)? Here, we address three issues of importance. The first is that such customization can lead to gray markets, in which customers who buy at the low price resell to customers facing the higher price. The second is that an offering to one segment may cannibalize sales to another segment. Third, government regulation may limit the kinds of customization in which one can engage. Price customization is discussed in Chapter 6.

Finally, pricing in the presence of competition is discussed in Chapter 7. Here one can have one of two strategic goals: accommodation or elimination. We cannot say which of these goals is best; that is an exercise in judgment that requires an intimate knowledge of the environment. However, we can say which pricing strategy is appropriate for each goal. There is one unmistakable message, however, about competition: competition depresses prices, which benefits only the buyer.

Now, a warning. This book is not for the faint-hearted. It presumes a familiarity with what is typically covered in the quantitative core of a major MBA program. It requires the willingness to pursue logical arguments, some mathematical, to their conclusion. The reward for the effort is a clear understanding of the factors to consider in setting price, the conditions under which different pricing methods are optimal, and how to set prices under competition.

1.1 Genesis

This book grew from lecture notes the first author uses in an elective course in Pricing taught at the Kellogg School of Management. Portions of it have also been employed in the Managerial Economics course taught in Kellogg's Executive MBA Program.[7] This is complemented by the experiences of the second author, who runs the Kellogg executive program on Pricing Strategies and Tactics. The many years of teaching and interacting with industry participants in that program, as well as consulting for companies, provided a good understanding of issues and concerns that needed to be addressed.

In marked contrast to other books on pricing, this one is based on economic theory. This is not to deny the value to be had from looking at pricing through other lenses. It is simply that these other lenses do not yet provide a systematic and organized way to think about pricing. Economic theory does. Its power is not in the provision of to-do lists or the Gradgrind-like accumulation of facts.[8] Rather, it is in generating the right questions to be asked. Both our own experiences and those related to us by our students who have taken our classes has confirmed this view.

---

[7] A third audience are undergraduates in Kellogg's certificate program. For this select group, greater emphasis is placed on the underlying mathematics.

[8] Thomas Gradgrind, a character in Dickens's *Hard Times*, describes himself thus: "Now, what I want is, Facts. Teach these boys and girls nothing but Facts. Facts alone are wanted in life. Plant nothing else, and root out everything else. You can only form the minds of reasoning animals upon Facts: nothing else will ever be of any service to them."

A second point of contrast with other treatments of pricing is that we convey principles through stylized examples, rather than anecdotes. The simplicity of stylized examples allows one to see clearly which forces drive a particular outcome. It also makes errors in thinking harder to conceal. Complexity is introduced through the relaxation of the assumptions in the stylized examples or through the juxtaposition with reality. This approach has worked well, in our experience, with MBA students and executives.

Supplemented with suitable cases and problems, this book can be used in a quarter or semester long course on pricing strategy. A list of such cases and problems can be obtained from the authors.

1.2 Acknowledgments

As always in these matters, one's debts are many, and one forgets more of them than one should. While we remember, our thanks to Michael Sara who was enormously helpful in preparing this manuscript (diagrams, indexing, and typesetting). A nod to our many students who provided the impetus for this book with their questions. A bow to our immediate colleagues, as well as members of the wider company of scholars whose teachings allowed us to answer those questions. The suggestions and comments of the anonymous reviewers were very helpful in improving the book and avoiding confusion. Finally, thanks to the Kellogg School of Management. Without its commitment to the idea that "theory" matters, this book would not have been possible.

TWO

Buyer Behavior

To begin, we consider the simplest nontrivial pricing problem.

2.1 The Ultimatum

The world contains just two people: a buyer and a seller. The seller has a book that she values at zero that she wishes to sell to the buyer. It is the only book of its kind in the world and the buyer is fully aware of its contents and condition. The buyer values the book at $10, neither more nor less. Each is aware of how the other values the book. The seller has one chance to set a price. Once the price is fixed, the buyer has one chance to buy at the price posted or to decline. No other inducements, counteroffers, or promises are permitted. What price should the seller set to maximize her revenue?

The usual mysteries that cloud a pricing situation have been stripped away. There is no uncertainty about the nature or quality of the product. The value of the product to the buyer is known, as is the seller's opportunity cost. There are only one seller and one buyer. The dance between seller and buyer is limited to a single take-it-or-leave-it offer.

It is clear that the chosen price should not exceed $10, the value of the book to the buyer. Thus, the only question is just how close to $10 the seller can set the price and have the buyer accept. If one believes, as seems reasonable, that more money is better than less, any price below $10 will be accepted by the buyer, as it leaves the buyer with positive profit from the transaction. The largest amount the seller can charge (given that the smallest unit of currency is a penny) and still leave the buyer with a positive profit is $9.99.

It is possible that the buyer may view the $9.99 price as an outrageous instance of gouging. Refusing the book at that price means that the buyer is out a penny, but it is a small price to pay to make a point. If one believes fairness of the transaction, as measured by relative profits, is salient, a price lower than $9.99 is merited. One might argue that $5 is the only fair price.

Therefore, the price one chooses depends on how one believes a buyer will respond to that price. Hence, any discussion of pricing must begin with a model of how buyers respond to prices. In this book we adopt one particular model, called the **rational buyer** model. In the next section we describe it, warts and all.

2.2 Rational Buyer Model

The rational buyer model rests on three assumptions.

1. **Assumption 1**

   A buyer is able to assign a monetary value to each transaction and product, and that value is fixed and immutable. This value is called the buyer's **reservation price** (RP). It is the maximum price a buyer is prepared to pay for an additional unit of the product (or service). Determining a buyer's RP, though difficult, is not impossible; we discuss how this can be done in the next chapter.

2. **Assumption 2**

   A buyer evaluates a transaction in terms of its **consumer surplus**. Suppose a buyer's RP for one pound of sugar is $5 and we sell it to her for $3. If she buys the sugar from us, she will enjoy a consumer surplus of $5 − $3 = $2. In general, a buyer's consumer surplus is the difference between the RP and the price the buyer pays.[1] A buyer will never purchase a product that yields negative consumer surplus.

3. **Assumption 3**

   In choosing between transactions, the buyer will choose the transaction that maximizes consumer surplus.

   For example, suppose our buyer has a choice between a pound of sugar and a pound of salt. To make life simple, assume that she will buy one or the other, but not both. Let her RP for sugar be $5 and her RP for salt be $4. Sugar is sold at $3 a pound, whereas salt is sold at $3.50 a pound. Which will she acquire? We assume that she will choose the option that *maximizes consumer surplus*. In this case, the consumer surplus on sugar is $2, whereas on salt it is $0.50. Therefore, she will buy the sugar.

---

[1] Price is taken to mean the *full* price including switching costs, shipping costs, and so on.

Table 2.1. *A Choice*

	Option *A*	Option *B*
RP	$11	$15
Price	$6	$9
Surplus	$5	$6

To drive the point home, imagine a buyer who must choose between two options. The relevant information for each option is displayed in Table 2.1.

Observe that our hypothetical buyer has a higher RP for option *B* than for option *A*. This means that our buyer derives more value from option *B* than option *A*.

If our hypothetical buyer can choose, at most, one of option *A* or option *B*, she will choose option *B* because it has the larger surplus. Notice that she chooses the option with the higher price. This should not come as a surprise. A buyer is prepared to pay more if he or she gets more.

Consider now the seller of option *A*. How should he change his price to attract our hypothetical buyer? Clearly, he should lower it. How low? Until option *A* delivers at least as much surplus as option *B*.[2] Suppose, for illustration, that the seller of option *A* drops the price to $4.50. Consider Table 2.2.

Option *A* now delivers more surplus than option *B*. Our hypothetical buyer will choose option *A* in this case. Notice that she now chooses the option she considers inferior. Why? If it is priced low enough, it is good enough.[3]

The examples summarized in Tables 2.1 and 2.2 capture the idea that buyers make trade-offs. If one is not prepared to accept this, then one will learn little from this book.

Frequently, a buyer will purchase through an agent. Large companies, for example, employ purchasing agents.[4] In selling to agents, one should keep in mind that the agents' interests need not coincide with those of their lord

---

[2] The reader may wonder what happens in the event that option *A* and option *B* deliver exactly the same surplus. We consider this to be a knife-edge case that is not particularly relevant. After all, by changing one of the prices by a penny, we can break the tie. In this book we adopt the convention of resolving the tie in the way most convenient to make the necessary point.

[3] One can imagine extreme cases in which no matter what the price of option *A*, the buyer will never choose it. This can be accounted for in the rational buyer model. It corresponds to the case in which the buyer's RP for option *A* is $0.

[4] In some cases the seller must sell through a hierarchy of agents with varying degrees of authority and incentives.

Table 2.2. *A Choice Redux*

	Option *A*	Option *B*
RP	$11	$15
Price	$4.50	$9
Surplus	$6.50	$6

and master.[5] In the following text we assume that if a buyer works through an agent (who is entitled to make the purchase decision), then the relevant RP is not the buyer's, but the agent's.

2.3 Warts

We highlight some departures from the rational buyer model with a series of thought experiments from Thaler (1985).

1. You are lying on the beach on a hot day. All you have to drink is ice water. For the past hour, you have been thinking about how much you would enjoy a nice cold bottle of your favorite beer. A friend gets up to make a phone call and offers to bring back a bottle of your favorite beer from the only nearby place where beer is sold – a small, run-down grocery store. He says that the beer might be expensive and asks how much you are willing to spend. He says that he will not buy the beer if it costs more than the price you state. What price do you tell your friend?

2. You are lying on the beach on a hot day. All you have to drink is ice water. For the past hour, you have been thinking about how much you would enjoy a nice cold bottle of your favorite beer. A friend gets up to make a phone call and offers to bring back a bottle of your favorite beer from the only nearby place where beer is sold – a fancy resort hotel. He says that the beer might be expensive and asks how much you are willing to spend. He says that he will not buy the beer if it costs more than the price you state. What price do you tell your friend?

Of interest are those who respond with different prices. This is puzzling because the product being consumed is identical in both circumstances:

---

[5] In some industrial settings, for example, an equipment purchase locks the buyer into the purchase of spare parts and services. Suppose the buyer's agent is evaluated on initial expenditures. The shrewd seller will price the original equipment low and the spare parts high.

a bottle of beer on the beach. One cannot justify the difference in terms of the experience. The experience of drinking one's favorite cold beverage on the beach is worth something. Why should what it is worth depend on where the beverage is bought? When pressed, respondents who offer different prices typically explain the difference in terms of their expectations. They expect to pay more at the fancy resort hotel. But this begs the question. Why should *expecting* to pay more affect one's *willingness* to pay more?

Respondents who answer the preceding two questions differently violate the first of the three assumptions of the rational buyer model. Their RPs are not fixed. In fact, their RPs can be influenced by how the transaction is positioned and advertised.

1. You set off to buy a Cross ballpoint pen at what you believe to be the cheapest store in the area. On arriving, you find that the Cross pen you want costs $69, a price consistent with your prior expectations. As you are about to make the purchase, a reliable friend tells you that the very same Cross pen is selling for $10 less at a store approximately 10 minutes away. Do you go to the other store to buy the Cross pen?
2. You set off to buy a Sony camcorder at what you believe to be the cheapest store in the area. On arriving, you find that the camcorder you want costs $495, a price consistent with your prior expectations. As you are about to make the purchase, a reliable friend tells you that the very same camcorder is selling for $10 less at a store approximately 10 minutes away. Do you go to the other store to buy the camcorder?

Respondents willing to walk in one scenario and not the other violate the second assumption of the rational buyer model. If a buyer receives a surplus in the first case from walking, he or she would enjoy the same surplus from walking in the second scenario. When pressed, these respondents explain the discrepancy by pointing to the percentage savings to be had from walking. Thus, they do not evaluate the transaction on the basis of the absolute savings, but on the percentage savings. This particular violation of the model benefits the seller, as the seller can extract more from the buyer by playing on the percentages. Large-ticket items are particularly ripe for manipulation. Buy a car and then spend more for the factory-installed navigation system – it is only a negligible fraction of the price of the car.

The third assumption is violated because no buyer can possibly be aware of *every* option and its price. Thus, even if buyers sincerely desired the option that maximized consumer surplus, they would have to settle for the one that did so among the *limited* set of options of which they were aware. Nor can buyers recall exactly the price of all competing alternatives. Instead, they rely on an impression or expectation of what seems a reasonable price. This is called a **reference price**.[6]

2.4 Defense of the Rational Buyer Model

Economics starts with the assumption that humans are rational. A defense is easy. What is the alternative – Irrationality? It explains everything – and so, nothing. Humans may not be rational all the time, but they are not irrational all the time either. Further, even if humans occasionally depart from rational behavior, these departures can take many different forms. What determines when they depart from, and revert to, rational behavior? The answers to these questions would be very person-specific. The end result would be a theory of pricing that would depend intimately on the personalities of those involved. The rationality assumption allows one to develop a theory independent of the specific identities of buyers and sellers. Whether you should follow the predictions/prescriptions of such a theory in a particular situation will hinge on whether you think your intimate knowledge of the personalities of the players matters.

2.5 Price Setting

Price is the outcome of a negotiation between buyers and sellers. This is obviously true in the sale of a secondhand car or custom industrial equipment, but apparently not in the purchase of toothpaste. Do not be misled. Even though the purchase of toothpaste does not entail the haggling associated with the bazaar, it is the case that the seller is negotiating. The seller has adopted a particular negotiating strategy: a take-it-or-leave-it offer.

There are two aspects to every negotiation: the first is how to size the pie and the second is how the pie is to be divided between the parties. The size of the pie is determined by the seller's product or opportunity cost and the buyer's RP. If the buyer's RP is smaller than the product cost, no sale will occur. If the buyer's RP exceeds the product cost, a sale might occur

---

[6] If unawareness of other options is the result of the trade-off between search costs and potential benefits, then this is sensible and can be included in the model by adding search costs to the price. Sometimes, though, buyers are unaware of other options not because of search costs, but because of lack of imagination or faulty memories.

at a price that will fall between the product cost and the buyer's value. For instance, if we let $11 be the buyer's RP and $1 be the product cost, the pie that buyer and seller are haggling over is worth $11 − $1 = $10. Each clearly wants as large a share as possible. The division of the pie, or how large a share each obtains, depends on their **best alternative to a negotiated agreement** (negotiation aficionados call this BATNA). If, for example, the buyer can get the same product for $5 elsewhere, the buyer can guarantee a surplus of $11 − $5 = $6. It is clear the seller must offer at least that much in surplus. This shrinks the pie to $10 − $6 = $4. If our story ended here, the only unresolved issue would be how that $4 is to be divided between seller and buyer.

Establishing a BATNA itself may require a negotiation with someone else. Having established one, the next step is to credibly convey this information to the person with whom one is negotiating. An auction is an example of a negotiation strategy designed to do these two things simultaneously. The seller is negotiating with many buyers at the same time. The current highest bid represents the seller's BATNA in selling to those who have yet to raise the bidding.

Suppose now that the seller throws in a service contract with the product that has the following features: it costs the seller $1 to execute the service contract and the buyer's RP for the product–service bundle is $15. Furthermore, no other seller is offering to bundle services with the product in this way. Now, when it comes to haggling, the pie is of size $15 − $2 = $13. Because the buyer can buy the product alone for $5 elsewhere, the buyer is guaranteed a surplus of $11 − $5 = $6. This shrinks the pie to $13 − $6 = $7. Notice that the pie is now larger than before. How does this help the seller? A small share of a large pie may be more valuable than a large share of a small pie.

A study of all negotiating strategies for setting a price is beyond the scope of this book. Instead, we focus on what appear to be the three most popular strategies: posted price, auctions, and haggling.

A **posted price** is an instance of a take-it-or-leave-it offer. Variations of it, in which the posted price is contingent on outside circumstances such as the time of purchase are popular (frequently called **dynamic pricing**). With the advent of the Internet, **auctions** have become a popular price-setting strategy. This is a formalization of the often-used negotiating ploy: "I can get a better deal with Joe." A posted price and an auction limit the kinds of counteroffers a buyer can make. A posted price entertains no counteroffer. In an auction, a buyer can only respond with a better offer. **Haggling**, the oldest pricing strategy, allows the buyer and seller the opportunity to consider a richer set of offers and counteroffers. Sellers thinking about how to price something must think about which of these pricing methods to use. Having chosen, they must then decide, for example, the price to post, the auction design, or the kinds of offers and counteroffers to entertain. In this book, we examine the pros and cons of these three pricing schemes, but more emphasis will be devoted to the first two.

Two aspects of pricing are important, but we have very little to say about them. We mention these here so that you may keep them in mind.

The first is that a firm's price sometimes conveys a signal about the firm's quality or the nature of the product it is selling. Franco Bosisio, former head of the Swatch design labs, makes the point thus (see Taylor (1993)):

Price has become a mirror for the other attributes we try to communicate.... A Swatch is not just affordable, it's approachable. Buying a Swatch is an easy decision to live with. It's provocative, but it does not make you think too much.

Second, we assume that the seller is interested in a price that maximizes profit. Here we mean real or economic profit, and not accounting profit. In assuming profit maximization, we ignore the possibility that the price will be viewed as unfair by customers who then balk at buying. The fate of Robert Keayne, a seventeenth-century New England merchant, is instructive in this regard.[7] Keayne, the son of an English butcher, migrated to the New World in 1635. In New England he prospered as a merchant tailor, importer of manufactured goods, and leader in local affairs. In 1639 he was castigated by church and state for extracting too great a profit from the sale of a bag of nails, great gold buttons, a bridle, and a skein of thread. Narrowly escaping excommunication by the Puritan church, he was admonished

for selling his wares at excessive Rates, to the Dishonor of Gods name, the Offence of the Generall Cort, and the Publique scandall of the Cuntry.

Like Galileo, he was required to confess his sin to regain full membership in the Puritan church.[8]

2.6 Key Points

1. The reservation price (RP) for an offering is the maximum the individual is willing to pay for that offering.
2. The surplus of a transaction is the difference between the reservation price and the price charged for that transaction.

---

[7] See Bailyn (1955).
[8] "*E pur, si muove!*"

3. In choosing among the transactions before them, rational buyers choose the one that yields the largest surplus.

4. The reservation price may change depending on the context. Context effects include the purchase environment, the time of purchase, the dollar value of the purchase, the items being compared, and so forth.

THREE

Estimating Price Response

If one takes the rational buyer model seriously, the most important challenge for the seller is determining how a buyer will respond to a price. For this reason, we begin this chapter with a laundry list of methods for estimating how buyers will respond to price.

1. *Managerial judgment.* A simple way is to use the accumulated knowledge of product managers, salespeople, and members of the product engineering team to arrive at a demand curve for the product or service. Subjects are given a product book that provides information on items such as product sales and product price, as well as competitive sales and competitive prices. After digesting this information, the subjects are asked how much, in percentage terms, sales are likely to change for an X percent price increase where X is incremented in some fashion, say 2 percent, 4 percent, and so on, up to 10 percent, followed by the same questions for an X percent price decrease. Subjects should be asked to think about competitive response during the exercise, so the obtained demand curve reflects a realistic state of the world. For each price response, the subjects should identify a source-of-volume model, which is a way to describe how the composition of buyers (those who buy from this seller, those who buy from the competition, and those who currently buy from no one) changes as a function of a price change. For example, for a 10 percent price cut, subjects should identify how much of the sales increase is going to come from increased purchases by existing customers, how much by switching competitive customers, and how much from new customers. In the same way, for a particular price increase, subjects describe how much the seller is going to lose, and to whom. It is helpful to obtain responses from a number of individuals who are knowledgeable about the product in question and the market in which it competes. It is also useful for the individuals to provide a brief justification of their assessments.

Next, the information obtained from the different individuals is combined. In the first step, each individual provides his or her own data. In the second step, the individual data, as well as the justification, are provided to all the participating individuals without identifying any of them. Each individual is then asked whether he or she would change his or her assessment. The updated information is fed back again to the individuals. The goal of this cycling is to combine the received wisdom of the individuals. What one gets in the end is a demand curve along with lower and upper sales bounds for each price change. Essentially, this procedure yields management's best judgment of how its customers are likely to respond to price changes. This method is a variant of the Delphi technique.[1]

If the company has multiple products, it is instructive to compare the price response estimates across products. One can build a model that relates the characteristics of the different products to the varying price response estimates. For example, one would expect that sensitivity to price increases is higher in more competitive markets, when many substitutes are available, when relative marketing spending is low, and when the expenditure outlay by the customer is large.

When will this procedure work well, and when will it not? Even those close to the product are not conditioned to think of price response in this manner, so this method of eliciting response may be alien to some of them. The response is likely to reflect actual product behavior reasonably well in the case of well-established products, for which the respondents have observed sales changes as a result of price changes, and less well for newer products.

2. *Analogous products.* To understand the evolution of an nth-generation product, it is instructive to look at previous generations of the product. This works best for incremental innovations and when the competitive set does not change. The price of a previous generation serves as the benchmark for the new generation. Examples would be successive generations of the Intel Core-Duo processors, Canon PowerShot digital cameras, and newer generations of metalworking machines. The reference price is the price of the previous generation, and an estimate of the differential value is needed to obtain the reservation price.

---

[1] A forecasting method that combines the predictions of a panel of forecasters. Delphi itself is a town on the southwestern spur of Mount Parnassus in the valley of Phocis. According to legend, it was here that Apollo slew Python, protector of the navel of the earth. On that site was built the temple from which prophecies inspired by Apollo were issued.

Customers, on the other hand, may use a competitive product as the reference for the newer generation of the seller's product. If the competitive product is priced lower than the seller's previous-generation product, the new product would be overpriced for this customer. If the competitive product is priced higher than the previous-generation product, the seller is potentially leaving money on the table by underpricing its new product for this customer.

3. *Benchmarking.* In the previous case, we considered analogs to be the company's own prior-generation product. A more general case is to compare the company's product with competitive products in the market that are chosen as benchmarks. An analysis of price response of competitive products can provide an understanding of how the firm's product might behave. AMD, for example, could evaluate how the market responds to Intel's pricing; Marriott could benchmark appropriate Hilton properties.

Retailers such as Best Buy routinely monitor competitors' prices because of their price-matching guarantee on identical items. At some level, all products are benchmarked. Even at the concept stage, which could be three years prior to launch, car manufacturers identify the competitive set in terms of functionality and price. They aim for a target price at launch that is based on benchmarking the competition.

In the case of business-to-business (B2B) product pricing, participants could be shown a benchmark product and asked how much they would be willing to pay for improvement in features or performance. They could also be asked how much less they would pay for removal of features or decreases in performance. These data can be gathered through web-based surveys, mail surveys, or one-on-one interviews.

4. *Focus groups.* Focus groups are a widely used qualitative market research method to obtain reactions from the target market to a wide range of questions, from new product evaluation to customer service evaluation, to competitive product evaluation, and so forth. Although not typical, focus groups can also be used to obtain price ranges for products and services. These price ranges, however, will be affected by the way the products and services are described, and by what these items are compared to. Therefore, a richer understanding of price response can be obtained by changing the descriptions and the reference products across focus groups. In the hands of a skilled moderator, focus groups can yield insights about product usage, price response, and competition that can be very helpful in product positioning.

Focus groups have five disadvantages. First, sample sizes are small, typically eight to ten individuals per focus group. Second, focus groups are expensive, sometimes running about $5,000 per focus group.[2] Third, inter-action among group members can break down because of one or more intimidating participants, or low skill level of the moderator. Fourth, the artificial nature of the environment may cause group members to focus on features and functions of the product that they would place less weight on or ignore altogether in the field. Fifth, responses are sometimes motivated by a desire to please the moderator of the focus group.

5. *Surveys.* Purchase intention surveys can be used to obtain likelihood of purchase at specific prices. A demand curve can be generated by using differ-ent prices with different random samples. Rather than asking the respondent to react to multiple price points and creating an artificial demand effect, it is better to describe the product and ask about willingness to pay a specific price and rotate the prices across the random samples. The downside is that larger sample sizes would be required. An alternative and more efficient way of gathering data is to vary both the price and product features and obtain multiple responses from the same respondent. Another important consid-eration is that respondents typically overstate willingness to purchase at any specific price, so that sensitivity to price is understated. Market research companies gather such data using a five-point scale, called boxes, with a box score of 1 for definitely would not buy to a box score of 5 for definitely would buy; usually, only the top two boxes (scores of 4 and 5) are considered as a measure of purchase intent. In addition, the top two-box score is weighted by a number less than 1 to reflect the tendency by consumers to overstate interest. Although purchase intent data can overstate actual demand, it can still be used to obtain a reasonable estimate of purchase elasticity. (See Section 4.1.2 for details.)

6. *Experimentation.* Field experiments are a practical way of estimating price response. An alternative to field experiments is to evaluate consumer purchase in a simulated shopping environment. Here, a shopping aisle is set up and consumers make purchases as if in a grocery store. The price of the product in question is varied and the price response estimated. In a controlled field experiment, companies can evaluate advertising spend-ing levels, advertising copy, pricing, couponing, packaging, and so on. A pricing experiment may involve two or three representative markets. Man-aged carefully, price can be varied within the same market as well, to get greater variation. In estimating price response, it is important to control for

---

[2] Based on a 1998 survey of the Qualitative Research Consultants Association. The median cost for a typical two-hour focus group with seven to ten participants was between $4,000 and $5,000.

environmental and competitive effects. These effects may not be the same across markets. It is easy to see that such field experiments are elaborate, time-consuming, and expensive.[3] Car rental companies vary the price of supplementary insurance and cost of filling up the gas tank to evaluate consumer response. Airlines vary the price of an upgrade at check-in time, the price of moving to a seat with more legroom, and the price of various other amenities, to estimate price response.

7. *Historical data.* With good-quality sales data and data on one's own price and competitive prices, one can use regression analysis to estimate a demand curve. If the contemplated price changes are in the range of prices in the data, and if the competitive response does not change, the estimated price sensitivity is likely to be a good benchmark. (Details are discussed in Section 4.4.)

This seems straightforward, but there are practical considerations to worry about. For consumer packaged goods, the shelf price may not change very much over a period of time, say three to six months. On the other hand, promotions, when used, alter the price paid by quite a bit. It may be necessary to separate sensitivity to shelf price from sensitivity to promotions. It is also better for the regression model to incorporate the effect of competition. However, competitive behavior that mimics the company's behavior with respect to price and promotion can affect the precision of the parameter estimates because of multicollinearity. One solution to this problem is to combine cross-sectional data (i.e., sales and price data for the product and competitive products from different regions of the country) and time-series data and analyze these data using an appropriate regression model. It is not as likely that competitive behavior is similar everywhere, so combining time-series data with cross-sectional data increases the precision of parameter estimates.

Regression analysis is possible only if data are available. Companies will have current sales and price data but may not archive historical data. Furthermore, few companies track and record competitive information (on prices or other marketing activities) systematically. Data vendors such as Nielsen and IRI, which track volume, prices, and marketing activity for the retail industry (supermarkets, drug stores, club stores, and convenience stores), maintain extensive data bases. IMS maintains similar data on the pharmaceutical industry.

---

[3] Anecdotal reports exist of competitors sabotaging experiments by deliberately varying their prices or mounting aggressive advertising campaigns during the experimental period.

8. *Economic value to the customer* (EVC). This methodology is ideally suited to quantifying the value that customers place on a product or service. Because value is relative, the product (or service) in question is compared to a reference product the customer considers the benchmark. This could be a competitive product or the company's own previous-generation product. One can see that the relative value would be different depending on the product that is used as the reference. Quantifying the differential value is not a simple matter. One way is for the company to assess the difference based on comparative testing. Another way is to enlist the assistance of the customer to estimate the differential value through value-in-use analysis. A third way is for outside experts to assess the differential value. A more detailed discussion of EVC follows in Section 3.1.

9. *Conjoint analysis.* In conjoint analysis, subjects are provided a series of options and asked to make preference or choice judgments. For example, in a product category such as laptops, subjects could be presented a series of pairs or triples and asked to make a choice from each set. The laptops would be described on a variety of attributes such as price, size, weight, speed, brand, and memory. From the results of the choices, one can calibrate trade-offs subjects make between attributes of the product or service and price. The technique has been used to to design as well as price cars, mass transit, hotels, and appliances.

A variety of sources provide a richer account of each of these methods, so we refrain from a detailed discussion. See, for example, Anderson and Narus (2004) and Lillien, Rangaswamy, and De Bruyn (2007).

Table 3.1 lists the advantages and disadvantages of each approach. In this book we focus on the use of EVC.

3.1 Economic Value to the Customer

The goal of EVC is to monetize the additional value a product brings to customers above what they already receive from their present suppliers. It can be used to determine how much the customer will pay to switch from one product to another, so it is a useful tool for solving strategic pricing problems. EVC can also help a supplier discover which customer segments value its product most. EVC can help the supplier to segment the market more precisely, to design its product to meet the needs of the most profitable segments, and to charge those segments a premium for the extra value they receive.

The analysis begins with the choice of a particular customer segment to focus on as well as a reference product, often that of a competitor, that a

Table 3.1. *Methods for Estimating RPs*

Method	Advantages	Disadvantages	Where most helpful
Managerial judgment	Leverages accumulated wisdom	Tendency to overweight recent data; not a common way of thinking	B2B, used for brand-new products for which data are unavailable; managerial judgment used to obtain a proxy for a demand curve
Analogous products	Unless first-generation launch, other products in the line can serve as analogs	Does not work well for really new products	B2B, where companies launch products based on a platform; e.g., automobiles, microprocessors
Benchmarking	Competitors' products used to benchmark price and sales response	Does not work well for really new products	B2B and business-to-consumer (B2C) products; common to monitor competitive prices; pricing rules based on being within a certain range of competitive prices
Focus groups	Leverages interaction among participants to understand product usage and expected price response; can reveal surprising insights	Could be affected by herd behavior and an ineffective moderator; small and unrepresentative samples	In B2B, assembling a group of lead users or product experts to evaluate value; how much willing to pay for adding and deleting features; common in B2C to use focus groups to discuss product usage; obtaining price response less common

(continued)

Table 3.1 (continued)

Method	Advantages	Disadvantages	Where most helpful
Surveys	Potential to use large and representative samples to obtain price response	Response rates for mail and telephone surveys quite poor; difficult to explain certain kinds of products in a mail or telephone survey; personal interviews are expensive; web-based surveys are popular, but suffer from self-selection bias	Purchase intention surveys more common in B2C than B2B; in B2C mall-intercept surveys often used; opportunity to demonstrate product and obtain price response
Experimentation	Lab and field; lab allows greater control and isolation of price effects, field has external validity	Artificial environment of lab can produce unrealistic price response; usually confined to student subjects. Field is difficult, time consuming and costly to set up; price experiments in the case of consumer products require retailer cooperation; subject to disruption by competitors	B2C products; consumer packaged-goods (CPG) companies use field experiments to assess price, advertising, promotion, and package response; car rental companies vary the fuel surcharge and price of GPS systems to estimate uptake, etc.
Historical data	Prior sales and price data used to estimate price response	Cannot be used for new products; in some cases insufficient price variation to reliably estimate price response; competitive price data may be unavailable; estimating own price response alone is misleading in volatile markets in which company product sales is significantly affected by competitive price moves	B2B and B2C products; in many CPG categories, sold through supermarkets and drug stores, data are used to obtain response to temporary price promotions than to price per se

typical customer in the segment is assumed to be using. Finding the right reference product depends on how the choice is framed by the buyer. In some cases, it will be the product currently being used by the customer segment. In others, it may be the product of any particular competitor, or even the company's last-generation product. The company should not draw its candidates from too narrow a pool: any product the customer uses to satisfy the same underlying need that the given product satisfies is a valid choice.

The principle of EVC is that for any customer currently using the reference product, there are both benefits and costs from switching to the company's product. The company's product may have better functionality – maybe a more comfortable airplane, a faster computer, or a production line with lower error rates. In the B2B context, improved functionality might mean that the new product enables the customer to charge its own customers higher prices or reduce costs by working more efficiently. The new product might outstrip the reference product by placing lower burdens on the customer. On the flip side, the new product may impose switching costs (for example, requiring additional training.)

Suppose R_r is the RP for the reference product held by the buyer and p_r the price of the reference product. Let R_n be the reservation price of the new product and p the price that is contemplated for the new product. How large can p be to induce the buyer to switch from the reference product to the new product? The buyer will switch provided the surplus on the new product exceeds the surplus on the old. That is,

$$R_n - p \geq R_r - p_r.$$

Rearranging:

$$p \leq p_r + (R_n - R_r)$$

Hence, the most one can charge for the new product is the price of the reference product plus a premium equal to the value of the new product over and above the reference product. In other words:

$$EVC = \text{reference price} + \text{differential value}$$

Thus, start with the purchase price of the reference product and then add improvements in functionality and cost savings to the customer. The company is then left with the amount it should be able to charge customers for the new product and still take business away from the maker of the reference product.

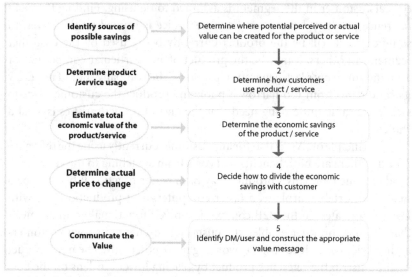

Figure 3.1. Steps in Value Pricing.

3.1.1 Five Steps

Executing an EVC analysis involves five steps, summarized in Figure 3.1.

Step 1: Identify sources of possible savings.
First, identify all sources of savings that could be realized by the customer through the use of the new product or service. A process-tracing approach is recommended to help in this identification. In this approach, a complete enumeration is made of the use of the product, who uses it and when, conditions of use, impact on secondary products and peripherals, cycle time, downtime, machine changeover time, environmental impact if appropriate, and so forth. Too often, only the obvious sources of savings are recorded. This might lead one to conclude there is not much difference between the new product and that of a competitor who is using the same basic criteria in selling its product.

- *Direct cost savings:* the vendor's value proposition to the buyer is that the vendor saves the buyer direct costs such as labor or materials.
  Qualcomm sells GPS technology to large trucking fleets and demonstrates that they can save the customer time and fuel through efficient re-routing; *Ariba,* using reverse auctions, claims to reduce procurement

costs; automation saves on labor costs; outsourcing converts fixed costs to variable costs, etc.

- *Convenience:* the value proposition is a process change that saves the buyer costs or enables the buyer to reach more of its customers than it could do before, thus enhancing revenue.

  Google's ad network and pay-per-click models have revolutionized the online advertising space, enabling users to more effectively use their ad budgets; vendors of online banking automation hardware and software sell convenience and cost savings to banks.

- *Durability and reliability:* the value proposition here is overall longer use of the product, longer time intervals between scheduled maintenance, and modular components to make repairs quick and efficient; the customer pays more but the savings provide a payback in a certain period of time, after which the customer is ahead.

  Some German manufacturers of machine tools, processing equipment such as roasting machines, and the like, have demonstrated value through superior durability and reliability.

- *Superior performance:* the value proposition is improved functionality; the buyer pays significantly more for the performance, but either saves costs by switching to the new product or is able to generate more revenue by switching to the new product.

  It is now commonplace in the marketing of medical devices and some pharmaceuticals to conduct pharmacoeconomics studies to demonstrate improved performance that results either in cost reduction, reduced mortality, or improved quality of life as a means of justifying a higher price. Companies such as EMC and SUN at their peak charged high prices for their data storage systems and high-end servers, respectively, because of superior performance.

- *Reduced risk* (perceptual, psychological): the value proposition offered by the vendor is reduced risk to the buyer from avoiding wrong decisions, and providing peace of mind, security, and high-quality service.

  Goldman Sachs, IBM, GE, McKinsey, and others are able to price their services above the competition because of psychological benefits to the buyer, as well as, of course, actual benefits.

Step 2: Determine product/service usage.
In some cases, there can be an interaction between the user and the usage situation that can provide an additional source of value.

- *Who is the user?*
  Consider a vendor of shipping industry news that provides worldwide

tracking of container cargo, ship registry, safety records, and so forth.
Customers are shipping companies. The vendor can sell two versions
of the information: one a detailed description of worldwide cargo for
the shipping manager, and the second an executive top-line version for
the CEO; the second version can be priced higher than the first because
of the implied value of the CEO's time.

- *What is the usage situation?*

Consider two customers of Caterpillar tractors, one in Chicago and
the other in the jungles of Borneo. Caterpillar should be able to charge
the customer in Borneo more for quick service because the cost of
waiting will be higher; in Chicago, the customer could more easily find
a replacement tractor and be up and running quickly.

Consider a vendor of pest control services, and two distinct customers, a hospital and a prison. The vendor could use the identical
pest control products in the two environments, but the hospital service is performed by workers in clean, white, professional gear, whereas
the prison service is less pristine. The vendor can charge more for the
hospital service because of the higher implied value of a pest-free
environment.

Step 3: Measure economic value.
After all the elements are identified in steps 1 and 2, the actual cost savings
or the revenue increases are computed for each element. Only the differential value is relevant. This means that an appropriate reference has been
identified. This depends on who the customer or customer segment is and
what product serves as the reference for this customer or segment. Thus,
the communication of value will differ, depending on the customer.

- Analyze the economic return of the product or service to the customer.

Companies such as John Deere and Case New Holland have developed innovative GPS-based farming systems for seeding and fertilizer
applications for large tracts of farmland; in a conventional seeding process, there is wastage of seed (or lack of seeding) because of incorrect
tracking of the machine routes. In addition, the soil quality can vary
in a large tract of farmland, which would need special treatment. The
"precision farming" methods overcome these deficiencies. Cost savings
and revenue enhancements can be quantified. John Deere identifies this
technology as a major source of revenue in the future.

Sealed Air Corporation conducts studies at the customer site to show
the economic value added of using its packaging materials versus those
of the competition.

Step 4: Divide up the savings.

From step 3 we have computed the differential value, and hence EVC, from the equation that EVC = differential value + reference price.

Example 1 *Suppose a pharmaceutical company is pricing a new drug to be sold to hospitals. The drug saves $6,000 of incremental hospitalization costs. Suppose that only 5 percent of the patients taking the current drug on the market will suffer a setback and incur the $6,000 incremental costs. Then the differential value of the new drug is 0.05 × $6,000 = $300. Suppose the price of the drug currently used is $50. This means EVC = $50 + $300 = $350. But if the company charges $350, the hospital is not better off and should be indifferent between continuing with the current drug or using the new drug. There are also other factors to take into account. First, costs are certain, but benefits are a promise. The new drug may not quite work as expected for the particular hospital: perhaps only 3 percent of the patients actually benefit instead of 5 percent, a larger fraction of the hospital's pharmacy budget is tied up in this new drug, and so on. All of these reduce the differential value. The pharmaceutical company has to share some of the surplus (or the savings) with the hospital to encourage the hospital to choose the new drug.* □

Example 2 *Another example is the pricing of synthetic motor oil for trucking fleets. Suppose a truck requires 10 quarts (Q) of motor oil plus a new oil filter at every oil change. Say the truck travels 120,000 miles per year; regular mineral motor oil is changed every 10,000 miles, whereas synthetic motor oil lasts three times as long, so it needs to be changed only every 30,000 miles. In addition to lasting longer, synthetic motor oil also makes the engine run cooler and avoids certain kinds of maintenance problems. Assume the maintenance savings amounts to $200/truck/year. How do we quantify the value of the savings by using synthetic motor oil instead of mineral motor oil and what can we charge for synthetic oil?*

- *Mineral/synthetic drain interval = 10K/30K miles*
- *So, EVC (synthetic oil/Q) = DIFF value + reference price = 2 × (reference price) + reference price = 3 × P(mineral oil/Q)*
- *Say, P(mineral) = $1.50/Q*
- *Ignoring maintenance cost savings, maximum price of synthetic motor oil is $4.50/Q*
- *Maintenance cost savings/year/truck = $200/truck*
- *Let total number of synthetic quarts used/yr = x*
- *Then, additional value due to maintenance savings = $200/x*
- *So, EVC/Q (synthetic) = P(mineral) + [2P(mineral) + $200/x]*

- *Because the truck requires 10 quarts/fill, synthetic requires 4 fills × 10Q = 40Q/year, mineral requires 12 fills × 10Q/year = 120Q/year*
- *EVC(synthetic)/Q = $1.50 + [2 × 1.50 + $200/40] = $9.50/Q*
- *Let us verify our computation. If synthetical oil is priced at $9.50/Q, the truck fleet operator should be indifferent between using mineral oil versus synthetic oil.*
- *Cost (mineral/year) to the truck fleet operator = 120Q × $1.50/Q + $200 (maintenance) = $180 + $200 = $380/truck/year*
- *Cost (synthetic/year) = 40Q × $9.50 = $380/truck/year*

As you can see, these numbers are the same. Therefore, synthetic motor oil has to be priced below $9.50/Q for it to be considered as a substitute for regular motor oil. Note that if the reduction in maintenance costs by using synthetic oil is ignored, the EVC of a quart of synthetic oil is only $4.50, but increases to $9.50/Q when the maintenance savings are factored in. This is why it is critical to use a process-tracing approach to make sure that all relevant incremental costs are considered. In the preceding computation, we have ignored the time saved by making fewer truck stops with the synthetic oil. The company selling synthetic motor oil filters can use a similar computation to price the synthetic oil filters. □

Unfortunately, we cannot provide a formula to divide up the surplus. The seller can keep more of the surplus when there are fewer options for the buyer, when the seller has a strong reputation in the market, and when there are many intangibles that cannot easily be quantified. In some cases, the seller is forced to share more of the surplus when a third party, such as an insurer or the government, pays for some or all of the costs.

A more complex situation arises when the benefits accrue not to the buyer directly, but to the buyer's customers. As an example, consider a meat-packaging company, such as Tyson, that sells chicken to supermarkets. The meat packager buys the shipping boxes from a paper manufacturer, such as International Paper. The shipping boxes are coated to protect the chicken from spoiling. The supermarkets cannot dispose of the boxes as normal waste, but must arrange for special disposal because of the coating. Suppose the paper manufacturer develops an innovative coating that is biodegradable, so the supermarkets can save the cost of arranging for special pickup of the boxes. The paper manufacturer would like to charge a premium for these new boxes. However, the value of the innovation does not accrue to the buyer, here the meat packager, but to the meat packager's customers, the supermarkets. How does one determine economic value?

In this case, the economic value must be determined at the end-customer stage. The value is the money saved in the disposal of the boxes. In the case in which the seller sells directly to the buyer, the surplus is divided between the two parties. Here, the surplus must be divided among three parties. The paper company should be able to charge a premium for its innovation to the meat packager, which in turn charges a premium for the chicken packaged in these new shipping boxes. The end customer, the supermarket, should be willing to pay more to the meat packager as long as the savings generated by regular disposal exceeds the premium the customer pays for the boxes. The paper company should educate the supermarkets about the availability of these new boxes, and the supermarkets in turn pressure the meat packagers to use the new boxes.

Step 5: Communicate the value.
Value pricing is a buzzword in the market place, particularly in the case of B2B markets. Every seller would like to practice it. However, both buyer and seller have to be better off. That means the value has to be communicated to the buyer who should be convinced that he or she is better off in switching to the seller's product. Talking about value is not the same as demonstrating value. We believe that value should be quantified to the extent possible, so that both seller and buyer understand the size of the surplus over which they are negotiating. Too often, in our view, salespeople and sales managers talk about value in a general sense, but to be meaningful it must be very specific.

It is also important to understand who the decision makers are, as well as who will receive the value in using the product or service. Executive-level decision makers in the buying organization may recognize the strategic value of making the purchase, but they are unlikely to have operational experience with the product or service. The actual users of the product should also be educated about the value; otherwise, they may not realize the full value of the product when using it. As a result, the product will not deliver the value promised. This can be accomplished, for example, through user training programs (in the case of B2B), video demonstration, and product demonstrations. The opposite can also happen where the users, say engineers, recognize the value but have difficulty convincing senior management to make the investment. This means that different value messages must be crafted for the different audiences.

3.1.2 Psychology and EVC

Our discussion of EVC has focused on the actual differential value. Perceived differential value matters as well. We list some factors that influence a buyer's perceived differential value upward.

- **Degree of product uniqueness (functional and perceptual)**
  The more unique the product or service is, the lower the price sensitivity and higher the price that can be charged. Unique value is also embodied in brand equity. Michelin tires are typically higher priced than other tires, Sunkist pistachio nuts are higher priced than generic nuts, clothes at Nieman Marcus are usually at the higher price points, Caterpillar tractors are more expensive than comparable tractors, Nike shoes are more expensive than other athletic shoes, and so on. Even though one can search online and find the identical book at a lower price than at Amazon, Amazon is the clear leader in selling books online. This is a combination of greater awareness of Amazon and unique value.
- **Knowledge of available alternatives (few versus many)**
  The greater the number of substitutes the customer is aware of, the greater the price sensitivity. In general, the customer is likely to be aware of more substitutes when search costs are low. Reducing the time available for the customer to indulge in searching lowers price sensitivity. This is one reason that retailers such as Best Buy and Abt in Chicago announce that they will match or beat the lowest competitive price, or why car dealers tell customers the price is good only for that day. Sustained marketing keeps awareness of one's product high at the expense of competitors that spend little on advertising. The Internet has lowered the cost of search in many cases, which does not bode well for sellers, unless they can create unique value in their site or customer interaction, as Amazon (see previous example) seems to have done.
- **Degree of product complexity involved (low versus high)**
  If different products are easy to compare, price could be expected to play a direct role in the choice. Introducing some complexity into the way products are described and presented can make product comparisons difficult and reduce the primary role of price. Bundling is one way of introducing complexity. Even though the competitors can also bundle, as long as one seller's bundle is different from the others, it is not easy for the customer to compare prices in a simple way. Using different terminology is another way of introducing complexity. Major sellers of HDTVs, such as Sony, Samsung, LG, and Panasonic, use different

trademarked descriptions of their products' performance, making it difficult for the consumer to line up the attributes side by side and make a comparison.

- **Urgency of the purchase (low versus high)**
  The greater the urgency of the purchase, the lower the price sensitivity. Airlines understand this by pricing last-minute tickets at a significant premium. Service companies charge a premium for emergency service. FedEx, for example, charges more for 8 A.M. delivery versus noon delivery.

- **Nature of the purchase environment and degree of confidence in the purchase (low end to high end, low to high level of confidence)**
  The environment in which a purchase is made can influence the customer's price sensitivity. A luxurious shopping environment and highly attentive customer service can reduce price sensitivity. Such a seller also incurs higher costs of serving the customer, but the valuation to the buyer of the same product, which could be purchased in a inferior selling environment, should not depend on the seller's costs. The buyer, however, is not just buying the product alone, but also participating in the service rituals and basking in the glow of the attention, which justifies the higher price in the customer's mind. The earlier example of paying more for a beer purchased from a fancy resort hotel versus a run-down grocery store is even more extreme because the consumer is not experiencing the ambience. Again, the consumer may justify the price difference by the cost difference of the two outlets.

  A seller can reduce price sensitivity by inspiring greater confidence in the purchase decision. There are many stores selling consumer electronics. A retailer such as Best Buy can reduce uncertainty in the buying decision through knowledgeable salespeople, installation services, extended warranties, and the like. The same is true of the Internet retail environment. A scan of HDTV prices for a particular model and make will reveal a wide range of prices, and typically lower prices on the web than those at a retail outlet. In this product category, retail sales currently dominate web sales because the retail environment provides greater confidence through personal attention. Even well-known brands such as Dell and HP have failed in their attempt to sell HDTVs through their web sites and have exited this market.

- **Dollar value of the purchase (large versus small)**
  The greater the price tag of the purchase, the more price-sensitive the customer will be. This is confounded by the income effect – extremely wealthy individuals will not be fazed by the price of a Ferrari. In

most cases, however, price sensitivity will increase with price. Creative financing can reduce the price effect. Leasing and deferred payments are one option. Another is to get the customer to experience the product free. As part of the launch of the Docutech product, Xerox persuaded a number of companies to serve as beta sites. The companies paid only for consumables. Xerox was successful in overcoming price resistance by demonstrating the value of the product. This type of *value in use* demonstration can be a key selling point in supporting high prices and lowering customer price sensitivity.

- **Proportion of the product's cost to the total cost incurred (low versus high)**
  Linear Technology sells analog chips to customers such as Agilent and Intermec. Agilent uses these chips in oscilloscopes that cost $100,000 a unit. Intermec, on the other hand, uses the chips in mobile data scanners that cost $2,500 a unit. The cost of the analog chip is a small fraction of the total cost of the oscilloscope while being a larger fraction of the cost of the scanner.[4] Hence, we expect Agilent to be less price sensitive to the price of chips than Intermec. Ski lift operators in popular resorts such as Vail and Aspen charge lower prices for use of the ski lifts to local residents than to out-of-towners. Why? For the local residents, the price of the ski lift is the total cost, so they are very price sensitive. For out-of-towners, the price of the ski lift is only one part of the total cost, which includes air fare, hotel, car rental, meals, and so forth. One also needs to factor in the total expenditure on the product. For example, a spark plug at 75 cents a plug is a very small fraction of a car's total product costs. But for a car manufacturer such as Toyota, which makes, say, 8 million vehicles a year, even a 5 cent increase in the price of a plug would mean 30 cents additional for a six-cylinder vehicle, and $2.4 million for the total production. Here, the total dollar value of the purchase becomes a factor.

- **How much of the cost is the customer's responsibility (low to high)**
  Price sensitivity is lower if the costs are shared with a third party. Consumers with drug prescription plans are less sensitive to the price of brand-name drugs than those without such insurance. Realizing this, insurance companies are now changing the blanket copayment amount to one that takes into account the difference between the generic price, if a generic alternative is available, and the branded price. Another

---

[4] These data are from a July 10, 2007 article from the *Wall Street Journal* by George Anders titled "In a Tech Backwater, A Profit Fortress Rises."

way of sharing in the cost and reducing price sensitivity is through buy-back plans that reduce the risk of obsolescence for the buyer.

- **Uncertainty about product quality (low to high)**

  In some cases, price can serve as a quality signal. This is particularly evident in the case of lawyers, consultants, cosmetic surgeons, clothing, hotels, and the like. After all, if a criminal defense lawyer were to charge $100 an hour, how good could he be? If the rate were $250 an hour you might notice. If it were $500 an hour, you may infer he must be pretty good. If he were to charge $1000 an hour, you will convince yourself that he will get you off from whatever predicament you find yourself in! If a hotel charges $500 a night, you infer it must be very good. A single-malt scotch at $100 a bottle or a vodka at $60 a bottle may lead you to think they must be of very high quality. Johnnie Walker has successfully introduced a range of scotch whiskeys labeled Red, Black, Gold, and Blue at successively higher prices. Vodka, which is nothing more than distilled grain, has seen an explosion in prices. Absolut, which was the first premium vodka, has now been surpassed by even pricier labels like Grey Goose, Belvedere, Citron, and Kettel One.

Some of these factors are correlated – for example, the greater the uniqueness of the product, the fewer the substitutes. Uniqueness is typically a combination of functional differences and perceptual differences. The former is created through research and development (R&D) and engineering and product design. The latter is created through brand advertising. Luxury goods command high prices because of both functional differences and perceptual differences, with the latter often being the dominant factor. More than a mere income effect (ability to pay) is at work here to support the higher prices. The psychological effect of exclusivity is a powerful inducement to buy.

The reference price is also a variable that the seller is in a position to influence. This view is supported by two findings from psychology. The first, called the **framing effect**, says that consumers react differently to losing, say, $50 versus winning the same $50.[5] That is, they are more unhappy at losing a certain amount than happy at winning the same amount. These findings have important effects on price communication. For example, a surcharge for using a credit card versus cash payment is framed as a loss and would be viewed negatively, whereas a discount for paying by cash instead of credit

---

[5] First documented by Tversky and Kahneman (1981).

card is a gain and would be viewed positively. This research also suggests that it is better to bundle losses and unbundle gains. Consumers react more positively to one large loss than to a series of losses totaling the same; hence, it is better to bundle losses. On the other hand, they seem to value a number of small gains more than a single large gain of the same magnitude; hence, it is better to unbundle gains.

The second finding is called **anchoring and adjustment**. Individuals make estimates of uncertain quantities by first anchoring on a quantity and then adjusting it. The choice of anchor can be influenced by context and other irrelevant cues. Adjustments from the initial anchor are usually insufficient. The anchoring and adjustment effect can also be linked to framing. Suppose you are in the market for a refrigerator. The store salesman starts you off with a high-end model and works down. Every feature you give up is a "loss" in exchange for saving money, which is a "gain." Because losses hurt more than gains, you are likely to stop sooner. Suppose the salesman starts you at the low end and works up. Every feature you add is a "gain" in exchange for spending more money, which is a "loss." Again, because losses hurt more than gains, you are likely to stop sooner and end up with a lower-priced refrigerator than in the other case. In an automobile selling context, the dealer would like to start with the manufacturer's suggested retail price (MSRP) and work down, whereas the buyer wants to start with the invoice and work up. This is a peculiar industry, in which the consumer knows the dealer's cost. After all, a consumer spending tens of thousands of dollars on high-end kitchen appliances does not know what the retailer paid the manufacturer.

Now, the higher the reference price, typically the higher the EVC. Therefore, it is in the seller's interest to influence what the customer uses as the reference, so that the seller can raise the EVC. There are four potential candidates for a reference price. The first comes from the price of an available substitute. The challenge for the seller is to influence the buyer to consider substitutes that would favor the seller. Discount merchandisers, such as Target and Kohl's, for example, attempt to do this by comparing themselves with higher-priced vendors. The second is to use the last price paid or some market price as a reference. If the buyer typically pays $10 for a glass of wine, that serves as a reference. Therefore, establishments serving more expensive wines must justify the difference in terms of added value. The added value comes from higher-quality wines, from using expensive stemware, from having the wine bottle uncorked and wine poured at the table, and so on. The third is from the seller himself or herself in the form of a suggested or list price. Some sellers post a price to set a reference and advertise to consumers to "compare at." This is common with office product vendors, office furniture catalog marketers, discount liquor stores, and the like. In the case of office products and office furniture sellers, the comparison price or "list" price is quite high and the advertised sale price is 50 percent to 75 percent below list, giving the customer the illusion of a great bargain. The seller sets the list price and sells at a discount to the catalog marketer, which in turn marks up the product to the end customer. The end customer does not know the price paid by the catalog marketer, but is quite taken in by the large discount. The fourth candidate is the seller's costs. Research shows that buyers are more willing to accept the seller's costs going up, rather than scarcity, as a justification for higher prices. Customers become incensed when the price of shovels goes up significantly after a major snowstorm, because in their minds the reference price has not changed. However, retailers who explain that price increases are due to cost increases (for example, coffee retailers have been known to post information about costs) bear much less of the customers' anger.

3.2 Key Points

1. This chapter highlighted a number of ways to estimate a demand curve or how sensitive buyers are to a price change.
2. A five-step approach to value pricing is described.
3. The goal should be to raise the customer's reservation price (or willingness to pay). Reservation price equals the reference price plus differential value. The higher the reference price used by the customer, typically the higher the reservation price. Marketing could influence which product is used as the reference. Differential value consists of objective (or actual) differences as well as subjective (or perceptual) differences. A number of different ways to influence the perceived difference positively are described.

FOUR

Uniform Posted Price

In this chapter, we examine the issues associated with setting the same posted price for all buyers. The first is the trade-off between margin and volume. A high price means a high margin but a low sales volume. A low price means a low margin but a large sales volume. Somewhere between the two is a "sweet spot," and it is natural to ask what that sweet spot depends on.

To think about the trade-off between margin and volume, it will be useful to ignore competition. Therefore, as we change our price we assume that the competition will not respond by changing its price, its offering, or both. Furthermore, to keep the arithmetic simple, we assume that the consumer surplus from buying a competitor's product is always zero.[1] What is restrictive about this assumption is that the consumer surplus *never* changes. In effect, the competition does not change its prices in response to us changing ours, or configuring its product differently. The economics shorthand for this assumption is that the firm setting prices is a **monopoly**.[2] We will adopt this shorthand in the text that follows. The assumption, though drastic, allows us to focus on the interaction between the seller and buyers to the exclusion of other issues. (The consequences of dropping this assumption are examined in Chapter 7).

Why choose to sell via a posted price? When one sells to many buyers at the same time, negotiating with each of them is costly. In this case, it is

---

[1] In particular, it means that as long as we offer the buyer the product at a price below the buyer's RP, the buyer will buy from us. If the consumer surplus from competing products was something other than zero, we would just have to check that the price offered was such that the consumer surplus on our product was at least as large as that on the competition's product.

[2] Monopoly comes from the Greek *monos polein*, meaning alone to sell. In this book, however, we do not use the word to mean sole seller, only that if there is competition, the competition does not react.

reasonable to assume the seller will adopt a posted price – that is, make a "take-it-or-leave-it" offer to every buyer. If the seller is selling through an agent, a posted price saves on having to offer detailed instructions on when, and by how much, to change the price on each transaction. A posted price also serves to reduce the possibility of collusion between the agent and the buyer.

4.1 Margin versus Volume

Assume a single divisible good, called SOMA, which is sold by the monopolist and whose qualities are known to all buyers.[3] The monopolist charges the same price per unit to all buyers and the buyers are price takers.

The monopolist incurs a total cost of $C(x)$ for producing x units of SOMA. The demand for SOMA as a function of the unit price p, called the *demand curve* or *function*, is $D(p)$. Where it comes from will be discussed later. For the moment, assume that it is given. The monopolist's problem is to choose both a price and a quantity to produce to maximize profit. Given the demand function, once one chooses p, one has implicitly chosen the quantity (x) to produce. This is because nothing is gained by producing an amount different from that demanded.

The monopolist's problem is to choose the price p at which to sell in order to maximize profit. The monopolist's profit as a function of the price p is $pD(p) - C(p)$. Let's do an example.

Example 3 *Suppose our monopolist has a production cost function, $C(x) = x$ that is, a unit cost of $1 a unit. Let $D(p) = 9 - p$. Once the monopolist chooses a price p, that determines the demand. The amount produced will exactly meet that demand. So,*

1. *Choose a price p.*
2. *At the chosen price, demand will be $9 - p$.*
3. *Thus, the monopolist will produce $9 - p$ units.*
4. *For this quantity choice, the revenue will be $p(9 - p)$.*
5. *The cost of producing this quantity will be $9 - p$.*
6. *Profit will be $(9 - p)p - (9 - p) = -p^2 + 10p - 9$.*

---

[3] Soma is a possibly fictitious plant whose juice was used in India to produce an intoxicating drug. It appears in Huxley's *Brave New World* as a narcotic that is distributed by the state to produce social harmony. More recently, the drug carisprodol has been marketed in the U.S. under the brand name Soma. It is a colorless, crystalline powder used as a muscle relaxant.

Table 4.1. *Price and Profit*

Price	1	2	3	4	5	6	7	8	9
Demand	8	7	6	5	4	3	2	1	0
Profit	0	7	12	15	16	15	12	7	0

There are at least two ways to find the profit-maximizing price. The first is trial and error.[4] *Table 4.1 summarizes the results of such an approach. Notice that there is no point in considering prices smaller than $1 or larger than $9.*

From Table 4.1 we see that the profit-maximizing price (to the nearest dollar) is $5 a unit. At this price, the quantity to produce is exactly the quantity demanded, 9 − 5 = 4. The profit obtained is $16.

The second approach is to use calculus. To find the price p that maximizes profit, we differentiate $-p^2 + 10p - 9$ *and set to zero, so* $-2p + 10 = 0 \Rightarrow p = 5$. *You should check that the second derivative is negative.*[5]

So much for the computations. To get some insight into what is going on, it helps to rewrite the profit function as

$$(p-1)(9-p).$$

The first term is just the margin or profit per unit, and the second is the quantity sold. Their product is the total profit. As one increases p, two things happen in the expression for profit. First, $p - 1$, *the profit per unit, increases but the volume sold,* $9 - p$, *goes down. If one decreases p, then the profit per unit goes down but the volume sold increases. The profit-maximizing price is chosen to balance these two competing tensions. What determines the balance point is discussed later.*

From Table 4.1 we see that the profit rises from 0 as p increases from $p = 1$, *reaches a peak at* $p = 5$, *and then declines to zero when* $p = 9$. *When the price is smaller than $5, say* $p = 2$, *the monopolist can increase profits by raising price. This is obvious from the table. Here is what is going on. As one raises price, the profit per unit increases, but the demand drops. However, the profit per unit is increasing faster than the demand is dropping. Past the peak, the demand is dropping faster than the margin is increasing.* □

4.1.1 Where Demand Curves Come From

When there are sufficient data, either from past sales or controlled experiments, regression can be used to determine a seller's demand curve.

---

[4] Start with a price of 0 and increment by $1 each time. For each price, compute the relevant profit.

[5] In fact, it will be -2. This ensures that the solution yields a maximand and not a minimand.

Regression techniques assume that the uncertainty in buyers' RPs can be modeled probabilistically.

Independent Private Values Model

In this model, a seller's uncertainty about a buyer's RP is probabilistic. Each buyer's RP is treated as an independent random variable drawn from some common distribution. For example, suppose the RP for one unit of SOMA of a randomly selected buyer from a certain population is a random variable with a uniform distribution between 0 and 10.[6] That is, the RP of a buyer selected at random is any number between 0 and 10 with equal probability. Two things should be noticed about this model.

First, no precise claim is made about a particular buyer's RP, only a statistical kind. Second, the assumption of a uniform distribution is made for arithmetical convenience only. One should not interpret this to mean that the distribution of RPs will always be uniform. Most likely they will be normally distributed, but this distribution makes for tedious computations.

Suppose the seller posts a price p for the good. Will a randomly selected buyer from this population buy the good? One cannot say for sure, but one can compute the probability of the buyer doing so. If the surplus from any substitute transaction is zero, the buyer will purchase at the price p as long as the RP exceeds p. The probability of that is[7]

$$Pr(RP \geq p) = 1 - Pr(RP \leq p) = 1 - 0.1p.$$

If the population consists of, say, 1000 buyers, then the expected demand at price p will $1000 \times [1 - 0.1p]$. In the preceding example, a particular population size was assumed. If there was uncertainty about the population size – that is, volume uncertainty – one would replace the 1000 by the expected population size. Thus, if N is a random number that represents the size of the population, the expected demand would be $E(N)(1 - 0.1p)$.[8] This last expression should remind the reader of the demand curves commonly exhibited in undergraduate economic courses. In fact, for any (reasonable) demand curve, there is a corresponding distribution of RPs that will give rise to it. That is, a demand curve can be

---

[6] If X is a random variable with a uniform distribution between 0 and a, then $Pr(X \leq t) = t/a$.

[7] If the surplus from a substitute transaction were s, the relevant probability would be $Pr(RP - p \geq s)$.

[8] It is assumed here that market size, N, is independent of the choice of p.

interpreted as a formula for the probability that the RP exceeds a certain price.

Actual demand is rarely the *expected* demand.[9] Therefore, why should one use the expected demand at a particular price as an indicator of the actual demand at that price? We cannot always do this. However, suppose the market we sell to is composed of thousands of individuals, each of whom has an RP for one unit of SOMA that is uniformly distributed between 0 and 10. Further suppose that these RPs are independent of one another.[10] Then, based on what we know about sampling, we can be fairly confident that the actual demand will be close to the expected demand.

If one is willing to ignore the issues associated with passing from a random number to its expected value, we can represent the way in which an individual's (or market's) demand for different quantities of a commodity depends on its price by a **demand curve** or **demand function**. An example would be something such as $100 - 2p$. If the price, p, is \$3, the demand will be $100 - (2 \times 3) = 94$ units. An important feature of a demand function is that as the price of the product rises, the demand for it decreases. The demand curve for a product is valid as long as the prices of all other goods stay fixed. In a market with many buyers, the total demands for a particular commodity at a price will be the sum of all the individual buyers' demands at that price.

Regression

A natural way to tease out such the relationship between expected demand and price is through regression analysis. The demand for a product depends on things other than the price of the product itself. The presence of a promotion or advertising are obvious examples. However, to avoid clutter we ignore these other variables and focus on the price of the product (and possible substitutes).

The obvious regression to run is a simple linear one of demand against price. Such an approach imposes two requirements (at least). First, one must believe that the relationship between expected demand and price is linear. The second is that one has lots of data in the form of demand price pairs. This second condition is met, for example, with the kind of store-level scanner data on supermarket sales of mayonnaise. One has prices for each week and the demand for that week.

---

[9] Our colleague, Scott McKeon, puts it this way: you are not entitled to your expectations.

[10] This means that knowing your RP does not tell me anything about the RPs of people with the same first name as you, for example.

When a linear regression is inappropriate,[11] it is usual to consider a log-log regression, or semi-log regression. In a log-log regression, one regresses the natural logarithm of demand against the natural logarithm of price. In a semi-log regression one regresses the natural logarithm of demand against the price.[12]

In sum, this gives rise to three classes of demand curves used in practice. These are listed below. Here, p_i is the unit price of product i, and $D_i(p)$ is the demand for product i, given the array $p = (p_1, p_2, \ldots, p_n)$ of prices.

1. $D_i(p) = a_i - b_i p_i + \sum_{j \neq i} b_{ij} p_j$.
   The coefficient $b_i > 0$ describes how the demand varies with a change in price of i, other prices fixed. The coefficients b_{ij} describe how demand for i varies with a change in price of product j. If $b_{ij} \leq 0$, then j complements i, and if $b_{ij} > 0$, product j is a substitute.

2. $D_i(p) = a_i p_i^{-b_i} \prod_{j \neq i} p_j^{b_{ij}}$.
   Here, $b_i > 1$.

3. $D_i(p) = e^{a_i} e^{-b_i p_i} \prod_{j \neq i} e^{b_{ij} p_j}$.

In the first case, the coefficients of the price variables are obtained from a simple linear regression. In the second case, the coefficients are obtained from a regression of the logarithm of demand against the logarithm of price (log-log). In the third case, the coefficients are derived from a regression of the logarithm of demand against price (semi-log).

A linear demand function, $D = a - bp$, corresponds to the assumption that RPs are distributed uniformly. The probability distribution over RPs that corresponds to a log-log regression, $\ln D = a - b \ln p$, is exponential. The probability distribution over RPs for a semi-log demand function, $\ln D = a - bp$, corresponds to a power law distribution; that is, $Pr(RP \leq p) = bp^{-(b+1)}$.

Sometimes one may wish to estimate the probability of purchase at a price p rather than average demand at price p. That is, rather than estimating $E(N)Pr(RP \geq p)$, we estimate $Pr(RP \geq p)$. This is done with a variation of regression known as **logit**.

Logit is a variation of regression to handle situations in which the dependent variable in the regression is a dummy/indicator variable (i.e., it takes on the value 0 or 1). An example will illustrate when the technique is to be used.

---

[11] For example, if there is a problem with nonconstant variance.
[12] To determine which regression model should be used, one can examine a scatter plot of the residuals of each regression to check for the absence of curvature.

Table 4.2. *Purchase Data*

Household ID	Discount	Purchase (Yes = 1, No = 0)
000	$5	1
001	$5	0
002	$10	1
003	$10	1
004	$20	0
005	$30	1

A seller selects 1000 households at random and divides them (again at random) into five groups of size 200 each. To each household in each group, the seller sends a coupon offering a discount on the price of the product. Different discounts are offered to different groups. Subsequently it is determined whether a household made a purchase, and this is recorded. A sample of the records generated is shown in Table 4.2.

An obvious problem with data such as these has to do with households that make a purchase without the coupon, but we ignore this possibility here.

Naturally, we would like to use the data to tell us how the "intention" to purchase is related to the price. The difficulty is that the variable we wish to predict is 0 or 1. In the language of regression, the dependent variable is a dummy variable. Logit is used in precisely this situation.

In our example, one begins by computing π_i, the proportion of buyers in the ith group who bought. Let X_i be the size of the discount offered to members of the ith group. This is summarized in the Table 4.3.

Next, regress the log of $\frac{\pi_i}{1-\pi_i}$ against X_i. The term $\frac{\pi_i}{1-\pi_i}$ is called the *odds ratio*.

One may be concerned that we have only five data points in the regression. This is true, but ignores the fact that each of the five data points comes from a sample of size 200. This is what logit exploits.

Table 4.3. *Redemption Rates*

Discount	No. of Households	No. of Coupons Redeemed	Proportion Redeemed
$5	200	30	0.15
$10	200	55	0.275
$15	200	70	0.350
$20	200	100	0.5
$30	200	137	0.685

For this data, the result of the logit is:

$$\ln\left[\frac{\pi_i}{1-\pi_i}\right] = -2.044 + 0.097\,X_i.$$

Rearranging terms, we get:

$$\pi_i = \frac{e^{(-2.044+0.097\,X_i)}}{1 + e^{(-2.044+0.097\,X_i)}}.$$

This is an example of a logit demand curve. The general form of a logit demand function is

$$\Pi(p) = \frac{e^{(a-bp)}}{1 + e^{(a-bp)}}.$$

Here $\Pi(p)$ is the probability of purchase at price p. The multiproduct version of a logit demand curve takes the form

$$\Pi_i(p_i) = \frac{e^{a_i - b_i\,p_i + \sum_{j\neq i} b_{ij}\,p_j}}{1 + \sum_j e^{a_j - b_j\,p_j + \sum_{k\neq j} b_{jk}\,p_k}}$$

where the b_js are positive parameters that measure the price sensitivity of the corresponding offering, with other prices held fixed.

The distribution over RPs that corresponds to a logit demand function is called the *logistic distribution*. It is similar to a normal distribution. It is natural to ask why not consider demand functions that arise from the assumption that the RPs are normally distributed. Indeed, this is sometimes done; the associated regression technique is called *probit*. However, the probit model is more cumbersome and because, in many cases, it gives results similar to the logit model, the logit model is more popular.[13]

4.1.2 Elasticity of Demand

In many textbooks and the odd conversation, one will hear the term **price elasticity of demand**. It is a measure of the sensitivity of demand to a change in price.[14] It is the percentage change in the amount demanded as a result of a really small percentage change in the price, *other things held fixed*. For the moment, let us overlook what it means to hold other things fixed and what a really small percentage change is. The notion of elasticity is sometimes

---

[13] Neter et al. (1996) provide a comprehensive treatment of regression.

[14] Of course, customer tastes and the availability of viable substitutes determine this sensitivity.

expressed as follows:

$$-\left(\frac{\%\ change\ in\ quantity}{\%\ change\ in\ price}\right).$$

Even though there is a negative sign in the expression for elasticity of demand, it is a non-negative number somewhere between 0 and infinity. This is because a percentage increase in price will result in a percentage decrease of demand, making the numerator negative. The negative sign makes everything positive again.[15] This particular definition of elasticity, though easy to digest, does not make explicit the fact that the elasticity of demand will vary with the current price. For example, if chocolate costs 1 cent a pound, we would not expect a 50 percent increase in price to have a significant effect on demand. On the other hand if it cost 1 dollar a pound, a 50 percent increase in price might have more of an effect on demand. Thus, the elasticity of demand depends not just on the change in price, but also on the base price from which a change is made.

Underlying every elasticity number is a time frame. To illustrate, consider the demand for gasoline after its price increases. In the immediate aftermath of the increase, we expect demand to change very little. In this sense, the elasticity of demand for gasoline at the initial price would be small. However, if the price increase is a sustained one, we expect buyers to organize their lives around the increase – for example, by changing vacation plans, carpooling, or switching to a more fuel-efficient car. Hence, over the long run, we expect the elasticity of demand to be relatively larger. Thus, when invoking an elasticity, the reader should have in mind a time frame in which it is relevant.

The gasoline example might lead one to conclude that the short-run elasticity of demand for a good or service will be smaller than its long-run elasticity. This intuition is flawed in the case of durable goods such as washing machines, automobiles, and houses. Their durability allows a buyer to postpone the purchase of a new car, say, initially. However, with age, the car wears out and postponement becomes expensive. In this case, buyers are less sensitive to a price change in the long term.

Now we turn to the issue of what a really small percentage change in price is. A formal definition is described in the technical aside that appears at the end of this chapter. For most practical purposes, a small change is 1 percent. In this book we define the elasticity of demand to be the **percentage drop in**

---

[15] Because an elasticity is a percentage divided by a percentage, it is a dimensionless number.

Table 4.4. *Regression Curves*

Type	Equation	Elasticity	Elasticity at Average Price
Linear	$3602 - 321.2p$	$\dfrac{321.2p}{3602 - 321.2p}$	2.156
Log-log	$10.976 - 1.989\ln p$	1.989	1.989
Semi-log	$9.026 - 0.269p$	$0.269p$	2.047

demand from a 1 percent increase in price. This definition of elasticity is an approximation to the genuine article, but good enough for our needs.[16]

Example 4 *Suppose demand, D, is related to unit price p by*

$$D = 100 - p.$$

As an illustration, we compute the elasticity of demand when the price p is $2.
At this price, demand is $100 - 2 = 98$. Increase the price by 1 percent. Thus, the price becomes $2.02. At this new price, demand is $100 - 2.02 = 97.98$. This is a $\frac{98 - 97.98}{98} \times 100 = 0.0204$ percent decrease. Thus, the elasticity of demand is 0.0204.

In this example, the procedure for computing elasticity of demand is exact. This is so because the demand curve is linear in price. □

If $D = a - bp$ where a and b are nonnegative numbers, the elasticity of demand is $\frac{bp}{a-bp}$. If the demand curve comes from a log-log regression that is $\ln D = a - b\ln p$ the elasticity of demand is just b. If the demand curve comes from a semi-log regression that is $\ln D = a - bp$ the elasticity of demand is bp. If the demand curve comes from a logit regression that is $D = \frac{e^{(a-bp)}}{1+e^{(a-bp)}}$ the elasticity of demand is $\frac{bp}{1+e^{(a-bp)}}$.

Example 5 *Table 4.4 lists the demand curves obtained from applying the three regression models to a particular set of price data to estimate sales. The elasticity of demand at the average price for each model is also reported. Figure 4.1 displays a plot of the actual sales against the estimated sales from each of the regressions.* □

As noted earlier, the definition of elasticity of demand we use here is an approximation. To see why, suppose that at a price of $1 a unit, the demand for a hypothetical product is D units. Suppose at this price the elasticity

---

[16] *Zero elasticity* at **all** prices means that the quantity demanded does not change with price. When the elasticity (at a particular price) is less (more) than 1, we say that demand is *inelastic* (*elastic*) at that price.

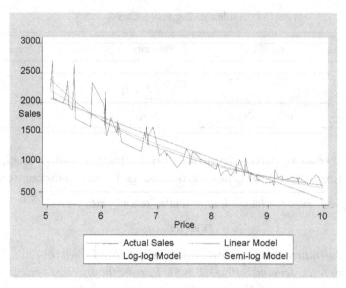

Figure 4.1. Plot of actual vs. predicted sales.

of demand is 2. Furthermore, suppose that the elasticity of demand is 2 for all prices between $0 and $2. With this information, we know that if the current price of $1 a unit is increased 1 percent, demand will drop 2 percent. What happens if the current unit price is increased another 1 percent, to $1.0201 a unit? This amounts to a 2.01 percent increase. It is tempting to say that the demand will drop about 4 percent. However, this is incorrect. Why? The first 1 percent increase will produce a price of $1.01 and a 2 percent drop in demand, leaving us with a demand of $(1 - 0.02) \times D = 0.98 \times D$. To get the price up to $1.0201, we have to increase price by another 1 percent. However, this results in a 2 percent drop on the new base demand of $0.98 \times D$. Thus, the new demand will be $0.98 \times 0.98 \times D = 0.9604 \times D$. This is a 3.96 percent drop in demand. Therefore, simply multiplying the elasticity by the percentage increase in price *overestimates* the resulting decline in demand. For a price drop, multiplying the elasticity by the percentage drop in price will *underestimate* the increase in demand. The difference between the actual change in demand and the estimated demand is analogous to the difference between compound and simple interest. The difference increases as the magnitude of the price change under consideration increases.

What is meant by "holding other things fixed"? In the real world, price changes do not occur in a vacuum. Promotions and advertising campaigns may be in force. Competitors may be adjusting their prices in response to one's price changes. Thus, observed changes in one's own demand is a function of one's own prices as well these other influences. This would seem to make elasticity of demand an idealization of no practical value. However, the same regression techniques that allow us to obtain a demand curve also permit us to estimate elasticities even when other things are not held fixed. The following example illustrates this principle.

Example 6 *Suppose that one has run two regressions to estimate the demand curve for one's product. The first is a log-log regression of one's own demand (D) against one's own price (p). The output of this regression is*

$$\ln D = 4.24 - 2.92 \ln p.$$

The second regression is a log-log regression of one's own demand (D) against one's own price (p) and the competitor's price ($\hat{p}$):

$$\ln D = 6.23 - 3.34 \ln p + 1.45 \ln \hat{p}.$$

The first regression finds that the elasticity of demand for one's product is 2.92, whereas the second finds that it is 3.34. The discrepancy is explained by noting that the first regression estimates demand without holding the competitor's price fixed. In the absence of information about a competitor's price, but assuming that the competitor changes its price in a way that is statistically similar to the way it has changed prices in the past, the estimate for elasticity that it yields is valid. The second regression estimates demand holding the competitor's price fixed. When data are available on competitor's prices, the elasticity estimate from the second regression is the right estimate. □

Estimates of the elasticity of demand may be found in a variety of sources. Blattberg and Neslin (1990), for example, report price (as well as promotion) elasticities for brands in four common grocery products: flour, tuna fish, bathroom tissue, and margarine.[17] The elasticities vary across brands, with the average around 2.5. A meta-analysis (Tellis (1988)) of a large number of research articles published in the *Journal of Marketing Research* finds the average elasticity to be about 1.8. The product categories included detergents, durable goods, food, toiletries, pharmaceuticals, and some unspecified categories.

Table 4.5 gives elasticity estimates (that hold in a narrow range around existing prices) from Gwartney and Stroup (1997) for various categories of goods.

---

[17] From Blattberg and Neslin (1990), pp. 355–356.

Table 4.5. *Elasticity Estimates*

Category	Elasticity (short-term)	Elasticity (long-term)
Airline travel	0.1	2.4
Gasoline	0.2	0.7
Tires	0.9	1.2
Automobiles	1.2–1.5	0.2

It is important to keep in in mind that the elasticity of demand for a product may be very different from the elasticity of demand for the version of that product sold by a particular seller. For example, the elasticity of demand for cars made by Toyota is likely to be quite different (higher) than that for cars made by Mercedes Benz.

Because the presence of substitutes and complements will affect the demand for a product, it is useful to know how sensitive the demand is to a change in the price of a substitute or complement. This is measured using **cross price elasticity of demand**. By analogy, it is the percentage change in demand for one's product from a 1 percent change in the price of another. Formally, the cross price elasticity of demand of product A with respect to product B is

$$-\left(\frac{\% \text{ change in quantity of } A}{\% \text{ change in price of } B} \right).$$

Unlike elasticity of demand, cross price elasticity can be a negative number.[18]

Using Purchase Intent

If historical data about price and demand are unavailable, one can use purchase intent surveys to estimate elasticities. As noted in Chapter 3, purchase intent surveys can overstate the actual demand. Nevertheless, the purchase intent at different prices can still be used to obtain a (unreliable) measure of purchase elasticity. Suppose that the average purchase intent at a price of $100 is 6 percent of the total market. At $150, the average purchase intent is 2 percent of the market. This means that a 50 percent increase in the price results in a 67 percent drop in demand. Thus, the elasticity at the $100 price is 1.33.

Suppose that the purchase intent overstates the actual purchase by a factor of 2. That is, suppose the truth is that only 3 percent would purchase the

[18] Why?

Table 4.6. *Survey*

Price	Purchase Intent
$50	12%
$75	10%
$100	7%
$125	3%

product at a price of $100, and only 1 percent would purchase the product at a price of $150. The purchase elasticity would be unaffected, as long as the overstatement factor is the same at the different prices. There may be psychological reasons for less of an overstatement at lower prices and more of an overstatement at higher prices in a survey – that is, in real life, fewer customers may purchase the product at the higher price. For example, suppose at the lower price of $100, the overstatement is a factor of 2, whereas the overstatement at the higher price of $150 is a factor of 3. The computed purchase intent price elasticity equals

$$\frac{[(6/2) - (2/3)]/3}{[150 - 100]/100} = \frac{14}{9} = 1.56.$$

The elasticity numbers are still quite close. One would get a better estimate if more price points had been tested. In practical surveys, generally no more than three price points are used. As an illustration, suppose four price points are used, and the data are as follows (Table 4.6):

A log-log regression of purchase intent against price yields a price elasticity of 1.40. Admittedly it is a regression with four data points, which is not recommended for statistical purposes. In this case, however, it is appropriate to do so to get a rough estimate of the elasticity. We are obtaining a price elasticity for purchase share, not demand. Demand at a certain price is share at that price multiplied by market size, which is constant. The log of demand is log of (share × market size), which equals log (share) plus a constant value. Thus, the price elasticity of demand is the same as the price elasticity of share. This is also the case for a linear demand function.

4.2 Margin and Elasticity

In Example 3, the monopolist's profit-maximizing price, $5, is *larger* than its unit cost of production of $1. In a perfectly competitive market, and when all firms have the same unit cost, a firm's selling price would be set by the market to *equal* its unit cost of production. In fact, it will always

Table 4.7. *Margin and Elasticity*

Price	1	2	3	4	5	6	7	8	9
Elasticity	1/8	2/7	3/6	4/5	5/4	6/3	7/2	8/1	∞
Profit	0	7	12	15	16	15	12	7	0

be the case that the monopolist's profit-maximizing price will exceed its unit cost of production. The magnitude of that difference will depend on the sensitivity of the demand to a change in price. How do we know this? The elasticity of demand at $p = 1$ is $1/8 < 1$.[19] Thus, if we increase price by 1 percent, demand drops by *less than* 1 percent. Because the margin is expanding faster than the volume is shrinking, the monopolist winds up better off. In general, if the elasticity of demand at a particular price is smaller than 1, it always pays to increase the price of the product. What one loses on volume is made up by what one gains in margin. In Table 4.7, the elasticity of demand at various prices for the monopolist of Example 3 is shown along with the corresponding profits.

At a price less than the profit-maximizing price, the elasticity of demand is less than 1. Thus, raising the price can only increase profit. At a price that exceeds the profit-maximizing price, the elasticity is more than 1. Hence, increasing the price by 1 percent results in drop in demand in excess of 1 percent. Thus, further price increases can only lower profits.

The relationship between the profit-maximizing price and the elasticity of demand is made precise with the markup formula:

$$\frac{p^* - c}{c} = \frac{1}{e(p^*) - 1}. \tag{4.1}$$

Here, p^* is the profit-maximizing price, c is the constant unit cost of production, and $e(p^*)$ the elasticity of demand at price p^*.[20] The left-hand side of equation (4.1) is the ratio of the profit margin to the cost, which is sometimes called the *percentage markup* (*over cost*). The term on the right-hand side is the reciprocal of the elasticity of demand minus 1. Therefore, the elasticity of demand at the profit-maximizing price must exceed 1. The larger the elasticity of demand (at the profit-maximizing price), the smaller

---

[19] The demand curve in Example 3 is $9 - p$. The elasticity of demand is $\frac{p}{9-p}$. At $p = 1$, elasticity is 1/8.

[20] The markup formula described here holds for the case in which the seller has constant unit costs. Further, it applies only to the profit-maximizing price. It is not a device for actually computing the elasticity of demand. For the precise conditions under which it holds, and for the derivation, see the Technical Aside at the end of this chapter.

the markup – that is, the smaller the margin per unit. The markup formula can also be stated in the following equivalent form:

$$\frac{p^* - c}{p^*} = \frac{1}{e(p^*)}. \tag{4.2}$$

In this case the left-hand side is the percentage markup over the sale price.[21]

The markup formula demonstrates that the power to sustain a price above marginal cost depends on the elasticity of demand of the relevant product or service. The elasticity term captures how buyers will respond to a change in the seller's price. This will depend on the value they place on the seller's product and the opportunity costs of using a substitute product. Because different products (or even the same product in different locations) will have different elasticities, they should not necessarily have the same markup.

It is useful to ask what happens to the markup if the elasticity of demand increases (at every price). The markup decreases. As customers become more sensitive to a price change, the margin per customer decreases.

The markup formula is relevant to a seller who is not a monopolist in two ways. First, it is possible to estimate the elasticity of demand to account for competition. Second, a seller in a competitive market cannot sustain a markup larger than a monopolist facing the same elasticity of demand. Thus, the relative markup formula gives an upper bound on the markup the seller in a competitive market can expect to receive.

Example 7 *Suppose our monopolist as in Example 3 has a production cost of $1 a unit. Let* $D(p) = 9 - p$. *We use the markup formula to determine the profit-maximizing price. We need the elasticity of demand as a function of price for this demand curve. It happens to be* $\frac{p}{9-p}$. *Therefore, if* p^* *is the profit-maximizing price,*

$$\frac{p^* - 1}{1} = \frac{1}{\frac{p^*}{9-p^*} - 1} = \frac{9 - p^*}{2p^* - 9} \quad \Rightarrow \quad (p^* - 1)(2p^* - 9) = 9 - p^*$$
$$\Rightarrow \quad p^* = 5.$$

It turns out that it is much more convenient to use the markup formula in its percentage markup over sales price form. In that case,

$$\frac{p^* - 1}{p^*} = \frac{1}{\frac{p^*}{9-p^*}} \quad \Rightarrow \quad \frac{p^* - 1}{p^*} = \frac{9 - p^*}{p^*} \quad \Rightarrow p^* - 1 = 9 - p^* \quad \Rightarrow p^* = 5.$$

□

---

[21] This is also called the *Lerner index*.

A derivation of the markup formula can be found in the Technical Aside at the end of this chapter.

4.2.1 Choosing Quantity

In our story of the profit-maximizing monopolist, we focused on the choice of a profit-maximizing price. We could just as well have started with choosing a quantity and letting demand set the price instead. The answer would be the same. We confirm this in the next example.

Example 8 *Suppose our monopolist has a production cost of $1 a unit. Let* $D(p) = 9 - p$.

1. *Choose a quantity x, in other words* $D(p) = x$.
2. *To sell this quantity, the price per unit must be* $9 - x$.
3. *For this quantity choice, the revenue will be* $x(9 - x)$.
4. *The cost of producing x units will be x because the cost is assumed to be $1 a unit.*
5. *Profit will be* $x(9 - x) - x = -x^2 + 8x$.

Again, there are two ways to find the value of x to maximize profit: trial and error and calculus. Either way, you should conclude that $x = 4$ *is the profit-maximizing output.* □

4.3 The Relevance of Costs to Prices

Is the unit cost of the product or service being sold relevant for setting the sales price? If one is free to charge different prices to different buyers, the answer is no. To see why this must be, consider again the ultimatum situation in Section 2.1. We argued then that the price the seller should set (assuming a rational buyer) was $9.99. Suppose the cost of delivering the book to the buyer was $1. Would that make a difference to the price that should be set? Would it make a difference if the cost were $2? In both cases, no. The price is determined solely by the value the buyer places on the book. The unit cost is relevant only for deciding whether a sale is worthwhile. If the most one can charge is less than the cost of delivery, there is no point in making the sale and thus no point in selecting a price. If there were many buyers, each with a different RP for the book, the seller would simply charge each buyer a price slightly below that buyer's RP. Again, the cost of delivering the book is irrelevant for deciding the price.

If one is forced to charge the same price to every buyer, then the unit cost of the product or service is relevant for choosing the price. We can see this from the relative markup formula. Recall that if p^* is the profit-maximizing price and c the unit cost of production,

$$\frac{(p^* - c)}{c} = \frac{1}{e(p^*) - 1} \Rightarrow p^* = c + \frac{c}{e(p^*) - 1} \Rightarrow p^* = \frac{c}{(1 - \frac{1}{e(p^*)})}.$$

The profit-maximizing price depends on the unit cost because it is performing double duty. The price affects the demand, which in turn affects the total cost of production. It is important to recognize that the price depends not on the unit costs alone, but on the elasticity of demand as well. Thus, different products (or the same product in different markets) carried by the same seller should not necessarily have the same markup.

What about fixed costs that are independent of the volume sold? These are irrelevant when deciding on the price because no matter what the price (and therefore the volume sold), these costs do not change. They are relevant for deciding whether the product or service should be sold, but not in deciding the price at which it should be sold.

4.4 Break-Even Calculations

When an estimate of the elasticity is unavailable, a break-even calculation is a simple and useful substitute for informing a judgment about how to set price. Such a calculation allows one to replace the question of what the elasticity of demand is with a simpler question: is the elasticity bigger or smaller than some particular value? First we describe the details of a break-even calculation under two simple but different scenarios.

In the first scenario, we contemplate a price change for an existing product or service. That price change may alter the sales volume, but that volume change will not result in a change in the fixed costs of operation. Let p be the current price per unit, c the cost per unit, and V the current volume of sales. We are interested in knowing whether increasing the price to $\bar{p} > p$ will be profitable. Such an increase will decrease the volume sold by Δ units. We are interested in the value of Δ so that the profit after the price increase is the same as the profit at the current price. Algebraically, we need the value of Δ that solves the following equation:

$$(p - c) \times V = (\bar{p} - c) \times (V - \Delta). \tag{4.3}$$

The left-hand side of equation (4.3) is the current profit (ignoring fixed costs). The right-hand side of equation (4.3) is the profit after the price increase (ignoring fixed costs that did not change). From equation (4.3), we find that that the break-even volume is

$$V - \Delta = \frac{(p - c)}{(\bar{p} - c)} \times V.$$

In other words, the break-even volume is obtained by multiplying the current volume by the ratio of the current margin to the new margin.

Solving equation (4.3) for Δ, we see that

$$\Delta = \frac{(\bar{p} - p)}{(\bar{p} - c)} V. \qquad (4.4)$$

We call $\frac{(\bar{p} - p)}{(\bar{p} - c)} V$ the *break-even volume decrease.* The break-even percentage drop in volume will be

$$\frac{V - (V - \Delta)}{V} \times 100 = \frac{(\bar{p} - p)}{(\bar{p} - c)} \times 100.$$

Suppose one knew the elasticity of demand at the current price p. Call it $e(p)$. Increasing the price from p to $\bar{p}$ corresponds to a percentage increase of

$$\frac{\bar{p} - p}{p} \times 100.$$

This means that the demand will drop by at least

$$e(p) \times \frac{\bar{p} - p}{p} \times 100.$$

If

$$e(p) \times \frac{\bar{p} - p}{p} \times 100 > \frac{(\bar{p} - p)}{(\bar{p} - c)} \times 100,$$

the actual drop in demand will exceed the break-even volume decrease. Thus, increasing the price to $\bar{p}$ will be unprofitable.

A similar calculation can be performed for the case of a price decrease to $\underline{p} < p$. The corresponding break-even volume increase will be

$$\frac{(p - \underline{p})}{\underline{p} - c} V$$

and the break-even percentage increase in volume will be $\frac{(p - \underline{p})}{(\underline{p} - c)} \times 100$.

Example 9 *Consider a base case in which the unit price is $100, and the cost per unit is $60, providing a unit contribution of $40. In Table 4.8, we record the break-even change in volume for four different price changes.*

Table 4.8. *Break-Even Changes*

	Base Case	20% Price Cut	10% Price Cut	20% Price Increase	10% Price Increase
Price	$100	$80	$90	$120	$110
Cost	$60	$60	$60	$60	$60
% Volume change	0%	100%	33.33%	−33.33%	−20%

In each of the four cases, it is assumed that the product is made the same way. That is why the unit cost does not change.   □

It is instructive to compare the break-even percentage volume changes when unit costs are a high proportion of the price to when they are a low proportion of the price. We will use equation (4.4). We write the new price $\hat{p}$ as a multiple of the current price p. Specifically, $\hat{p} = (1 + \alpha) \times p$. If $\alpha > 0$, this corresponds to a $\alpha \times 100$ percent increase in the price. If $\alpha < 0$, this corresponds to a $\alpha \times 100$ percent decrease in the price. Suppose the unit cost $c = (1 - \beta) \times p$. For this to make sense, we need $\beta < 1$. This means that unit costs correspond to a $\beta \times 100$ percent decrease in the unit price.

Suppose first that $\alpha > 0$ (this corresponds to a price increase). Substituting this into equation (4.4), we get

$$\Delta = \frac{((1 + \alpha) \times p - p)}{((1 + \alpha) \times p - (1 - \beta) \times p)} V = (\frac{\alpha}{\alpha + \beta}) \times V.$$

Fix an $\alpha \times 100$ percent increase in the price. As β decreases, the percentage drop in volume needed to break even goes up. Thus, when variable costs are a large fraction of the selling price (i.e., β is small), a price increase disproportionately increases the contribution, allowing for a much bigger volume decrease. On the other hand, when the variable costs are small (large β), a price increase does not increase the contribution that much, thereby allowing only a small decrease in volume.

Similarly, when $\alpha < 0$ (this corresponds to a price decrease), we get that the increase in demand needed to break even is[22]

$$\Delta = (\frac{-\alpha}{\alpha + \beta}) \times V.$$

When variable costs are a high proportion of the selling price (small β), the contribution is small, and a price cut shrinks the contribution a lot more,

---

[22] This quantity is nonnegative because $-\alpha > 0$ and $\alpha + \beta > 0$, because prices should exceed costs – that is, $(1 + \alpha)p > (1 - \beta)p \Rightarrow \alpha + \beta > 0$.

Table 4.9. *Volume Changes (V = 2100)*

	20% Price Increase, $\alpha = 0.2$	10% Price Increase, $\alpha = 0.1$	10% Price Decrease, $\alpha = -0.1$	20% Price Decrease, $\alpha = -0.2$
Cost 30% of price, $\beta = 0.7$	−466.67	−262.5	350	840
Cost 70% of price, $\beta = 0.3$	−840	−525	1050	4200

requiring a large volume increase to compensate. On the other hand, when the variable costs are small (large β), the contribution is large, and a price cut does not change the contribution that much, requiring only a small volume increase to make up for the price cut.

Table 4.9 illustrates this point numerically by displaying different values of Δ for various combinations of α and β assuming $V = 2100$. A negative value of Δ corresponds to a volume drop.

The analysis and the table suggest that cutting price when the variable cost is a high proportion of the price (small β) is unlikely to be profitable because the large volume increases necessary to make up for the price cut may not be realized. Raising price, on the other hand, may bear examination. This is because volume has to drop by quite a bit (see Table 4.9) before contribution is affected. No one likes to give up customers, but the customers who will leave will be the price-sensitive ones. Of course, the number of customers one has to start with matters. If one is serving a few large customers, the power resides in the hands of the customer. In the automotive industry, the parts and component suppliers are very much at the mercy of the large and few automotive manufacturers. Differentiation of the products also matters. The more differentiated and less substitutable the product, the greater the ability to raise price. In the case of commodities such as coffee, tea, aluminum, bauxite, tin, steel, and the like, the variable cost is a very large fraction of the selling price. There are many suppliers and the margins are very small; price reductions are devastating, whereas price increases may be profitable. It is very difficult to raise commodity prices, however, except when there is a supply–demand imbalance.

Airlines, software, and pharmaceuticals are examples of industries for which the variable cost is a small fraction of the selling price. The variable cost of flying a passenger from Chicago to Frankfurt is a small fraction of the price of the ticket. The variable cost of another pill or pressing a software CD is again a small fraction of the price of the pill or the software. In these cases, the volume increase necessary to make up for the price cut is not high.

As shown in Table 4.9, a 10 percent price decrease when the variable cost is 30 percent of the price ($\beta = 0.7$) requires about a 17 percent increase (350/2100) in volume to break even, compared with about a 50 percent increase (1050/2100) when cost is 70 percent of price ($\beta = 0.3$). One might expect the use of price cuts to stimulate volume. Price increases, on the other hand, are not likely to be advantageous because only small decreases in volume are tolerated.

In the second scenario, we contemplate the introduction of a new product at price p. Let c be the unit cost of the product and C be one-time fixed costs associated with the introduction (e.g., new equipment, new space). We seek the volume V needed for the seller to exactly break even on the new product. Thus, V must satisfy the following equation:

$$(p - c) \times V - C = 0. \tag{4.5}$$

Solving equation (4.5) for V we determine that the break-even volume V is given by $\frac{C}{(p-c)}$. The higher the fixed costs, C, the larger the break-even volume. The break-even volume is useful for conducting a sanity check. For example, if $\frac{C}{(p-c)}$ exceeds the estimated size of the total market for this product (and its substitutes) over its lifetime, then we know that the choice of price p is impractical.

4.5 The Sin of Cost-Plus Pricing

Cost-plus pricing comes in two varieties, naive and sophisticated. Naive cost-plus pricing consists of two steps. First, a total cost per unit[23] of each product is computed. Next, the price is determined by using a markup over total cost per unit, determined by purely internal considerations – for example, a rate of return hurdle. In the sophisticated version the markup chosen is influenced by external market considerations as well. Either prescription for pricing is at variance with the markup formula that says that the price should depend on the variable cost and elasticity of demand (which, in turn, depends on market conditions). For this reason, it is a sin.[24]

Even though it is widely acknowledged that cost-plus is not the right way to set prices (and we explain why later), old habits die hard. A survey of pricing practices by Noble and Gruca (1999) found that cost-plus pricing

---

[23] Also called absorption or fully allocated costs per unit.
[24] A venial one. Unlike the mortal variety, it does not lead to eternal damnation in hell.

was used by 53 percent of the respondents to their survey.[25] Earlier surveys also find a majority of respondents using cost-plus pricing. Even in the luxury goods segment, cost-plus pricing is popular. Christie, Vongkiatkachorn, and Gersch of Simon-Kucher & Partners claim that as many as 50 percent of price-setting decisions are based on manufacturing costs.

Cost-plus pricing seduces with simplicity. It is much easier for a business to total its costs than to assess customer value. Its simplicity is also its Achillies heel. A stylized example will convey the point.

Example 10 *We consider the operation of a dramatically simplified hair salon. Its fixed costs, such as rent, utilities, waste pickup, and so on, are $5,000 a month. It employs a manager (at $2,000 a month) and four hair stylists, each paid $600 a month. In addition, each stylist receives $20 for each customer's haircut. Whatever tips are received belong to the stylist and are not shared with the business.*

Thus, variable costs (per haircut) are $20 a unit and total fixed costs are $5000 + $2,000 + (4 × $600) = $9,400. We now need to determine a total cost per haircut – that is, how much of the fixed cost to be allocated to each haircut. To do this, assume that the salon is open 5 days a week for 9 hours each day. Each stylist gets an hour off for lunch. Thus, each stylist works for 8 hours a day. Assume each haircut takes an hour. Each stylist can process a maximum of 8 customers per day, for a total of 32 haircuts/day. Assuming 22 working days per month, the maximum number of haircuts possible is 22 × 32 = 704 haircuts a month.

To determine a price via cost-plus, we need to pin down the volume of business. Suppose, for no reason at all, that on average only 60 percent of the stylists' time is utilized at current prices. This means the salon processes 0.60 × 704 = 422 haircuts in a typical month. To cover all costs, the salon has to charge:

$$\frac{9,400}{422} + 20 = 22.47 + 20 = 43 \quad \text{(rounded up)}$$

per haircut.

The "plus" part of the cost-plus pricing rule is to add a markup to the costs. The markup can depend on a variety of factors, including the location of the salon, its ambience, the skill of the stylists, prices charged by competitors, and intangibles. As one can see, the markup takes into account competitive prices, as well as some sense of customer value. Suppose the salon determines the

[25] We suspect this is an underestimate because practitioners would like to be seen as using the more sophisticated value pricing method.

markup (as a percentage of cost) to be 100 percent (i.e., double the cost). This would mean that it would charge $43 + $43 = $86 for a haircut. The profit per haircut is $86 − $43 = $43, and the profit per month is $43 × 422 = $18,146.

Suppose the actual demand at the $86 price is not 60 percent of capacity, but 50 percent of capacity. The salon now processes 352 haircuts a month (0.5 × 704). The fixed contribution per haircut rises to $9,400/352 = $26.70. The total cost per unit increases to $46.70. Applying the same markup will result in a price of $93.40. The resultant increase in price may push demand down even further, causing the salon to raise prices again. This kind of pricing could lead to a death spiral.   □

The problem arises because the business must estimate the fixed cost component per unit to compute absorption or fully allocated costs per unit. To estimate the fixed cost component per unit, one must forecast sales volume. However, the realized sales volume depends on the price of the product. The price computed by the cost-plus method need not correspond to the price that yields the estimated sales volume. Suppose the cost-plus pricing method yields a price higher than the price that can generate the target sales volume as in example 10. The higher price will lead to a lower sales volume. This lower sales volume will lead to a higher allocated fixed cost per unit, which will in turn lead to a higher price, which will lead to lower sales, and so on. Thus, the biggest problem with cost-plus pricing is that it ignores the demand curve (or price elasticity). Further, in a multiple product case, the fixed (or overhead) costs are allocated to each product according to some rule. These allocation rules can lead to perverse results.

The tale of how Wang Laboratories cost-priced the world's first word processor drives this point home. Introduced in 1976, the word processor was a hit in the marketplace. Competition from PCs eventually eroded the market share, however. As Wang sold fewer word processors, each word processor sold had to "carry" a larger share of the overhead costs, thereby pushing up the selling price and diminishing volume even more.

Because cost-plus pricing relies on allocating fixed costs among the units sold, a careless seller can be misled about a profitable pricing opportunity. The following example illustrates this.

Example 11 *A company with the capacity to produce 120,000 widgets a year currently produces 100,000 widgets a year that sell for $10 each.[26] The fixed*

---

[26] The *Oxford English Dictionary* defines a widget to be any gadget or mechanical contrivance. The plastic devices at the bottom of some beer cans that are used to produce a head of beer are called widgets as well.

cost of running the plant is $250,000, and the fixed selling cost is $80,000. The variable manufacturing cost is $5 a unit. For simplicity assume all other costs are zero. This yields an operating income of ($10 − $5) × 100K − $250K − $80K = $170K. The $10 price per widget is comfortably above the total cost per unit of $5 + $330K/100K = $8.30.

Suppose a customer offers to buy 15K units at $7 per unit. The $7 offered by the customer does not cover the total unit cost of $8.30, and so does not meet the markup requirement of the seller. A slavish adherent of cost-plus pricing would most likely reject the offer. In reality, however, the seller will make another $30K of profit by accepting the offer. The fixed cost of $330K ($250K + $80K) does not change because of the new order.[27] □

We close this section with a description of pricing at Parker Hannifin.[28] Parker Hannifin is an 89-year-old industrial parts manufacturer. It makes about 800,000 different parts (e.g., heat-resistant seals for jet engines, steel valves that hoist buckets) and, until the turn of the century, it used cost-plus pricing to price all of them. The cost to make and deliver each product was calculated and a 35 percent markup applied. Thus, custom parts received the same premium that standard parts did. Parts for which Parker Hannifin was essentially a monopoly seller were priced in the same way as components that were commodities.

In 2001, Donald Washkewicz took over as CEO of Parker Hannifin. Troubled by the use of cost-plus pricing, he instituted a move toward value-based pricing. Parker Hannifin's vast range of offers were classified into one of four categories, depending on the intensity of competition. At one end was category A, consisting of high-volume commodity items for which there was at least one other big competitor. At the other end was category D, which consisted of "specials" and "classics" that only Parker Hannifin produced. It was discovered that 28 percent of the parts produced by Parker Hannifin were in markets with little or no competition or for which the company offered a unique value (e.g., faster delivery). Prices on these parts were raised by at least 3 percent and as much as 60 percent. Some parts outside this group saw price decreases of as much as 15 percent. The company claims that this change in pricing policy has increased operating income by $200 million since 2002.

---

[27] There are other reasons that the manufacturer might reject the $7 offer, which are discussed in the next section.

[28] It is based on an article by Timothy Aeppel that appeared in the March 27, 2007 issue of the *Wall Street Journal*.

4.6 Credibility

What this discussion of posted prices obscures is the importance of the seller's credibility. A price is "posted" only if the seller is committed to that price. The buyer must be convinced that the seller will not budge from that price. To make this point about credibility clear, consider the seller of a durable good, one whose lifetime is longer than the period between price changes. Examples are compact discs and handguns.

Suppose there is a monopoly seller of widgets. There is no other seller of widgets and the unit costs of production are zero. For simplicity, suppose we are at the beginning of the year. At the end of the year, no matter when they are bought, these widgets become obsolete.

There are two potential buyers for the product, each of whom will buy at most one widget. The RPs of the buyers for one full year's use of a widget are $800 and $250, respectively.

If the monopolist chooses to sell widgets in January only, the profit-maximizing price is $800 and the total profit is $800.[29] At this price, the buyer with a RP of $250 for a year's use does not buy. Thus, the monopolist sells to half the market only.

Now July arrives. There is one buyer bereft of a widget. Because the cost of production of a widget is zero, any price that a widget can fetch goes straight to the bottom line. Why not attempt to sell a widget to the one remaining buyer? If a buyer chooses to buy a widget in July instead of January, the RP is reduced by a half, because the buyer obtains only half a year's use. Thus, by dropping the price in July to $125, our seller can sell one more widget. Therefore, at year's end, the seller collects $800 + $125 = $925.

At the end of the year, the widgets held by the two buyers become obsolete. In January of the next year, the widgets are again priced at $800. Now what happens?

If buyers know or believe that the monopolist will sell again in July at reduced prices, some who bought in January may switch to buying in July. To illustrate, consider the buyer with an RP (for the year) of $800. Call her Cassandra. Cassandra now has three choices, compared with the two from the previous year. She can not buy, buy now, or buy in July. Which will she do? It will depend on the surplus she will enjoy from each option.

If Cassandra decides not to buy, her surplus will be zero. If she buys in January, her surplus will be 0. If she decide to postpone her purchase to July, her RP becomes $400; that is, she gives up $400 in value. Therefore,

---

[29] You should be able to work this out.

postponing the purchase is not costless. Her surplus will depend on the price she anticipates the seller will set in July. Suppose Cassandra expects a price of $125. Then her surplus will be $400 − $125 = $275, more than 0. If Cassandra believes the monopolist will sell for $125 in July, she will switch from buying in January to buying in July. In making this switch, the supplier loses $800 − 125 = $675.

What happens in July? Our seller faces two buyers, one with an RP of $400 and the other with an RP of $125. What price will the seller pick? Clearly, $400. Notice that this price is much higher than the one anticipated by Cassandra. Look at things from the point of view of the seller, however. In the previous year, the seller generated a profit of $925. Now the seller's profit is $400. A seller with no competition is suffering a decline in profit.

The lesson here is that every seller competes against itself. In our story of the widgets, the seller is competing against its future self. This future self is born of the buyer's anticipation of a price cut. In our example, the monopolist's profits are eroded because there is an expectation of future price cuts. This behavior is not uncommon. Many firms regularly drop their prices at the end of the quarter to meet sales and revenue targets. Buyers learn to anticipate this, and they purchase accordingly. Not only does this play havoc with profits, but it also complicates production planning, as the seller must now plan for demand that is "bursty" rather than smooth.[30]

In other cases, sellers compete with their past selves as well – for example, secondhand goods and previous generations of an operating system. Let us say one must wait a year for secondhand versions to appear. Buying a used U2 CD a year after release for $7 rather than a new release for $14 means forgoing a year's worth of listening pleasure to save $7. Buying now means that a year's worth of listening is worth more than $7. Because secondhand CDs are a substitute for the virgin product, the elasticity of demand for new CDs would be higher than they otherwise would be, limiting the monopolist's profit.

In each case, the relative cost of postponing the purchase for buyer and seller determines the intensity of competition between the selves of the seller. If the buyer has a lower cost of postponing the purchase (delay, making do with an inferior model) than the seller (inventory, staff salaries), the buyer has the bargaining power.

How does the seller deal with this? With credibility on either price or supply. In the first case, this means announcing a price and sticking to it.

---

[30] A 1992 article from the *New York Times* says it best: "Merchants now treat their shoppers to a rich diet of one day-sales, pre- and post holiday sales, seasonal sales, clearance sales, sacrificing their profit margins in the process."

In the second case it means restricting supply. Ferrari, for example, does this by committing to producing a limited number of cars each year, safe in the knowledge that no buyer can reproduce a Ferrari in his or her home office. Textbook publishers do this by offering new editions that make earlier editions obsolete, thereby reducing the supply from the secondhand market. Erwin Cohen, an executive for the Academic Press, said the following:

Publishers release new editions of successful textbooks every few years not to improve content, although that may be a byproduct, but to discourage the sales of used books by making them seem obsolete.

4.7 Selling to One

The trade-off between margin and volume appears, in disguised form, when selling to a single buyer. The price at which the transaction will be consummated will be smaller than the buyer's RP and no smaller than the seller's opportunity cost. In the absence of any other structure, exactly where it will fall between these two numbers is hard to say. Suppose, then, that the seller is able to make a "take-it-or-leave-it" offer.[31] The success of such an offer depends on the credibility of the seller. In effect, we assume that the buyer will not respond with a counteroffer after the seller sets the price. The assumption is not entirely unrealistic. Many firms choose to sell through agents that do not have the power to rescind the take-it-or-leave-it offer. Vending machines are an example of this. You can buy the drink for 60 cents or walk away, but rail as you like, you can't inveigle the thing to part with the product for less.

Let's assume this and ask the following: if we are going to make a take-it-or-leave-it offer eventually, let's make it at the beginning. If so, what should the offer be?

The answer is easy. If you, the seller, know the buyer's RP, offer a price a hair below the buyer's RP. If the buyer believes that this is indeed a take-it-or-leave-it offer, the buyer will accept and close the transaction at the price quoted. Thus, the question of what take-it-or-leave-it offer to make is interesting only when the seller does not know the buyer's RP.

We model the uncertainty about the buyer's RP using the independent private values model. Suppose the seller believes the buyer's RP to be a random variable, X, uniformly distributed between 0 and 10. If the seller offers a price p, the buyer will accept provided $X \geq p$. The chance that this

---

[31] In this environment, it turns out that among all selling schemes, a take-it-or-leave-it offer is the best one for the seller to use.

will happen is:

$$Pr(X \geq p) = 1 - p/10.$$

The expected revenue of the seller will be

$$p[1 - p/10].$$

The higher the price, the lower the probability of the buyer buying at that price. The lower the price, the higher the probability of the buyer buying. Thus, the seller must trade off margin against the probability of a sale. The price that maximizes expected revenue is $p = 5$.

At the \$5 price, there is a chance that the buyer will not accept. In fact, the probability of this is exactly one-half. Thus, there is a 50 percent chance that the deal will not be consummated, even when both parties would benefit from the trade. For example, there is a 90 percent chance that the buyer's RP is larger than \$1 and \$1 is better than nothing for the seller. This risk of no trade is a direct consequence of the uncertainty in the buyer's RP. The seller can reduce the risk of no trade, but only by lowering the price.

If the transaction is consummated at the \$5 price, the seller knows that the buyer's RP is at least \$5. In fact, it is uniformly distributed between 5 and 10, which means that on average it is \$7.50. Thus, the seller knows he or she could have charged more, and feels remorse.[32]

4.8 Many Products

When a monopolist sells two or more related products, the price of one should not be set in isolation from the others. There are three ways in which the products can be related. The first is when the two products share a common resource for their production. If the products are priced in isolation from each other, it is possible that the demand for both will exceed the common resource used for their production.

The second way is when the two products complement each other but do not share a common resource. In this case, lowering the price of one stimulates demand for the other. Suppose we only had one product A, and the optimal markup of selling product A in isolation is m_A. Suppose we

---

[32] Many years ago, the Wharton School tempted the noted economist, Sanford Grossman, into leaving Princeton for Wharton. Wharton's salary offer was so large as to beggar the imagination not only of academics but the general public. When Grossman arrived at Wharton, the dean at the time, Russell Palmer, greeted him with a smile. Grossman is rumored to have responded, "If you're still smiling, it means I should have asked for more."

also have another product B, which is a complement to product A, whose optimal markup in isolation is m_B. Selling B along with A will result in an optimal markup for A lower than m_A. Stated differently, the sum of the optimal prices of A and B sold together will be lower than the optimal prices of A and B sold in isolation.

Frank Hruska, a former student, relates a tale that illustrates this point. His brother, a young sailor on leave in Cairo, was offered a camel ride into the desert for (U.S.) $10. Thinking the price too high, Hruska bargained the camel owner down to $5, whereupon he was led into the desert on the camel's back. In the middle of the desert, away from obvious landmarks, the camel owner ordered his beast to sit down. He then turned to Hruska and made an offer that couldn't be refused – $10 to return to Cairo. The forward and return trip are complementary products.[33] An extreme version of this complementarity is seen with *loss leaders*. One product is sold at a loss to stimulate sales of another. The following example illustrates the issues involved in choosing a loss leader.

Example 12 *A hypothetical company is the monopoly seller of printers (a durable good) and the ink cartridges (a consumable) that are used with the printer. For simplicity, suppose that only the company's cartridges can be used with the company's printers.[34]*

Each printer costs $150 a unit to produce and generates $35 of cartridge sales per year over three years. Discounted at 10 percent per year, this yields a net present value (NPV) of $87. For convenience, assume the cost of cartridges is zero. Suppose the elasticity of demand for the printer (holding the cost of cartridges fixed) is 2.5 (independent of the price of the printer).

If we ignore the revenue stream from the cartridges, the markup formula would tell us to set a price p^* for the printer to satisfy

$$\frac{p^* - 150}{p^*} = \frac{1}{2.5} \Rightarrow p^* = 250.$$

We can take into account the revenue stream from the sales of cartridges by using them to offset the cost of the printer. Because each printer costs $150 and generates an NPV of $87 in cartridge sales, the effective cost of a printer is $150 − $87 = $63. Using the markup formula, the new profit-maximizing

---

[33] Hruska might argue, however, that had he paid the $10 to begin with there was no guarantee that he would not have been asked to pay $10 for the return trip anyway.

[34] Later in this book we will examine the consequences of relaxing this assumption.

price of the printer, p', must satisfy

$$\frac{p' - 63}{p'} = \frac{1}{2.5} \Rightarrow p' = 105.$$

With the second price, $p' = 105$, the printer is sold at a loss.

At the price of $p^* = 250$, the company makes a margin of $250 - 150 + 87 = 187$ for each printer sold. At the price of $p' = 105$, the company generates a margin of $105 - 150 + 87 = 42$ for each printer sold. Therefore, to match the profit at the \$250 printer price, the drop in printer price must more than quadruple demand. This illustrates that for a product or service to be a loss leader, its demand must be very sensitive to a change in price.

The drop in printer price from \$250 to \$105 is about a 60 percent drop. Given our assumption that the elasticity of demand is 2.5, this suggests that demand will rise 150 percent, less than is needed. However, this is incorrect once we recall that this approach to estimating the change in demand generates an underestimate of the actual increase in demand. ☐

More interestingly, if the firm exercises monopoly power over one product (a copying machine, for example), but not over a complementary one (say, repair services), it can extend its monopoly power from one to the other. For example, a firm could lease the copying machine and, as part of the terms of the lease, require that service be provided by itself or its authorized agents. Such a move allows the firm to extend its monopoly power from one offering into the complementary offering (whether this is more profitable than other options is discussed later). Bundling the machine and service together in this way is illegal, however.

The third way two products can be related even when they do not share a common resource is when they are substitutes for each other. Thus, the price of one product can influence the demand of the other. In this case, a seller can stimulate the demand for one product by raising the price of the other. Thus, the markup for each product will be greater than the markup formula would suggest if each product was treated in isolation from the other. Suppose we only had product A. Say the optimal markup suggested by the formula is m_A. Now, suppose we also sell product B, which is a substitute for product A. Let the new markups be m_A^* and m_B. Selling the substitute allows $m_A^* > m_A$. An example of this is a phenomenon known as *sleeping patents*. A monopoly may acquire the patent for a close substitute to its offering, and then not produce the substitute (in effect, assigning a price so high that demand for the substitute is zero). No one else can manufacture the substitute. We examine the pricing of substitutes in more detail in Chapter 6.

4.9 Negotiation

When does it make sense to sell by negotiation?

1. When the buyer is uncertain about whether his or her needs can be met and when the seller is uncertain about the needs of the buyer. Here, the negotiation provides an opportunity for each party to both explore and specify those needs.
2. When there are joint gains. As we have conceived of pricing thus far, it is a zero-sum game. Any profit made by the seller is at the expense of the buyer. Thus, the possibility of gains is excluded. However, when the seller or buyer has access to nonpecuniary inducements, there may be a possibility for joint gains. For example, an employer may be unable to concede on salary to maintain parity with other employees but may be willing to be flexible on when the employee must report to work.
3. It allows the seller to charge different prices to different buyers, enhancing profitability. The flip side is that if the seller gets a reputation for dropping the price, the buyer has an incentive to wait (provided the buyer is patient enough) to force a concession.

4.10 Selling through an Intermediary

In many cases, a seller sells not directly to the end user, but through an intermediary. That intermediary can be a full-time employee of the seller with little or no discretion, or an independent agent, such as a retailer. Because the incentives of the intermediary need not align with the seller's incentives, it is important that the seller's pricing policy recognize this. In this section we will examine two stylized vignettes of this misalignment. We have chosen them because the issues raised apply to a wide range of situations.

4.10.1 First Vignette

Our first vignette involves a monopoly seller selling through a sales agent who is compensated on the basis of percentage revenue (i.e., sales). Imagine two scenarios: one in which the seller sets the price, the other in which the agent sets the price. Would they choose different prices? If so, who would choose a higher price?

The seller is concerned with setting a price that will maximize profit. The agent, on the other hand, is focused on maximizing revenue. This difference in objectives leads directly to the conclusion that they would prefer different prices.[35] To determine who would prefer the higher price, we assume the conditions for the application of the the markup formula (4.2) hold. If $c > 0$ is the unit cost of production of the seller, the seller would choose a price p^* to solve

$$\frac{p^* - c}{p^*} = \frac{1}{e(p^*)}.$$

The left-hand side of this expression is strictly less than 1. Thus, $\frac{1}{e(p^*)} < 1$, implying that $e(p^*) > 1$. Hence, at the price p^* that the seller would select to maximize its profit, the elasticity would exceed 1.

Now, turn to the agent. The agent would prefer a price that maximizes revenue. Maximizing revenue is the same as maximizing profit when costs are zero. Therefore, according to formula (4.2), the price $\hat{p}$ that maximizes revenue must satisfy

$$\frac{\hat{p} - 0}{\hat{p}} = \frac{1}{e(\hat{p})} \Rightarrow e(\hat{p}) = 1.$$

In other words, the agent would choose a price at which the elasticity is exactly 1. Thus, the agent prefers a price at which the elasticity is lower than the elasticity of the profit-maximizing price. Algebraically,

$$e(\hat{p}) = 1 \le e(p^*) \Rightarrow \hat{p} \le p^*.$$

Thus, the agent prefers a price no larger than that of the seller, and in some cases strictly less.

This analysis suggests that a salesperson who is compensated on the basis of percentage revenue (i.e., sales) has an incentive to choose a lower price than the seller, who is responsible for both revenues *and* costs. This will manifest itself in appeals for exceptions to the posted or list price, usually justified by special circumstances. The justifications for a price exception may be valid, but in the absence of other information, one cannot rule out the fact that they are also self-serving. This incentive problem is compounded

---

[35] Except, of course, in the case in which costs are zero. In this case, profits are the same as revenues.

when one relies on one's sales force for most of one's market intelligence (disposition of customer, nature of competitor's offers, etc.).[36]

An apparently obvious fix would be to align incentives perfectly and compensate the agent based on profitability. However, this is problematic because compensation is now tied to a component, cost, over which the agent has no influence. Alternatively, one could fix the compensation of the agent, but this reduces the agent's incentives to expend effort in the sales process. Indeed, there really is no compensation scheme that will align incentives perfectly and be practical. Nevertheless, the analysis suggests a guideline. Specifically, as the fraction of the agent's compensation linked to revenue increases, the less discretion the agent should be given to determine the price. Furthermore, it is important that market intelligence be collected from independent sources to verify the claims of the agent. At day's end, the challenge is to get the agent to see the trade-offs between price and cost that the seller must make. One practical way to do this is to respond to every request for a price exception by pointing out the break-even volume needed to accommodate the proposed price cut. Then follow this up by asking whether the agent can increase the volume of business brought in by this amount.

4.10.2 Second Vignette

In many industries, it is common for an intermediary, such as a retailer, to determine its price by simply doubling the wholesale price.[37] One problem with such a rule, already discussed, is that it ignores the fact that the markup should be sensitive to the elasticity of demand of the market in which one is selling. There is another problem, and a stylized example will reveal it.

Suppose a monopoly manufacturer (M) sells to a monopoly retailer (R), which in turn sells into a downstream market. The demand in the downstream market as a function of R's unit price p is $1000 \times (10 - p)$. M's unit cost of production is $1 a unit. M sells the product to R at a wholesale price of w per unit. For simplicity, we assume that R incurs no other costs beyond the wholesale price of w per unit.[38]

---

[36] Furthermore, this intelligence is usually gathered at the time a contract with a customer is up for renewal – i.e., when a deal is being discussed.

[37] There is nothing special about doubling the wholesale price. Our discussion will apply to any fixed factor such as 125 percent or 150 percent of the wholesale price.

[38] These other costs could be incorporated, but they would clutter the analysis without adding insight.

Suppose M could sell directly downstream into the market (equivalently, M and R work to maximize joint profits). What price would M pick to maximize profit? We can determine this using the markup formula. Because demand as a function of price, p, is $1000 \times (10 - p)$, the elasticity of demand will be $\frac{p}{10-p}$. By formula (4.2) (with $c = 1$), the profit-maximizing price p^* must satisfy

$$\frac{p^* - 1}{p^*} = \frac{10 - p^*}{p^*}.$$

Solving for p^*, we determine that $p^* = 5.50$. Demand equals $1000 \times (10 - 5.50) = 4,500$. At a price of \$5.50 per unit, M would realize a margin of \$5.50 − \$1 = \$4.50 a unit. Hence, M's profit will be \$4.5 × 4,500 = \$20,250. Therefore, the maximum profit to be extracted from this market (using a uniform price) is \$20,250.

Now we examine what happens when M sells to R and R, in turn, sells downstream. Suppose first that R follows a simple doubling rule to set the price. Thus, if M sets a wholesale price of w per unit, R charges a price of $2w$ per unit downstream. At a price of $2w$ per unit, R will see a demand of $1000 \times (10 - 2w)$. Because R must buy every unit it sells from M, it means that R will order $1000 \times (10 - 2w)$ units from M. Therefore, if M sets a wholesale price w, it will see a demand of $1000 \times (10 - 2w)$. Again, we can use the relative markup formula to determine M's profit-maximizing wholesale price. Because the demand curve that M now faces is $1000 \times (10 - 2w)$, the elasticity of demand will be $\frac{2w}{10-2w}$. By formula (4.2), the profit-maximizing value of w must satisfy

$$\frac{w - 1}{w} = \frac{10 - 2w}{2w} \Rightarrow w - 1 = \frac{10 - 2w}{2}.$$

Solving for w, we determine that $w = \$3$. This means that the price R will charge is \$6.

R's margin on each unit is \$6 − \$3 = \$3, and the demand it sees is $1000 \times (10 - 6) = 4000$. Thus, R's profit is \$3 × 4000 = \$12,000. Now, M's margin is \$3 − \$1 = \$2, so its profit will be \$2 × 4000 = \$8,000. In total, the two firms make \$12,000 + \$8,000 = \$20,000. This is \$250 less than before. The point is that when R follows an unvarying markup rule, the result is that M and R leave money on the table. The market had the capacity to generate \$20,250 in profit, but R and M jointly capture only \$20,000.

Now, suppose R chose the price to the downstream market that would maximize its profit. If M set a wholesale price of w, this would become R's unit cost. Therefore, by the markup formula (4.2), the profit maximizing

Table 4.10. *Price and Profit Comparisons*

	M sells directly	Via R, R doubles w	Via R, R chooses optimal markup
Wholesale price	n.a.	$3	$5.50
Downstream price	$5.50	$6	$7.75
M's profit	$20,250	$8,000	$10,125
R's profit	n.a.	$12,000	$5,062.50
Total profit	$20,250	$20,000	$15,187.50

price p^* would be set so that

$$\frac{p^* - w}{p^*} = \frac{10 - p^*}{p^*} \Rightarrow p^* = \frac{10 + w}{2}.$$

Therefore, the downstream demand would be

$$1000 \times (10 - p^*) = 1000 \times (10 - \frac{10 + w}{2}) = 1000 \times (5 - \frac{w}{2}).$$

Because R must order from M, this is also M's demand. This implies an elasticity of demand of $\frac{w/2}{5 - (w/2)}$. The profit-maximizing value of w for M will, by formula (4.2), be

$$\frac{w - 1}{w} = \frac{5 - (w/2)}{w/2} \Rightarrow w - 1 = 2 \times [5 - (w/2)].$$

Solving for w yields $w = \$5.50$.

If M sets a wholesale price of $w = \$5.50$, then R will set a price equal to $\frac{10 + w}{2} = \$7.75$. At this price, R will generate a margin of $\$7.75 - \$5.50 = \$2.25$ a unit and demand of $1000 \times (10 - 7.75) = 2,250$. Thus, R's profit will be $\$2.25 \times 2,250 = \$5,062.50$.

M's margin is $\$5.50 - \$1 = \$4.50$. Hence, M makes a profit of $\$4.50 \times 2250 = \$10,125$. Therefore, the total profit made by R and M is $\$5,062.50 + \$10,125 = \$15,187.50$. This is far less than the maximum possible profit to be extracted, which is $\$20,250$.[39] In adddition, the downstream price, $\$7.75$, is far higher than in the very first scenario. Table 4.10 summarizes the relevant figures.

The last row of Table 4.10 shows that when M and R choose prices independently, they leave money on the table, compared with the case in which M sells directly (or, equivalently, M and R coordinate on price). Why

---

[39] This phenomenon is called *double marginalization* in the economics literature. See Tirole (1988).

does independent pricing diminish joint profits? R's price determines the *size* of the pie to be shared between R and M. The *share* of the pie that M obtains is determined by its choice of wholesale price, w. However, w influences the choice of R's downstream price. The larger w is, the higher the downstream price that R sets, dramatically reducing the volume of sales. In other words, M obtains a larger share of a shrinking pie.

When M and R set price independently, R would prefer to commit to a markup rule such as doubling the wholesale price, rather than setting the price based on the optimal markup using the elasticity of demand. R committing to a markup rule is like making a take-it-or-leave-it offer. As discussed in section 4.6 of this chapter, if such a commitment as credible, it confers enormous bargaining power on the person who makes the offer. If M knows that R is following such a rule, it discourages M from setting a relatively high wholesale price. A high wholesale price would be doubled downstream, thereby choking off demand. On the other hand, when M sets the price first and R responds, bargaining power shifts to M and M is better off.

The lesson for M is that when negotiating w with R (or any more elaborate price schedule) it must be aware of the impact this will have on R's choice of a downstream price. Ideally, M would like the ability to control the downstream price. Indeed, our second vignette explains why, in some cases, M would like to set a price ceiling on R's price.

Resale Price Maintenance
As noted in the previous example, in some circumstances a manufacturer has an incentive to place a ceiling on the price charged by a retailer. There are also many cases in which the manufacturer would desire a price floor. Sellers of luxury items are a particular example. For them, the price is used as a signal of quality. A low price would suggest low quality.[40]

Imposing restraints on downstream prices is known as **resale price maintenance**. Its legal status in the United States has been murky. From 1911 to 1975, it was viewed as an instance of price fixing, which was outlawed by the Sherman Antitrust Act. However, a variety of ad-hoc exceptions were enacted at both the state and federal levels. In 1975, the U.S. Supreme Court finally ruled that resale price maintenance was per se illegal. That is, the act of limiting downstream prices itself is illegal. In short, no appeal to

---

[40] Kolcraft Enterprises Inc., a Chicago-based supplier of bassinets and strollers, uses price floors. In its pricing agreement, the company states that it does so "to protect all Kolcraft and Kolcraft-licensed brands from diminution."

offsetting benefits or mitigating circumstances could be used to justify the practice.

Nevertheless, manufacturers are able to influence downstream prices through other means – for example, informing buyers about the manufacturer's suggested retail price. In June 2007, the U.S. Supreme Court overturned the original 1975 ruling that deemed resale price maintenance per se illegal. Henceforth, it was subject to the *rule of reason*.[41] That is, judges should weigh the costs and benefits associated with resale price maintenance in making a determination. The cost to society of a price floor, for example, is reduced competition, which harms consumers. A price floor, on the other hand, encourages retailers to engage in promotional activities such as advertising and improved service.[42] In the absence of a price floor, some retailers may free-ride on the efforts of others. This diminishes the incentives of retailers to provide service or even carry the particular offering, thereby harming consumers. As a practical matter, the 2007 ruling by the U.S. Supreme Court means that resale price maintenance will return in most commercial situations. However, in other parts of the world, resale price maintenance is still illegal in many circumstances.[43]

Over the years a cottage industry of firms, such as NetEnforcers Inc., has sprung up whose purpose is to monitor the prices at which their clients' products are sold.[44] These companies monitor web sites, newspapers, and retail outlets to identify sellers selling below the floor specified by the manufacturer. If the retailer is an authorized dealer, the manufacturer can force compliance by threatening to terminate the retailer's contract. For example, when AceToolonline was discovered to be selling below the floor set by Black & Decker, it had to forfeit some advertising support from Black & Decker. In addition, Black & Decker stopped routing customers from its own web site to AceToolonline for thirty days. If the retailer is an unauthorized dealer, the manufacturer may allege that use of the product's name or image constitutes trademark or copyright infringement. Tod Cohen, eBay's vice-president for global government relations, notes that "manufacturers and agencies like NetEnforcers are increasingly getting more aggressive policing the prices of our sellers."

The greater aggressiveness on the part of manufacturers to enforce compliance with price policies has encouraged some major discounters, such

---

[41] For more details, see Henry and Zelek (2003).

[42] If one cannot reduce the price to boost volume, one must resort to other means.

[43] Certain European countries, such as Germany and France, permit exceptions for offerings with a cultural value. Others, such as Finland, grant exceptions on a case-by-case basis.

[44] Other firms include MAPtrackers Inc., Cyveillance Inc., and Brand Protection Agency.

as Costco, to call for new laws to limit resale price maintenance. Others, such as Target and Sears, have taken the battle to state courts. Maryland, for example, passed legislation in 2007 making it illegal for manufacturers to stipulate minimum prices. The legislation also applies to goods purchased over the Internet.

4.11 Adverse Selection

Thus far, the discussion of the trade-off between margin and volume has assumed that the change in the volume of buyers produced by a price change does not result in a change in their mix. To illustrate, consider the interest rate on credit cards. A drop in a card's interest rate will attract more customers. This is the volume effect. There is a second effect, though: the mix of new customers may be skewed toward customers with higher credit risks. This change in the mix increases the card issuer's cost of doing business. In this case, the seller cares not just about the effect on volume, but the effect on the mix of customers as well. In contrast, consider the business of selling, say, apples. Assuming sales are for cash only, a change in the mix of customers would be irrelevant for evaluating the consequences of a price change.

The term **adverse selection** refers to changes in the customer mix that adversely affect the seller. In the case of the credit card company, it might mean an increase in the proportion of high-credit-risk customers. Credit card and insurance companies are well-known examples of sellers that face adverse selection problems, but they are not the only ones. Imagine, for example, a gas station with an on-site convenience store. Looking at current data, the owner might conclude that a drop in the price of gas would be more than offset by increased traffic drawn to the convenience store. However, that analysis assumes that the mix of customers after a price drop would remain the same. Perhaps the price drop will attract a higher proportion of price-conscious customers who are unlikely to make use of the convenience store. If so, dropping the price would be a bad idea.

Pricing in the face of adverse selection is a more complex task. In this book, we do no more than warn the reader to keep it in mind. The remainder of the book largely ignores the issue.

4.12 The Price Waterfall

The price a customer pays, sometimes called the **pocket price**, may differ from the list price. The difference between the list and the pocket price was dubbed the **price waterfall** by Michael Marn and Robert Rosiello of the McKinsey consulting company.[45]

A product or service typically starts with a list price. General Motors, for example, has an MSRP for each of its vehicles. Boeing has a list price for each of its planes, a machine tool manufacturer has a list price for each of its machine tool offerings, and so on. How does a company arrive at a list price? In an ideal world, the list price reflects the true value of the product from the seller's point of view, taking into account competitive factors and customer response. An Armani suit priced at $2,000 at Neiman Marcus presumably is what Neiman Marcus (and Armani) believe reflects the true value of the suit. In many cases, however, the list price is simply a starting point from which discounts are offered to the customer.

The first discount is the *on-invoice discount* to arrive at the invoice price. Components of this on-invoice discount include standard dealer or distributor discounts that every channel partner or customer receives, special dealer/distributor discounts applicable to particular customers, order size discounts to encourage larger orders, and the like. Company accounting systems are typically designed to handle discounts off-list, which show up on the invoice. Next, there can be a series of discounts that are negotiated between the salesperson or account representative servicing the particular account, which do not directly show up on the invoice. These are called *off-invoice discounts*. Examples of off-invoice discounts include discounts for cash payment, co-op advertising in which the seller shares the cost of certain kinds of advertising, a bonus for specific promotions run by the customer, product-line rebates where the buyer is encouraged to buy more of the items in that seller's product line, an annual volume bonus or rebate provided when the buyer reaches a specified target volume purchase, discounts off the standard freight charges, and cost of carrying receivables shifted to the seller. These types of discounts are treated off-invoice because they are idiosyncratic to the particular transaction and depend on the relationship between the seller and the buyer. Subtracting the off-invoice discounts from the invoice price yields the pocket price.

Figure 4.2 shows the "waterfall" effect of prices falling from the list price to the invoice price to the pocket price. When the product being sold is standardized and costs do not vary by account, the pocket price at the account level is enough to assess profitability. On the other hand, if there is significant customization involved, it is helpful to create a **profit and loss** statement (P&L) at the specific account level. This would require knowledge

---

[45] See Marn, Roegner, and Zawada (2004).

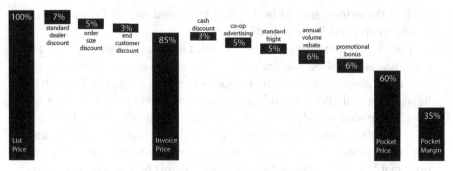

Figure 4.2. Price waterfall.

of all the variable costs that are specific to the transaction. Subtracting the direct product cost and these transaction-specific costs yields the pocket margin. Next, fixed costs are allocated to compute the desired pocket margin to break even at the current operating level.

Managing the pocket price is important. This is the revenue that the seller receives, not what shows up on the invoice. As we have seen earlier, a 1 percent improvement in the price, all else equal, has a rather large impact on margin. As an example, the list price is $100, the invoice price is $85, the pocket price is $60, and the pocket margin is $35. If the seller can save 1 percent in the off-invoice discount so the pocket price improves to $61, the margin improves to $36, or by 2.9 percent. A 2 percent reduction in the off-invoice discount, improves the margin by 5.7 percent.

4.12.1 Using the Price Waterfall Methodology

The ability to manage the variety of discounts and the depth of discounts depends on the power relationship in the channel, as well as the degree of autonomy granted to the salesperson or account manager. Most companies will provide a range for the different discounts that the salesperson cannot cross without permission from his or her superior. An analysis of the discounts provided by each salesperson is a helpful first step in rationalizing the discounts across the sales force. Identifying the salespersons who are on the high end of the discounts range, as well as analyzing the accounts themselves – for example, the size of the accounts and the extent of competition for the accounts – is a second step to understanding the heterogeneity among salespersons and the accounts. Plotting the pocket price paid by each account against account size can also be quite revealing. One might expect that the large accounts are the ones receiving the larger discounts because of competition from other sellers. This may not be true in practice because of relationships between the salespersons and the accounts. The manager should sit down with each salesperson and analyze the accounts one by one to see where pricing power can be improved. In some cases, the customers are not sophisticated enough to break out and understand the dizzying number of discounts being provided. Deleting some discounts and consolidating others so that the discount magnitudes look larger are some ways to manage such accounts. The best accounts are those that are paying at the higher end of the pocket price. Analyzing who these customers are and seeing how to increase sales to these accounts is a profitable move. At the same time, tightening up the excessive discounts offered to the low pocket price customers, or even dropping some of these customers, is also a move to improve profitability.

The process described here seems easy, but unsustainable, because every seller could do the same thing. It is not, however, simple to do. First, one needs a very good accounting system that tracks all these discounts, particularly the off-invoice discounts, and assigns them to each account instead of lumping them into a cost pool. Second, one needs management discipline to hold fast to the discount structure and not cave in to customer demands. Third, one needs to understand that matching competitive discounts should be avoided if the product is differentiated, and a business case can be developed that shows that the buyers can pass along the higher price to their customers. Nike, for example, does not provide the same magnitude of discounts to retailers as its competitors, insists that the retailers take a number of their shoes and not just the best sellers, cautions retailers against discounting the retail price too much, and so on. It is able to hew to such a course because it has built a strong brand and engages in significant pull advertising to drive consumers to the retail stores.

The price waterfall method starts with a list price, works down to the invoice price, and finally reaches the pocket price. This method is useful in industries in which there are myriad discounts to manage. For example, in the grocery retailing industry, there are a variety of discounts and shared payments between the manufacturer and the retailer having to do with case discounts, in-store promotions, local feature advertising, slotting allowances, and so forth. We have explained how the seller can manage the discounts to achieve a higher price. How can buyers exploit the waterfall? First, buyers need to itemize the different discounts separately so that they understand the value of the different components. Second, buyers must

assess which of the functions for which they receive a discount they can perform more efficiently than the seller. For example, in the toy industry, sellers
often offer a long repayment period to induce buyers to buy early. If the
buyer's cost of capital and storage costs are low, the buyer could decline this
waterfall component and instead negotiate a lower invoice price. A buyer
who is flush with cash and can obtain better freight charges on its own can
negotiate with the seller to move the freight discount waterfall component
to the cash discount waterfall component.

Clearly, the waterfall methodology is not useful in every situation. It does
not apply, for example, to products sold directly by Dell to end consumers,
to products purchased through auctions, and in industries with very few
and transparent discount components.

4.13 Key Points

1. This chapter explains the interaction between price and volume, shows
   how to compute profit, demonstrates the application of regression
   analysis, and explains price elasticity of demand.
2. The profit-maximizing price (p^*) is computed as a function of the
   unit variable cost (c) and the price elasticity ($e(p)$). It is given by
   the markup formula: $p^* = \frac{c}{[1 - 1/(e(p*))]}$. The relationship between price
   and elasticity given in the markup formula applies only to the profit-
   maximizing price. The markup formula applies only to the case of a
   monopolist. In a competitive environment, the estimate of p^* will be
   an upper bound on the price.
3. Break-even is explained and the relationship between break-even volume and price changes is demonstrated. Specifically, if α is the percentage change in the price ($\alpha > 0$ for a price increase and $\alpha < 0$
   for a price decrease) and $1 - \beta$ is the ratio of variable cost to price,
   then $\frac{\alpha}{\alpha + \beta}$ represents the volume decrease that can be tolerated for an
   α percent price increase, and $-\frac{\alpha}{\alpha + \beta}$ represents the volume increase
   needed when price is decreased α percent.
4. The problem with cost-plus pricing is that it ignores demand-side
   information and hence leads to suboptimal pricing.
5. When selling complementary goods, as in a printer and ink cartridge,
   the price of one good can be lowered because of revenue from the
   other.
6. The optimal price will be higher when profit is the criterion than when
   revenue is the criterion. That is why salespeople who are compensated

on how much revenue they produce prefer a lower price than does the company, which is focused on profit.

4.14 Technical Aside

4.14.1 Elasticity of Demand

Let $D(p)$ be the amount demanded at price p. Then, the elasticity of demand is $-(p/D)(dD/dp)$. Here $\frac{dD}{dp}$ stands for the derivative of the demand function with respect to p. Notice that, as defined, elasticity of demand is a positive number, because we expect $\frac{dD}{dp}$ to be negative.[46]

To see precisely why the definition of elasticity we use in the main body of the chapter is an approximation, consider a specific demand curve: $D = \frac{K}{p^b}$. Here, K and b are positive constants. The reader can readily verify that the elasticity of demand at all prices is b. Suppose the initial price is p_0 per unit and at that price, demand is $D_0 = \frac{K}{p_0^b}$. If the initial price is dropped by x percent to $p_1 = (1 - \frac{x}{100})p_0$, the new demand will be $D_1 = \frac{K}{p_1^b}$. Observe that

$$\frac{D_1}{D_0} = \frac{p_0^b}{p_1^b} = \frac{p_0^b}{[(1 - \frac{x}{100})p_0]^b} = \left(\frac{1}{1 - \frac{x}{100}}\right)^b = \left(1 - \frac{x}{100}\right)^{-b}.$$

Now, for x sufficiently small, $(1 - \frac{x}{100})^{-b}$ is approximately $1 + b\frac{x}{100}$.[47] In other words, D_1 is obtained by increasing D_0 by a factor of $b\frac{x}{100}$. This is precisely how we would have computed D_1 from D_0 using the (not quite correct) definition of elasticity in the main body of the chapter.

4.14.2 The Markup Formula

Here we derive the markup formula. Consider a monopolist whose cost for producing x units is $C(x)$. At price p per unit, the demand the monopolist faces is $D(p)$. The problem of computing the profit maximizing price is:

$$\max \; pD(p) - C[D(p)]$$
$$\text{s.t. } p \geq 0.$$

Assuming that the profit function is concave in p and differentiable, we can compute the price that maximizes profit by equating the first derivative of

---

[46] Others adopt a different convention, in which the elasticity is a negative number.

[47] In fact, $(1 - \frac{x}{100})^{-b} > 1 + b\frac{x}{100}$.

the profit function to zero and solving for p.

$$D(p) + p(dD/dp) - (dD/dp)C'(D(p)) = 0$$
$$\Rightarrow p - C'(D(p)) = -(D(p)/D'(p))$$
$$\Rightarrow [p - C'(D(p))]/p = 1/e(p)$$

where $e(p) = -(p/D(p))(dD/dp)$, is the elasticity of demand.

FIVE

Auctions

Auctions are a venerable selling institution, in use since the time of Herodotus. The word comes from the Latin *auctus*, meaning to increase. An obscure term for auction, one guaranteed to impress friends and neighbors, is the Latin word *subhastare*. It is the conjunction of *sub*, meaning "under," and *hasta*, meaning "spear." After a military victory, a Roman soldier would plant his spear in the ground to mark the location of his spoils. Later, he would put these goods up for sale by auction.[1]

Perhaps the most engaging tale about auctions is the sale of the Roman Empire to the highest bidder. It is described in Edward Gibbon's account of the decline and fall of the same.[2]

In 193 A.D. the Praetorian guard[3] murdered the emperor Pertinax. Sulpicianus, father-in-law to Pertinax, offered the Praetorians 5,000 drachmas per guard to be emperor. Realizing they were onto a good thing, the guard announced that the empire was available for sale to the highest bidder. Didius Julianus outbid all comers and became emperor for the price of 6,250 drachmas per guard. The description by Gibbon is worth a read:

This infamous offer, the most insolent excess of military license, diffused an universal grief, shame, and indignation throughout the city. It reached at length the ears of Didius Julianus, a wealthy senator, who, regardless of the public calamities, was

---

[1] The highest bidder was called the *emptor*, whence the term *caveat emptor*.

[2] "It was at Rome, on the 15th of October 1764," Gibbon writes, "as I sat musing amid the ruins of the capitol, while the bare-footed friars were singing vespers in the temple of Jupiter, that the idea of writing the decline and fall of the city first started to my mind." Seventy-one chapters, 2136 paragraphs, a million and a half words, 8000 footnotes, and one American revolution later, Gibbon produced *The Decline and Fall of the Roman Empire*. The incident of the auction is described in chapter V, volume I.

[3] Bodyguard of the Emperor.

indulging himself in the luxury of the table. His wife and his daughter, his freedmen and his parasites, easily convinced him that he deserved the throne, and earnestly conjured him to embrace so fortunate an opportunity. The vain old man hastened to the Praetorian camp, where Sulpicianus was still in treaty with the guards, and began to bid against him from the foot of the rampart.

He was beheaded two months later when Septimus Severus conquered Rome.

In our discussion of auctions, we focus first on the case of a seller wishing to sell a single object to two or more bidders.[4] In general, it makes sense to run an auction only when the available supply of what is to be sold is less than the potential demand for it. In other words, to sell by auction presumes some form of monopoly power. In the absence of such power, there is nothing to compel the attendance of bidders at an auction.

Four popular auction forms are used in the sale of a single object.

1. **English ascending**

   This comes in two versions. The first is an *open cry auction*, in which bidders cry out their bids, with each bid being higher than the previous bid. The auction ends when no participant is willing to bid further, at which point the highest bidder wins the object and pays the price bid.

   The second, called a *clock auction*, involves an auctioneer setting the price. The price is initially set to zero and subsequently raised. If bidders desire the object at the current price they raise their hands. If the price exceeds what bidders wish to pay they need only drop their hands to exit the auction. A bidder who exits the auction is not permitted to participate again. As long as as at least two bidders have their hands raised, the price continues rising. The price stops rising the moment exactly one bidder remains with a raised hand. The remaining bidder wins the good at the terminal price.

2. **Sealed-bid second price**

   Bidders submit sealed bids. The highest bidder is awarded the good and charged the the second highest bid. This auction is also called the *Vickrey auction*, in honor of the Nobel laureate William Vickrey, who is credited with its invention and analysis. However, such auctions were

---

[4] The discussion applies, with obvious modifications, to procurement auctions. However, procurement introduces wrinkles not typically present in sales situations. For this reason we defer a discussion of auctions in procurement to Chapter 7.

in existence before Vickrey wrote about them. They were and continue to be used for the sale of rare stamps, for example.

3. **Sealed-bid first price**
   Bidders submit sealed bids. The highest bidder is awarded the good and pays the bid.
4. **Dutch descending**[5]
   The price is initially set at some large number, one that exceeds the RPs of all bidders and then declines. The first bidder to call out "stop" gets the good at the price at which a stop was called.

It is possible to both imagine and point to auctions for the sale of a single good that differ from these four. These differences are usually cosmetic and, in any case, tend to be quite rare. The obvious question to be answered is which of these auction forms is best for the seller. This is the focus of this chapter.

Two aspects of an auction deserve comment. First, the auctioneer plays an important role. A good auctioneer drums up excitement for the object being sold[6] and decides whose bids are recognized and whose are not. In this way, the auctioneer can favor a "regular" bidder/customer over an occasional bidder.[7] Second, careful thought must be given to the terms of sale. As an illustration, we reproduce the terms of sale from an eighteenth-century auction.[8]

1. The high bidder is the buyer. If a dispute arises as to which bid is highest, goods will be put up for sale again.
2. No bidder may advance another's bid by less than six pence when the amount offered is less than one pound, or by less than one shilling when the price is one pound or more.
3. Merchandise for sale is warranted as perfect, and before removing goods from premises, any buyer may accept or reject them.
4. Each buyer must give his name and make a deposit of 5 shillings on each pound sterling (if demanded); no deliveries will be made during the sale.

[5] This type of auction is called Dutch descending because it is used to auction tulips in Holland.
[6] This is true even in the online setting, in which the auctioneer designs the interface and thereby affects the attractiveness the site.
[7] Some auctioneers also "invent" bids. This is called "pulling a bid off the wall" and, in more aristocratic settings, as "pulling a bid off the chandelier."
[8] Adapted from Cassady (1979).

5. All purchases must be taken away at the buyer's expense, and the amount due shall be paid within three days of purchase.
6. Any would-be buyer unable to attend the sale may have his commission executed by a representative of the auction firm.

Item 1 recognizes the possibility that things can, and do, go wrong in an auction and specifies what will be done in such an eventuality.[9] Item 2 specifies an increment rule to ensure that an auction progresses with reasonable celerity. Item 3 specifies who is responsible for verifying the quality of the asset sold. In item 4, a deposit is required to screen out bidders who are not serious or lack the money to bid seriously. Item 5 specifies who is responsible for delivering the item. Item 6 allows a buyer to use an agent.

5.1 The Benchmark Model

How should one bid, and what is the revenue that the auctioneer will obtain? The second question cannot be answered before the first. To answer them requires a model of how bidders value the object and their attitude to risk. We describe this in the **benchmark model**.

1. Because some auctions (as we will see later) involve a degree of risk, we must specify the risk attitudes of the buyer and seller. We assume that both buyer and seller are risk neutral. This means they evaluate and select among risky choices according to the expected payoffs those choices will yield.
2. Bidders' RPs are private information to themselves and independent draws from some distribution (the independent private values model). The independence condition means that knowing one bidder's RP gives no clue about another's RP. Furthermore, should a bidder discover another bidder's RP, that would not influence his or her own RP. Knowing another's RP may influence a bid but not the RP's value. These assumptions hold when the object sold is for private consumption only. An example of such a situation might be bidding for the chance to dine with Queen Elizabeth II.[10] Different people will value this opportunity differently. Discovering that one's neighbor likens the experience to a reading of Vogon poetry is unlikely

---

[9] Other examples include what is to be done in the event of a tie or a winning bidder subsequently withdrawing.

[10] Assuming, of course, that such a right was not transferable.

to influence the monetary value that one attaches to such an opportunity.[11]

3. Bidders are homogenous in the sense that all bidders' RPs are drawn from the same distribution. This is a technical condition whose meaning will become clearer later.

4. The auctioneer and bidders obey the rules of the auction. Thus we rule out, for the moment, the possibility of collusion among the bidders and cheating on the part of the seller.

5. The auction occurs in a vacuum. This condition allows us to ignore the effects of an active secondary market for the good where the winner of the auction might resell to one of the losers or the possibility of future auctions involving the same set of bidders.

Next, one must understand what constitutes a bidding strategy. A *bidding strategy* is a rule that specifies the bid one should submit as a function of one's RP. Thus a strategy is not a single number, but a rule. This seems odd. If one's RP for the object is $10, is this not the only number that should influence one's bid? No. It matters also how others will bid and that, in turn, depends on what their RPs are. Thus, one needs to put oneself in their shoes and ask, given *their* RPs, how they would bid. One way we get a handle on this is to ask how we would bid if our RP was different from $10.

In the following sections we assume that the number of bidders is n and therefore there are up to n different RPs in the room. Denote by v_n^1 the largest RP from this set of RPs and by v_n^2 the second largest RP.

5.1.1 English Ascending

The simplest of the four popular auctions to analyze under the benchmark model is the clock variant of the English ascending auction.

What bidding strategy should one adopt in an English auction? Under the independent private values model, the identities of bidders who are still active in the auction is entirely irrelevant. All that matters to a bidder is the current price. As long as that price is below one's RP, one should keep one's hand raised. The instant the price slides past one's RP, drop out. The

---

[11] According to *The Hitchhiker's Guide to the Galaxy*, "Vogon poetry is . . . the third worst in the Universe. The second worst is that of the Azgoths of Kria. During a recitation by their Poet Master Grunthos the Flatulent, of his poem 'Ode to a Small Lump of Green Putty I Found in My Armpit One Midsummer Morning,' four of his audience members died of internal hemorrhaging, and the president of the Mid-Galactic Arts Nobbling Council survived by gnawing one of his own legs off.

auction stops when there is exactly one bidder left. This happens the first time the price inches past v_n^2. Assuming the price increments in the English auction are vanishingly small, it means that the auction terminates with a price of v_n^2, the second highest RP. The bidder with the highest RP wins the auction and pays v_n^2.

5.1.2 Sealed-Bid Second Price

This auction has the curious property that one's bid does not determine one's payment. The bid, however, does determine the chance of winning. The higher the bid (other bids held fixed), the higher the chance of winning. These two observations conspire to yield the conclusion that the right bidding strategy is to bid one's RP.

To understand why, consider two cases. First, suppose one bids below one's RP – of v, say. This can only lower the chance of winning the object and cannot influence the payment one makes conditional on winning. Now, suppose one bids an amount $b > v$. The only way this could be an improvement over bidding v is if one wins the object with a bid of b and loses it with a bid of v. If this is the case, someone must have submitted a bid x such that $b > x > v$. Therefore, when one bids b and wins, one must pay at least $x > v$, which is more than it is worth to oneself.

Logic dictates that everyone else will follow the same strategy. Therefore, the bidder with the highest RP wins the auction and pays the second highest bid, which in this case will be v_n^2. Notice that this auction and the English ascending both generate a revenue of v_n^2 for the seller.

5.1.3 Sealed-Bid First Price

The analysis of the sealed-bid first price auction is more complicated. If one's RP is v, clearly one should not bid above v. What about shading one's bid down? This reduces the probability of winning. However, if one wins, one pays less than one otherwise would. Thus, there is a trade-off to be made between the probability of winning and the payoff to be obtained conditional on winning.

To think about how much one should shade down from one's RP, one can assume that one's RP, v, is the largest (if this assumption is false, it does not matter). If one's RP is the highest, guess the value of the second highest RP and bid a shade above that. Because RPs are random variables in our model, we can replace the operation of guessing by computing an expected value.[12] The important point is to compute the expected value of the second highest RP conditional on one's RP being the largest, and bid a hair's breadth above that. Formally, one should submit a bid of $E(v_n^2|v_n^1 = v)$. The analysis that supports this conclusion can be found in the Technical Aside that appears at the end of this chapter.

The expression $E(v_n^2|v_n^1 = v)$ increases with v. If a bidder employs this bidding strategy, the higher the RP, the higher the bid. If all bidders employ this strategy, bidders with higher RPs submit higher bids than those with lower RPs. Why all bidders should follow this same strategy is not entirely obvious and is discussed in the technical aside at the end of the chapter. However, supposing they do, the bidder with the highest RP will submit the winning bid, which, on average, will be $E(v_n^2)$. Thus, the seller makes $E(v_n^2)$ in revenue.

The amount by which a bidder should shade down depends on the distribution of the RPs and the number of bidders. In general, as the number of bidders increases, the amount one should shade down declines. This is to be expected, as an increase in the number of bidders increases competition. Thus, shading down can only decrease the probability of winning as the number of bidders increases.

5.1.4 Dutch Descending

The Dutch descending auction, though cosmetically different, is equivalent to the sealed-bid first price auction. Why? In the Dutch auction, each bidder must decide in private when he or she will call out "stop" and must do so at the moment the price drops to that level. Imagine that each bidder were to write down on paper the price at which he or she would call a stop. Instead of running the auction, we could just examine the slips of paper and award the object to the bidder who wrote the largest number on their slip and charge that amount. The outcome would be identical to running the auction itself.

5.1.5 Revenue Comparison

The revenues to be had from the four auctions is summarized in Table 5.1.

Under the benchmark model, all four auctions award the object to the bidder with the highest RP. Therefore, in expectation, all four auctions

---

[12] Recall from statistics that the best estimate of the value of a random variable is its expected value.

Table 5.1. *Auction Revenues*

Auction	Revenue
English Ascending	v_n^2
Sealed-Bid second-price	v_n^2
Sealed-Bid first-price	$E(v_n^2)$
Dutch Descending	$E(v_n^2)$

generate the same revenue, $E(v_n^2)$. Thus, under the benchmark model, there is no reason to prefer one of the four auctions to another. A common feature of all four auctions is that the expected revenue increases with the number of bidders. This is intuitive; more competition means higher prices.

The reason all four auctions generate the same expected revenue is that bidders adapt their bidding strategies to the rules of the auction. This is something commonly overlooked by naive observers of auctions. To illustrate the error this leads to, suppose a seller ran a second-price auction in which the two highest bids were $2,000 and $1,500. In this case, the seller obtains a revenue of $1,500. Could the seller not have done better by running a first-price auction instead, so gaining $2,000? No, because the bidder who submitted the $2,000 bid in a second-price auction would submit a different (lower) bid when faced with a first-price auction.

Using a Reserve
Can one do better in terms of revenue than the preceding four auctions? Yes, provided the seller is willing to assume more risk by withholding the good. This can be done by announcing a reserve price (called the *reserve*).[13] If no bid exceeds the reserve (which is set in advance), the good is not sold. In the event that the winning bid exceeds the reserve, the winning bidder must pay an amount no smaller than the reserve. One can think of the reserve as a bid by the seller. Any winning bid must exceed the seller's bid. This increases competitive pressure on the buyers and drives up expected revenues. The drawback is that there is a chance that the object will go unsold if no bid exceeds the reserve. To see how a reserve may help, suppose two bidders with RPs of $5 and $8. A seller using a second-price auction clears a revenue of $5. However, if the seller had chosen the reserve to be $6, say, the seller would have cleared $6 instead. On the other hand, had the RPs been $5 and $4 instead, no sale would have taken place.

---

[13] Not to be confused with reserv*ation* price.

If the reserve chosen is too large, then with high probability the object will be unsold, reducing expected revenues. If the reserve is too small, it becomes irrelevant. The optimal choice of the reserve strikes a balance between these outcomes. It should be chosen to be the price the seller would quote if there was a single buyer. In other words, it is the optimal posted price to a single buyer. One way to see why this is reasonable is that one cannot be certain about the number of bidders who will turn up. Therefore, one should guard against the possibility of only a single bidder turning up. In this case, one would wish to sell by posted price (see Section 4.7).

To state this formally, let F be the distribution of RPs. Next, determine the value of p that maximizes $p(1 - F(p))$. Call it p^*. This is the optimal choice of a reserve. In fact, under the benchmark model, the auction design that maximizes expected revenue to the seller is a second-price auction with the reserve set at p^*. Why this is so is beyond the scope of this book.

As the number of bidders gets large, the reserve price p^* loses its bite. This is because as n gets large, the second highest RP, v^2, will exceed p^* with high probability. Thus, a reserve price matters only in auctions with a small number of bidders – and it can matter a lot. In the last decade of the twentieth century, New Zealand used a second-price auction without a reserve to sell spectrum licenses. In one of the auctions, an incumbent license holder bid NZ $7 million but had to pay only the second highest bid of NZ $5,000.

Is there a benefit to setting a reserve but keeping it secret? Within the confines of the benchmark model, no. If one steps outside the benchmark model, there are reasons to keep the reserve secret; we discuss these later. Should one set the reserve after seeing all the bids? If the bidders are aware that the seller will do this, they incorporate it into their bidding by bidding less aggressively. On balance, the seller probably winds up worse off. Can one set a reserve price after the bids are in but without informing the bidders of this? Yes. In practice this is accomplished through the use of a counterfeit or *shill* bid, and is usually illegal.

5.1.6 Auctions versus Posted Price

A rather obvious question is whether a seller would better off selling a product via an auction or a posted price. We answer this question in a limited way by comparing a second-price auction with a posted price under the benchmark model.

For simplicity, assume that there are three bidders with RPs independently and uniformly distributed between 0 and 1. Let v_1, v_2, and v_3 be the RPs of buyers 1, 2, and 3 respectively. A risk-neutral seller is selling one unit of SOMA. If the seller chooses a posted price p, the probability that at least one person will buy at that price will be

$$1 - Pr(v_1, v_2, v_3 < p) = 1 - Pr(v_1 < p)Pr(v_2 < p)Pr(v_3 < p) = 1 - p^3.$$

Thus, the seller's expected revenue will be $p(1 - p^3)$. The revenue-maximizing price will be $(1/4)^{1/3} = 0.63$. Expected revenue will be 0.47.

In the second-price auction, the unit of SOMA will sell for the second highest RP. With three bidders, the second highest RP is the median of $\{v_1, v_2, v_3\}$. The expected value of the median of three numbers uniformly distributed between 0 and 1 is $1/2$. Thus, the one unit of SOMA sells on average for 0.5, yielding an expected revenue of 0.5.

Thus, the auction yields a lower expected price than posted price (0.5 versus 0.63) but a higher expected revenue (0.5 versus 0.47). How can that be? Risk. In an auction, when the object sells at a particular price, it *sells at that price*. With a posted price, there is no guarantee that the object will be sold. In fact, in this example, the probability that the unit of SOMA is sold at the price 0.63 is 0.75 $(= 1 - (0.63)^3)$. A posted price strategy must live with the uncertainty about the buyer's RP. Auctions, through competition among buyers, reduces this uncertainty and results in higher expected revenues. However, as the number of bidders increases, the gap in revenue between posted price and auction diminishes. Thus, an auction (without reserve) dominates selling by posted price only when there are few bidders (but at least three).

5.1.7 Auctions versus Posted Price (Encore)

We revisit the comparison, but this time allow the seller the flexibility to choose the number of units of SOMA to offer. In particular, the seller can produce as many units as there are buyers. To keep the arithmetic uncluttered, assume the unit cost of SOMA is zero.

Assume n bidders, each wanting at most one unit of SOMA, with RPs independently and uniformly distributed between 0 and 1. If the seller posts a price p per unit of SOMA, each buyer will purchase with probability $(1 - p)$. Hence, the expected revenue will be $np(1 - p)$. The price that maximizes expected revenue will be $p = 0.5$, yielding an expected revenue of $0.25n$.

Suppose the seller decides to run an auction and, for simplicity, suppose the seller runs a $k + 1$st price auction. In such an auction, k units are offered, the k highest bidders win a unit each but pay the $k + 1$st highest price. This auction is the natural generalization of the second-price auction and has the same incentive properties. Each bidder bids truthfully. If the seller offers k units, the seller makes in revenue k times the $k + $1st highest RP. It turns out that the expected value of the $k + $1st highest RP is $\frac{n-k}{n+1}$. Thus, the expected revenue from auctioning off k units in this way will be $\frac{k(n-k)}{n+1}$. To maximize expected revenue, the seller must choose k to maximize $k(n - k)$.[14] This last expression can be rewritten as $nx(1 - x)$ where $x = k/n$. Now, compare $nx(1 - x)$ with $np(1 - p)$. The expected revenue from both the auction and the posted price are the same.[15] Thus, there is no reason to prefer the auction over the posted price.

How do we reconcile the two conclusions? The reconciliation hinges on the supply that the seller controls. If supply is fixed and less than the potential demand over the relevant time horizon, then the seller is better off with an auction. Unique works of art are obvious examples and, indeed, these are usually sold at auction.

Tickets for certain sporting events should also be sold at auction, according to the analysis advanced here. Indeed, this is starting to happen. In March 2009, the Chicago Board of Exchange offered tickets via auction for the 71 seats it has in the stadium where the Chicago Cubs play.[16]

The supply of hotel rooms and cinema and airplane seats is also fixed over the short term. One cannot rustle up an additional hotel room just to accommodate an extra guest. Therefore, in these cases they should be sold at auction – and in fact are, but not in a form easily recognized. The auctioneer initially sets the price low. As demand increases, the price rises to the point at which demand just meets supply. Yield management systems for pricing airline seats follow a similar logic (but are more elaborate in their implementation). In both cases these are auctions similiar to the clock version of the English auction, in which the seller calls out the price and bidders register their demand.

Cinema tickets would also seem a natural candidate for sale by auction. Indeed, the *Financial Times* on April 3, 2003, reported the following:

Like other Easy-branded ventures, EasyCinema will adjust prices according to demand, with charges of 20p for those prepared to book online a month in advance for a Tuesday afternoon performance. For last-minute bookings, prices will rise to

---

[14] Because $n + 1$ is a constant, maximizing $\frac{k(n-k)}{n+1}$ is the same as maximizing $k(n - k)$.

[15] If you are worried that this might be an artifact of the choice of auction, rest easy. It is not.

[16] The Cubs are a major league baseball team based in Chicago. Apparently, the team was once cursed by a goat and is doomed now to never win the World Series. The 71 seats are adjacent to the Cubs' dugout on the third-base line. This is an unnecessary detail needed to give color to what would otherwise be a dull and uninspiring narrative.

nearer 5 pounds. Costs will also be kept down by doing away with a box office, admissions staff and popcorn counters.

Although the number of seats in the cinema is fixed, viewers are sufficiently flexible about when they attend, so the supply is not limited with respect to the demand.[17] In addition, there is a possibility that the clearing price at auction would be used to infer the quality of the movie. This would be a more compelling signal than a movie review. As it happens, EasyCinema had a rough time of it because distributors were not prepared to release new films to the company. In part this is because a low price for seats at a movie would serve as tangible signal of the quality of the movie. EasyCinema's choice not to sell popcorn or drinks to patrons also reduced its revenue. The cinema lasted three years, closing in 2006. The company continues as a movie rental service.

If supply is flexible – think cars and diapers – it makes no difference which method is chosen. Either one is choosing a price and letting the market decide the quantity, or one is choosing a quantity and letting the market decide the price. In both cases, the expected revenue is the same.

5.1.8 An eBay Interlude

eBay is the largest online auction marketplace in the world. In 1998 it had 2 million registered users. At the end of 2010, the number had grown to 94.5 million active registered accounts globally; these are users who have bid on, bought, or listed an item in the most recent twelve-month period.

In an eBay auction, the seller can post a single item or multiple units of the same item. For an additional fee, the seller can set a reserve price that can be kept secret or made public. Starting in late 2000, the seller could also sell the item at "buy-it-now" or fixed price.[18] The buy-it-now option is not available once the auction starts.

The simplest form of an eBay auction begins with the seller specifying a start time, end time, opening price, and bid increment. The auction itself is like the clock version of the English auction conducted through agents. In the offline world, a bidder can choose to turn up at the auction in person or send an agent on his or her behalf. Typically, the instructions for the agents would specify the maximum amount they should bid (the ceiling). At the auction, the agent would simply remain active in the bidding until

[17] This is also true of some airline passengers. See the section on yield management to see how this is handled.
[18] The "buy-it-now" feature had been introduced earlier by other auction sites, such as U-bid.

the price exceeded the given ceiling. On eBay, the role of the agent is played by a program that will bid on the bidder's behalf. To initiate the program, it suffices to set a ceiling (called the *proxy bid*).

At the start of the auction, the "clock" will display the opening price set by the seller – say, for example, $100. Suppose the bid increment chosen is $5. When the first bidder arrives, the bidder enters a proxy bid, say, $250. There is no change in the price displayed on the clock. If no other bids are entered during the remainder of the auction, the lone bidder will secure the object for sale at a price of $100. Suppose a second bidder arrives. This bidder will see two items of information: the current price on the clock and the number of bidders who have bid so far. Suppose the second bidder enters a proxy bid of $125. The price on the clock now moves upward to one increment above $125 – that is, $130.[19] Suppose a third bidder arrives and submits a proxy bid of $300. Then the price on the clock would rise to $255. At any time, the price on the clock registers one increment above the second highest proxy bid.

At any time during an auction, a bidder can revise his or her proxy bid. In our example, the second bidder to arrive could, if he or she wished at some later time (before the end of the auction), revise the proxy bid upward. If the bidder did so after the third bidder arrived and changed it to $335, the price on the clock would increase to $305. In short the eBay auction is an example of a second-price auction in which the winning bidder pays the price bid by the second highest bidder (plus an increment).

Let us see how the conclusions of the benchmark model coincide with the behavior one sees on eBay. The most benign and uncontroversial of those conclusions is that increasing the number of bidders can only increase revenue for the seller. Consequently, we would expect to see individual sellers making investments to increase the pool of bidders that bid on their items. We see this, for example, in the way products are described and displayed.

What about the use of a reserve price? Because many auctions have only a small number of bidders (as discussed later), the benchmark model says that a reserve price should be used.[20] This is the case with a large number of auctions using a reserve.[21] In some cases, the reserve is kept secret (some estimates put it at about 14 percent of cases). Recall that

---

[19] If a new bidder submits a proxy bid below the current clock price, it is ignored.

[20] Although the opening price can act as a reserve price, a seller can set a reserve that exceeds the opening price.

[21] The evidence for this is anecdotal.

under the benchmark model nothing is gained (or lost) by keeping the reserve secret. Sellers sometimes prefer a secret reserve so as not to deter potential buyers who are uncertain about what the item on sale is worth to them. A low opening price (but not so low as to raise suspicion) may attract a buyer to submit a bid. Then, one hopes that the excitement of bidding (a phenomenon known as *competitive arousal*) takes over, causing them to up their bids. To ensure that the item is not sold for a song, the seller sets a reserve that exceeds the opening price. Had the seller published the reserve, this hypothetical bidder may have been deterred from bidding in the first place. The empirical evidence in support of this, however, is weak.

It was argued earlier that under the benchmark model, selling by auction dominates posted price when the supply was limited. If so, why did eBay introduce the option of selling by posted price, the "buy-it-now" option? For rare items such as works of art and antique weapons, the buy-it-now option should not be offered or fixed at a level at which it is unlikely to be used.[22] What about commodity goods in large supply, such as books, laptops, and camcorders? Although any one seller may have a limited supply of these items, from the point of view of the buyer, the number of different sellers selling the same item means that the supply is unlimited. If a buyer does not win the laptop of choice in the current auction, there is always another auction taking place for the same item. Indeed, how should a buyer choose which of the many auctions for the laptop of interest to participate in? Controlling for the quality and reliability of the seller, the buyer should bid in the auction that has the fewest number of bidders, as that will have the least competition. If the supply of laptops exceeds the demand, there will be a small number of bidders (two or three) at each auction, so the laptops are essentially sold at the reserve price.[23] Thus, for all practical purposes, the items are sold at posted prices. In fact, a June 2008 article in *Business Week* notes that eBay's chief, John Donahoe, believes that fixed price items are essential to future growth.[24] The buy-it-now option merely recognizes this fact. A second reason is that some buyers are impatient. This option allows them to purchase immediately without waiting until the end of the auction. In this case, the buy-it-now price should include a premium for allowing

[22] Think of it as a sucker's price.
[23] This estimate of the number of bidders per auction is based on half a million auctions on both the U.S. and Korean eBay sites. The data can be found in Kahng and Yang (2006).
[24] As of December 2010, fixed price sales were about 60 percent of eBay's gross merchandise volume.

a buyer immediate purchase. All of this seems to be well understood by experienced eBay sellers, as evinced by the following:[25]

"If you sell an item or class of items (say, clothing or CDs) which you have a lot of and which you list and sell at a predictable price, then take-it prices make a lot of sense," said Dave Michmerhuizen, who sells postcards on eBay. "A bidder is often willing to pay a few dollars more to eliminate competition and get the item sooner."

But for more individual or rarer items, the auction model works out best for the seller, he said.

"If you sell collectibles, take-it prices make less or no sense. Often these sellers have no good idea what an item is worth. Instead, they just start it and let the auction format determine the worth," he said.

Given that eBay runs a second-price auction, should one submit a single proxy bid with a value equal to one's RP? For commodity items, such as CDs and cameras that closely approximate the independent private values assumption, the answer is yes. Does it matter when one submits one's proxy bid? In theory, no. However, in the presence of bidders who revise their proxy bids during the course of an auction, there is a slight advantage to submitting one's bid at the last minute (called *sniping*). Doing so does not allow such bidders a chance to top one's bid. If one waits till the last minute, however, there is a chance that one's bid may not "get through." On balance, it appears one winds up ahead, but the benefit appears to be slender at best.

5.2 Beyond Benchmark

Under the benchmark model there is no reason for a seller to prefer one of the four popular auctions to the other. If one departs from the benchmark model, differences between the four auctions reveal themselves. It is these differences we examine in this section.

5.2.1 Risk

A risk-averse agent is one who would pick a certain outcome over a risky prospect even if the expected payoff from the risky prospect was higher than the certain outcome. For example, if option A involves a sure return of \$45 and option B involves a payoff of \$100 or nothing with equal probability, a sufficiently risk-averse agent would pick option A over option B. In

---

[25] From a January 28th, 2000 column by Margaret Kane in *ZDNET.co.uk* titled "Is eBay moving beyond auctions?"

other words, this agent is willing to trade higher expected returns for lower variance or, equivalently, more certainty.

If bidders are risk-averse rather than risk-neutral, the first-price or Dutch auction generate a higher expected revenue for the seller than the English or second-price auction. The intuition is that risk-averse bidders are willing to sacrifice profitability for an increased chance at winning the auction.

If a seller is risk-averse, then she will prefer the first price and Dutch auction to the other two as well. Even though all four auctions generate the same expected revenue, the English and second-price auctions have a higher variance. In the English and second-price auctions, the winning bidder pays v_n^2, whereas in the other two the winning bidder pays $E(v_n^2)$. The first is the random variable itself, and the second is the expectation of that random variable, which has a lower variance.

5.2.2 Common Values

The polar opposite of the independent private values is called *common values*. Here, all bidders would agree on the value of the asset being sold, but none knows what that value is. However, each is in possession of information (called *signals*) that allows them to estimate the true value of the asset. Because the signals bidders may have differ, the estimates they form may be different. A toy example will clarify the setup.

Imagine an opaque box containing 1000 marbles colored red and blue. Each red marble is worth \$1 and each blue marble is worth nothing. Thus, the value of the box depends only on the number of red marbles it contains. Imagine now that the box is to be sold at auction, by, say, a sealed-bid second-price auction to bidders, none of whom knows what has just been described. In particular, none knows the quantity of red marbles in the box. Observe that if the contents of the box were revealed, bidders would agree on the value of the box – hence, the "common" in common values.

Suppose that before the auction began, each bidder was allowed to scoop up 100 marbles selected at random, and then replace them. The proportion of red marbles in the sample would be the only clue the bidder would have to the actual number of red marbles in the box. A bidder who obtains a sample with a large fraction of red marbles will have a higher estimate of the number of red marbles in the box than a bidder who draws a sample with a small proportion of red marbles.

A real-life version of the auction of the opaque box involves bidding on oil leases. Such leases entitle the holder to a portion of the revenues from oil pumped out of the ground from a specified tract of land. Once pumping begins, bidders will agree on the value of the lease. Before that event, none knows the value of the oil that resides below the surface. Frequently, the seller of the lease will allow potential bidders to survey the tract in question to estimate its revenue potential. Because survey methods and how the results are interpreted differ, bidders may draw different conclusions about the revenue potential of the lease.

A particularly vivid example of an auction with a large common values component is the sale of spectrum licenses. The value of a license is a function of the traffic that will travel on that portion of the spectrum. Bidders have different estimates of this traffic volume based on different information sources.

Although there is a common values aspect to this environment, it is far from being a pure common values environment. The value of the license also depends on how the relevant portion of spectrum is priced and managed by the owner. These are things that are idiosyncratic to each bidder, introducing a private values component. These are not the only complications. In practice, multiple licenses are to be auctioned. Thus, the value of a license will also depend on the competition between eventual winners of other licenses. This means that bidders care not just about what they win, but also about what their rivals win as well. A full discussion of these added complications is beyond the scope of this book.

Let us return to our auction of the opaque box and suppose that there are just two bidders. Assume that the first bidder draws a sample with a small fraction of red marbles and the second bidder draws a sample with a large fraction of red marbles. Then, in the auction, the first bidder's bid is likely to be much smaller than the second bidder's bid. The second bidder wins and potentially pays a song for the box. Contrast this with what might happen if the box were sold in an open English ascending auction. The first bidder, seeing the second bidder outbid him, may be influenced to raise his or her bid. The logic is that the second bidder must have seen more red marbles than the first bidder did, so causing the second bidder to revise upward his or her estimate of the number of red marbles. In this case, good news (a large number of red marbles in a sample) for one is good news for all. In this environment, an open ascending auction generates a higher expected revenue than a sealed bid auction. If one sees one's rivals bidding aggressively, it must be because they have a high signal. This suggests that they possess good news. Knowing this, one should revise one's own estimate of the value of the good. In a sealed-bid auction, the information that others have is not revealed to others.

Inexperienced bidders participating in an auction with a large common values component are susceptible to a phenomenon known as the **winner's curse**. The winner is cursed because on winning the object, the winner realizes that it is worth far less than what was bid for it. To see why this is the case, imagine a transparent jar filled with pennies that is to be auctioned off to the highest bidder, who will pay that bid. A popular bidding strategy begins by estimating the value of the pennies found in the jar and then submitting a bid below this estimate. The degree by which one shades down depends on the perceived intensity of competition for the jar. If every bidder follows this strategy, the bidder with the largest estimate of the value of the pennies will probably have the highest bid and win the jar. However, the largest estimate from among a large group of bidders will probably be a gross overestimate of the value of the pennies. Thus, the winning bidder is likely to have overpaid for the jar. The following example is more explicit.

Example 13 *Cato owns a company whose exact value is known only to him. Pliny wishes to buy the company. Under Pliny's management, the company will be worth 1.5 times more than it is worth under Cato's management.[26] For example, if the company is worth $20 million under Cato, it will be worth $30 million under Pliny.*

Pliny makes a take-it-or-leave-it offer to Cato for the company. If the offer exceeds what the company is worth to Cato, Cato will accept and sell the company to Pliny. The difficulty is that Pliny does not know the current worth of the company.[27] What price should Pliny offer?

Suppose that Pliny's uncertainty about the current value of the company can be modeled as a random draw from a uniform distribution between 0 and $100 million. According to this assumption, the company under Cato's management is worth, on average, $50 million.[28] Thus, it seems natural to make an offer, at or under $50 million. However, the lower the offer, the lower the chance of Cato accepting it. A naive Pliny might construct Table 5.2 to assess the tradeoff.

The first column lists the possible bids Pliny is considering. The second column lists Pliny's assessment of the chance that Cato will accept the offer. The

---

[26] Perhaps Pliny is a better manager, or there are synergies to be found, and so on.
[27] In practice, Pliny would investigate the company he is intending to buy before making an offer. The information gleaned from such an exercise will reduce, but can never eliminate entirely, the uncertainty associated with the worth of the company.
[28] Which means that, on average, the company is worth $75 million to Pliny.

Table 5.2. *Naive Trade-Off (M = million)*

Offer	Probability of Cato Accepting	Expected Profit
$50 M	1	$(75 - 50) \times 1.0 = \$25$ M
$40 M	0.9	$(75 - 40) \times 0.9 = \$31.5$ M
$35 M	0.75	$(75 - 35) \times 0.75 = \$30$ M
$30 M	0.5	$(75 - 30) \times 0.5 = \$22.5$ M
< $30 M	0	0

last column is the expected profit of the corresponding offer. This table suggests that an offer of $40 M is best.

However, the table seriously overstates the profit that Pliny will make. To see why, suppose Pliny makes an offer of $40 M, which is subsequently accepted. In the instant that it is accepted, Pliny learns that the company is worth less than $40 M; otherwise, Cato would have declined the offer. Knowing now that the company is worth less than $40 M, we know that on average the company must be worth $20 M. Thus, on average, the company, under Pliny's management, will be worth $1.5 \times \$20$ M $= \$30$ M, less than what he paid for it. Therefore, on average, Pliny loses money. This is the winner's curse.

The mistake is to base the offer on the expected value of the company under Cato's management. This is incorrect because it ignores the information revealed when Cato accepts an offer. What Pliny should be trying to estimate is the expected value of the company given that Cato accepts an offer of $40 M. With this in mind, Table 5.2 should be amended to Table 5.3.

In other words, if Pliny wins, he loses. □.

Sophisticated bidders make bids that account for the winner's curse. When thinking about submitting a bid, b, say, the sophisticated bidder asks, "What would I conclude if b is the highest bid?" Presumably the other

Table 5.3. *Sophisticated Trade-Off*

Offer	Probability of Cato Accepting	Expected Profit
$50 M	1	$((\frac{50}{2}) \times 1.5 - 50) \times 1 = -\$12.5$ M
$40 M	0.9	$((\frac{40}{2}) \times 1.5 - 40) \times 0.9 = -\$9$ M
$35 M	0.75	$((\frac{35}{2}) \times 1.5 - 35) \times 0.75 = -\$6.56$ M
$30 M	0.5	$((\frac{30}{2}) \times 1.5 - 30) \times 0.5 = -\$3.75$ M
< $30 M	0	0

bidders had much lower estimates of the value of the asset. This causes our sophisticated bidder to lower his or her own estimate of the value of the asset. The net effect is that the sophisticated bidder bids more cautiously. If all bidders are sophisticated, the winner's curse becomes a seller's curse instead, in that bidders submit bids well below the expected value of the asset, conditional on their information.

5.2.3 Heterogeneous Bidders

In the benchmark model, it was assumed that the RPs of all bidders were drawn from the same distribution. When this is not true – for example, when some bidders' RPs are in the interval from 5 to 10, whereas others are in the interval 0 to 5, say – bidders are said to be *heterogeneous*.

Such heterogeneity can reduce a seller's revenue. Bidders with relatively low RPs do not provide competitive pressure on bidders with relatively high RPs. As an extreme example, suppose one bidder has an RP between 5 and 10, and all other bidders have RPs between 0 and 5. The lone bidder with the relatively high RP knows that a bid slightly above 5 will secure the object no matter which of the four auctions is used.

When it is possible to link this difference in bidders to observable characteristics such as age, minority status or company type, the seller can do better through the selective use of subsidies or reserve prices. Specifically, the seller should subsidize bidders who are likely to have relatively low RPs and/or impose reserve price on bidders who are likely to have relatively high RPs. By favoring bidders with low RPs, the seller encourages bidders with high RPs to bid more. This is essentially a form of price discrimination done via the medium of an auction. In the U.S. auction for spectrum licenses from the last decade of the twentieth century, minority-owned companies were subsidized. The subsidy took the form of discount off their bid for a license, should they win it. These subsidies allowed the minority-owned companies to bid more aggressively, thereby putting competitive pressure on the nonminority bidders, causing them to bid more.

5.2.4 Violating the Rules

All four popular auctions are vulnerable, in varying degrees, to collusion among the bidders. Collusion by bidders will involve an agreement among a subset (called a *bidding ring*) that exactly one of them will participate seriously in the auction, and that sole participating bidder will compensate the others upon winning.[29] Nonparticipation can take two forms. The first is the obvious one of not submitting a bid at all. The second is to submit a bid so low that there is no realistic chance of winning. In both cases, the effect is to reduce competition and thereby lower the seller's revenue. Such collusive agreements can be sustained only if members of the ring are able to monitor their mutual compliance. For example, a sealed-bid auction in which the winner is not publicly announced may hinder such collusive agreements.[30]

A dishonest seller has the potential to manipulate the outcome of an auction through the use of false or shill bids. For example, in the sealed-bid second-price auction, the seller can claim that the second highest bid is only slightly under the highest bid. In the English auction, the seller can plant a fake bidder to drive prices up. These possibilities can be eliminated if bidders insist on some mechanism to verify the validity of the bids submitted. Notice that the sealed-bid first-price auction cannot be manipulated by the seller through shill bidding.

5.2.5 Multiple Objects

When auctioning multiple objects, the most obvious question is whether to auction them off separately or all at once. Answers to this and similar questions vary depending on how one models preferences of bidders. The simplest case involves multiple units of the same object, with each bidder wanting at most one unit, and independent private values. The sealed-bid second-price auction can be generalized to this case. Bidders submit bids, and the K, say, objects are awarded to the K highest bidders, all of whom pay the highest losing bid. Like the sealed-bid second-price auction, it results in an efficient outcome, and no bidder benefits by bidding below his or her valuation. Under the benchmark model, a broad class of auctions generate the same expected revenue. This equivalence holds whether the K objects are sold at once or sequentially.

A revenue-maximizing auction in this environment does use a reserve price. In this case, it is easier to see why. Suppose there were five bidders for four objects. Because the supply of units is close to the demand for units, an

---

[29] Compensation rarely involves a monetary transfer. Rather, the members of the ring take turns being the lead bidder at different auctions.

[30] However, it is not unheard of for bidders to employ private detectives to determine whether a member of the ring has violated the agreement.

auction will not bring in a large sum. By instituting a reserve price, though, the auctioneer prevents winning at a low price.

The next level of complexity involves multiple units of the same objects, with some bidders wanting two or more units. In this model, one must specify how each bidder values the first unit, the second unit, and so on. Thus, a bidder's valuation is now a vector. An extension of the sealed-bid second-price auction to this case is known. Unlike the single-good case, it is not the case that the generalization of the second-price auction charges the same price per unit to all bidders. Indeed, doing so would encourage bidders to "game" the auction. To explain why, we consider an "intuitive" auction for selling multiple units of the same object that charges the same price per unit to all bidders. In the auction, the auctioneer raises the price per unit (in a continuous way) and asks bidders to state how many units they want at the current price. If the sum total of requests exceeds the available supply, the auctioneer continues to raise the price. As the price rises, bidders decrease their demands. Eventually a price is reached at which the available supply equals the demand. The problem with such an auction is that it gives bidders an incentive to understate their demand. By reducing the amount demanded at any price, a price rise can be arrested. Although a bidder suffers by getting fewer units, this will be compensated for by a lower price per unit. This phenomenon is known as *demand reduction*. It is commonly associated with auctions of multiple units that have all winning bidders pay the same price per unit. This is not merely a theoretical possibility. There is strong evidence that it was present in California's power auctions at the tail end of the twentieth century.

With some exceptions, less is known about how to auction off heterogeneous objects. In this case, bidders attach values to different combinations of objects. A pair of objects that complement each other in the eyes of one bidder may be substitutes in the eyes of another. The difficulty is in designing the auction to allow the bidders the flexibility to express their preferences over different subsets of items. Once they have expressed their preferences over subsets, finding the optimal way to divide the objects among the bidders becomes an integer programming problem. To get a sense of the difficulties, imagine that one must auction off a dining room set consisting of one table, and four chairs. Some bidders want the entire set, others just the table, and others just a chair or two. Should one auction off each part of the set separately? What about the entire set as a single object? What about two separate auctions, one for the table and the other for a lot of four chairs? A full discussion of these matters is beyond the scope of this book.

5.3 Key Points

1. Four auctions – the English ascending, the sealed-bid second price, the sealed-bid first price, and the Dutch descending – are described. In the benchmark setting, the expected revenue to the seller is the same under all four auctions. In all cases, expected revenue increases with the number of bidders.
2. When supply is fixed and less than the potential demand, the seller is better off selling via auction than posted price.
3. If supply is flexible, in the benchmark model, an auction and posted price will yield the same expected revenue. In such a case, use of posted prices is more practical (e.g., products sold in supermarkets or department stores).
4. When the number of bidders is very small, the seller benefits from the use of a reserve price. The reserve price should be chosen to be the best take-it-or-leave-it offer one would make to a single buyer.
5. In a common values setting, it is possible for inexperienced bidders to bid too aggressively and end up with a "winner's curse," paying more than the item is worth.

5.4 Technical Aside

5.4.1 Sealed-Bid First Price

To determine what strategies bidders will use, we model the auction as a game between the bidders.[31] The equilibrium of the relevant game will be the recommendation for how to bid.

For ease of calculation, we assume the distribution of RPs is the uniform distribution on $[0, 1]$ and there are only two bidders. Let v be the RP of bidder 1 and w the RP of bidder 2. What bid, should bidder 1 submit? The first thought is to submit v itself (bidding truthfully). Might submitting a bid $u \neq v$ generate even higher expected payoff? For any bid, there are two possibilities: winning at bid u or not. If $P(u)$ is the probability of winning at bid u, the expected payoff is $(v - u)P(u)$. Thus, the optimal bid u maximizes $(v - u)P(u)$. But what is $P(u)$? It must depend on bidder 2's bid – and that bid will depend on bidder 1's bid. We exit this logical impasse by treating the auction as a game and determine the equilibrium of the game.

[31] See the Appendix (Chapter 9) for a brief primer on game theory.

In this context, a strategy will be a function B that assigns a bid to each RP. If bidder i uses a bid function B_i, bidder 1's expected payoff will be:

$$(v - B_1(v)) \int_0^1 P(B_1(v) > B_2(t))\, dt.$$

An equilibrium of this game will be a pair of bid functions, B_1^* and B_2^*, such that

$$(v - B_1^*(v)) \int_0^1 P(B_1^*(v) > B_2^*(t))\, dt \geq (v - B(v)) \int_0^1 P(B(v)$$

$$> B_2^*(t))\, dt\ \forall B \neq B_1^*$$

as well as a similar condition for bidder 2. How do we find such an equilibrium? Assume there exists an equilibrium bidding function B^*, where $B_1^* = B_2^* = B^*$ and B^* is strictly increasing. Next, use the equilibrium condition to derive an equation for B^*, which one then solves. Consider the preceding equation again. It can be rewritten to read:

$$B^* \in \arg\max_B \{[v - B(v)] \int_0^1 P(B(v) > B^*(t))\, dt\}.$$

By strict monotonicity of B^*, we can find an x for each v such that $B^*(x) = B(v)$, thus:

$$v \in \arg\max_x (v - B^*(x)) \int_0^1 P(B^*(x) > B^*(t))\, dt.$$

However, $P(B^*(x) > B^*(t)) = P(x > t) = x$, because t is uniformly distributed. Thus, to find B^* we focus on $\max_x (v - B^*(x)) \int_0^1 x\, dt$. The first-order condition for optimality implies that

$$(B^*)'(v) = \frac{(v - B^*(v))}{v}.$$

This differential equation with boundary condition $B^*(0) = 0$ has the solution

$$B^*(v) = E[t|t \leq v] = v/2.$$

Thus, in equilibrium, each bidder behaves as if his or her RP is the higher of the two and computes the expected value of the second highest RP. This estimate of the second highest RP is this bidder's bid. Thus, each bidder in this example *shades* the bid downward from the true RP by 50 percent. The revenue to the seller will be $E(\min\{v, w\})$, the expected value of the second largest RP.

If in our example we had $n \geq 2$ bidders, then, in equilibrium, a bidder with an RP of v should bid $(\frac{n-1}{n})v$. Thus, the bidder shades down by $\frac{v}{n}$. As n gets large – that is, as the number of bidders increases – the amount by which a bidder shades the bid down decreases.[32]

---

[32] For an in-depth treatment of auction theory, see Krishna (2002).

SIX

Price Discrimination

It is not uncommon for different customers to value the same product differently. This difference in valuation allows one to earn a greater profit by matching the price to a customer's RP – in other words, selling the same product or service to different buyers at different prices. In many cases, some modification of the product or service is needed to be able to charge different prices. The practice is called *price discrimination*.[1] To see why the practice is more profitable than charging a uniform price, an example is helpful.

Example 14 *Recall the monopolist from Example 3 in Chapter 4. The demand for the monopolist's product is described by the demand curve* $9 - p$. *Such a curve can arise in the following way: Suppose there is one customer with a RP of 8, another with a RP of 7, and so on. When the monopolist was restricted to charging a single price, we determined that the price should be $5 a unit, yielding a profit of $16. Suppose the monopolist could get away with charging a different price to each buyer, say, $7 to the buyer with a RP of $8, $6 to the buyer with a RP of $7, and so on until the buyer with a RP of $2.[2] The profit would be* $6 + 5 + 4 + 3 + 1 = 19$. □

Examples of price discrimination abound. Most movie theaters, for example, offer student discounts. Thus, filmgoers who qualify as students get a different price from those who do not. Certain tourist attractions in India charge foreigners higher entrance fees than natives. For example, at the Ajanta Cave monument, the price of admission for foreigners is *Rs.* 250,

---

[1] It raises some legal issues that are discussed later. Suffice it to say that for the kinds of examples we have in mind, they can be safely ignored.

[2] The monopolist could charge up to $8 to the buyer with an RP of $8 and so on. The buyer with an RP of $1 can be ignored, as the unit cost is $1.

whereas for natives it is *Rs.* 5.[3] Price discrimination will be unpopular with buyers who face the higher of the prices quoted. An October 2007 article appearing on Sify.com quotes Joseph Ramos of the Philippines, visiting India for the first time, as saying, "I am a guest in this country, so why am I being charged high prices at every place I visit?" Thus, as a practical matter, the seller should be prepared with a justification for the policy beyond simple profit seeking. In this case, for example, the director general of the Archaeological Survey of India (ASI), which is responsible for the care of Indian monuments, responded, "The reason for charging more from foreigners and less from Indians is because our national heritage belongs to us and locals should not pay more."

Price discrimination is vulnerable to attack on two fronts. The first is competition from another seller. Competition in the Indian airline market is an example. Prior to 2007, Jet Airways, Indian Airlines, and Air Sahara charged foreigners in U.S. dollars. These dollar fares were generally priced about 50 percent above the normal rupee fare. However, in an effort to attract customers away from competitors, these airlines have eliminated this dual pricing strategy.

The second front is arbitrage, of which there are two kinds. The first is associated with the **transfer of the commodity**. For example, the students who buy cinema tickets at the discounted price could resell them to nonstudents. Arbitrage of this kind is typically associated with gray markets, which are discussed later in this chapter. In some cases, the arbitrage opportunity is not exploited because the transaction costs of resale of the commodity from one buyer to another are large relative to the gains. If the gains from arbitrage are large, however, the seller must have a strategy to mitigate the effect of arbitrage. A popular way to do this is to convince buyers who face the higher price that they are getting something that those who face the lower price do not. This is usually accomplished by adding or subtracting features from some basic configuration of the product or service. Deluxe versions of music CDs or DVDs, for instance, add liner notes, a booklet providing background on the music or movie, interviews, bonus tracks, and outtakes. The trick, of course, is to do this in such a way that the price differential between the two versions is substantially larger than their cost differential. Thus, a number of examples of price discrimination involve the seller selling apparently different products. An example of this is in the market for laser printers. All printers are born fast. The manufacturer adds

---

[3] These were the rates in place in October 2007.

a line of code to slow them down. By offering both a slow and a fast printer, the printer manufacturer is able to charge different prices for what is, from the manufacturer's point of view, the same product.

The second kind of arbitrage, which is more subtle, is associated with the **transfer of consumption** between different packages or bundles offered to the customer. There is no transfer of goods between buyers in this case. We will defer an example of this until later.

Price discrimination comes in three varieties. In **first-degree price discrimination**, the ideal,[4] the firm identifies the RP of every buyer and prices accordingly. This is unlikely to exist because of arbitrage and the absence of perfect information about buyers' tastes.

Second-degree price discrimination identifies, imperfectly, the RPs of the buyers through a form of self-selection. Buyers choose among different packages of goods offered by the seller – that is, a menu – and in doing so they reveal something about their RPs. The trick is to match the package with the RP. Our previous printer example is an instance of second-degree price discrimination. Fast and slow printers are available to any buyer who wishes them. However, some buyers choose the fast version and others choose the slow version. Another example involves the use of coupons in Sunday supplements. Every reader of the Sunday paper is offered the coupons, but not all choose to use them.[5]

Third-degree price discrimination involves the use of a customer signal (such as age, occupation, usage, income, or race) to discriminate. The student discount is an example.

One can also imagine hybrids of the two. On the Dell web site, for example, one must first place oneself into one of a number of categories, such as student, small business, government, and the like. This is third degree. Next, one is presented a menu of various laptops plus add-ons (this is second degree).

6.1 The Third Degree

The basic logic is to charge higher-valuation customers (alternatively, less price-sensitive customers) more than lower-valuation customers (more price-sensitive customers) for the same product.[6] How does one tell a high-valuation buyer from a low-valuation buyer? In third-degree price

---

[4] For the firm, not customer.

[5] Coupons serve other uses as well – for example, in price experiments.

[6] This amounts to an income subsidy to the lower valuation customers.

discrimination, this is done using some observable signal. We provide several examples here.

1. **Demographic Variables**
   - Age
     Movie ticket discounts for seniors and/or children under 12 is an example. Seniors with fixed discretionary income are likely to be price sensitive; children's tickets are discounted to encourage parents to take children to the movies and reduce the dollar value of the purchase.[7]
   - Income
     Northwestern University charges higher medical insurance premiums to higher-income employees. The basis is that higher-income employees are less price sensitive than lower-income employees.[8]
   - Employment status
     Examples are student and teacher discounts, or discounts for non-profits versus corporate customers. Software prices are lower for schools and universities as compared with corporate customers; the former have lower valuation and would be more willing to wait for prices to come down.[9]

2. **Location**
   Supermarkets in different locations within the same city charge different prices for items such as milk and bread. These differences take into account that neighborhood incomes, as well as the degree of competition, vary from one location to another. A celebrated example of this was the Victoria's Secret catalog, which varied price according to zip code.

3. **Purchase History**
   Car companies, such as GM and Ford, give discounts to first-time buyers. Why? First-time buyers (e.g., college students) are likely to be income constrained. Car companies also entice owners of competitive cars with a discount. The logic here is that an owner of a competitive car has a lower valuation for a particular company's car, or the price is too high.

---

[7] By encouraging parents to bring their children, the cinema generates additional revenues from the sale of drinks and popcorn.

[8] However, higher-income employees are likely to be older, and thus greater consumers of health care.

[9] There may also be an externality effect in charging educational institutions a lower price in the form of positive word of mouth for the product.

4. **Firm Size**

In B2B settings, a seller will set prices based on the size of the purchasing firm. Oracle, for example, sells essentially the same enterprise software at a substantially lower price to midmarket customers compared with large-enterprise customers. Oracle has a definition of midmarket clients that depends on factors such as annual revenues, assets under management, or the size of the client's customer base.

5. **Application**

Kevlar, a fiber developed by DuPont, is lighter and stronger than steel and now has applications in a number of product categories, from bulletproof vests to packing material, hulls of fishing and racing boats, high-end tires, and racing shoes. The valuation of the product is different in the different applications. DuPont is able to charge different prices for Kevlar depending on the end-use application. There is no good substitute to Kevlar for bulletproof vests, and the valuation, protecting a human life, is high. For the hulls of fishing and racing boats, steel, wood, aluminum and fiberglass are substitutes, and the valuation for Kevlar is lower. For packing material, a number of substitutes exist, some of which are at low prices. Thus, Kevlar would be a viable option only when the product being shipped is of high value.

In many of these cases, there is a potential arbitrage opportunity. In some, the transaction costs are large relative to the gains, so arbitrage is essentially nonexistent. We do not, for example, see senior citizens selling their discount cinema tickets to non-senior citizens. Presumably the costs of waiting in front of the cinema to sell one's tickets exceed the profits to be had from resale. In other cases, the seller explicitly forbids resale or limits the quantities that an individual can purchase. Companies such as Microsoft and Dell, which sell to universities at discounted prices, have explicit rules prohibiting resale of these items to buyers outside the university. In the case in which price is a function of the way in which the product will be used, the seller can engineer the product for one application so as to be unusable in another application.[10]

Situations in which prices are negotiated in person, such as in automobile buying, allow for third-degree price discrimination. Here price can be based on race, gender, age, education, and so on. In a carefully researched study

---

[10] Some believe that services lend themselves more easily than goods to price discrimination. In part, this may be because services are impossible to resell. Further, because of the subjective component in many services with a large human component, it may be easier to extract a higher price.

using a large data set on automobile transactions, Morton, Zettelmeyer, and Silva-Risso (2003) found that women paid slightly more than men (about 0.2 percent), older consumers paid more (about 0.21 percent) than younger consumers (as age increases from 20 to 64 years), and African Americans and Hispanics paid 1.5 percent and 1.1 percent, respectively, more than whites. These results controlled for income, education, occupation, and wealth. The premium jumped to 2 percent for African Americans and 2.3 percent for Hispanics when these other variables were not controlled for. Next, the researchers investigated the impact of using the Internet on the gender and minority premium. The results indicate that using Autobytel.com wiped away most of the premium. For example, the premium paid by African Americans was reduced from 1.5 percent to 0.3 percent, and that of women reduced from 0.21 percent to 0.09 percent.

6.2 The Second Degree

In second-degree price discrimination, the seller offers a menu of choices to the buyer, from which the buyer selects. Buyers with low RPs will choose the inexpensive offerings on the menu. The trick is to encourage those with a high RP, to choose the expensive items from the menu. This is accomplished through a combination of carrots and sticks. The expensive items on the menu are laden with carrots to make them attractive to those with a high RP, whereas the inexpensive items are bundled with sticks to make them less attractive. The idea is not new, as can be seen from the writings of Dupuit (1844), a nineteenth-century Belgian railroad engineer:

It is not because of the few thousand francs which would have to be spent to put a roof over the third class carriages or to upholster the third class seats that some company or other has open carriages with wooden benches.... What the company is trying to do is to prevent the passengers who can pay the second class fare from traveling third class; it hits the poor not because it wants to hurt them, but to frighten the rich... And it is again for the same reason that the companies, having proved almost cruel to third class passengers and mean to second class passengers, become lavish in dealing with first class passengers. Having refused the poor what is necessary, they give the rich what is superfluous.

The two most popular instances of the menu idea in practice are **versioning** and **bundling**, which we discuss in detail.

6.2.1 Versioning

The problem with offering the same product to all buyers is that not all of them value all the features of the product in the same way. For this reason,

Table 6.1. *RPs for Printers*

	Fast	Slow
A's RP	$100	$40
B's RP	$49	$30

it is useful to add or subtract features of the product in different ways, to offer multiple versions of the same basic product. Different versions of the same product are customized to different buyer segments. In deciding on the number of versions of a basic product and how to price them, the firm needs to worry about the costs of producing and distributing the variety of products chosen and the consequent cannibalization of sales. The latter occurs when a product intended for one segment attracts buyers from another segment. This is the second form of arbitrage alluded to earlier (arbitrage of consumption). A simple numerical example illustrates the trade-offs involved.

Example 15 *Suppose you are the monopoly seller of two kinds of printers, fast and slow. For simplicity, assume the unit cost of each type is zero.[11] There are two customer segments, A and B, of equal size (suppose one of each). The RPs of each segment for each type of printer are shown in Table 6.1.*

As the seller, you cannot tell by looking at a buyer whether he or she belongs to segment A or B. In other words, there is no observable signal (such as gender or age) that indicates the segment to which a buyer belongs. This rules out the possibility of third-degree price discrimination.

You have three options to consider. First, price and sell the fast version only. Second, price and sell the slow version only. Third, offer both versions simultaneously. To determine which option is best, we calculate the profit consequence of each.

If you were to sell only the fast version, only two prices are worth considering: slightly under $49 and slightly under $100. At a price below $49, both segments will purchase, because the surplus offered is positive. At a price between $49 and $100, only segment A will purchase. However, any price well below $100 leaves money on the table. Finally, at a price that exceeds $100, no one will buy. Hence the two prices: slightly under $49 and slightly under $100. (To avoid having to write and read the phrase "slightly under" repeatedly, we simply drop it.) In other words, if buying confers a surplus of zero and not buying confers a surplus of zero, we assume that the buyer will break the tie in favor of buying.

[11] As pointed out earlier, fast and slow printers cost the same to make.

Table 6.2. *Revenue from Fast*

Price	Demand	Revenue
$49	2	$98
$100	1	$100

Table 6.2 lists the demand and revenue consequences from charging each of the two possible prices. Recall that because costs are zero, profit is the same as revenue.

Therefore, if you sell the fast version only, it should be priced at $100.

Now let us repeat the same analysis for the slow version.

In this case, a price of $30 for the slow version would maximize revenue (Table 6.3).

Of the two options considered so far, the best is to sell the fast version only and price it at $100. In this case, you shut out the B segment completely. To make more money, you must sell to both segments but get the A segment to pay more than B. How do you do that?

The idea is to offer both printers, and charge a higher price for the fast printer. Clearly, the fast version should be directed to the A segment, whereas the slow version is directed to the B segment. To squeeze the A segment, the fast version should be priced higher than the slow one. However, if the fast version is priced too high, the A segment will switch down to buying the slow version (this is arbitrage associated with the transfer of consumption). To illustrate, suppose the fast is priced at $100 and the slow is priced at $30. When faced with these two versions, a buyer in the B segment will choose the slow version. A buyer from the A segment will also choose the slow version. Why? Consider the surplus that such a buyer obtains from each version. The surplus on the fast printer will be $100 − $100 = $0. The surplus from the slow one will be $40 − $30 = $10 – in other words, the surplus on the slow version is larger. If you find this odd, keep in mind that the rational buyer model assumes that buyers make trade-offs. In this case, if a slow printer is priced low enough, it looks fast.

Table 6.3. *Revenue from Slow*

Price	Demand	Revenue
$30	2	$60
$40	1	$40

Table 6.4. *Modified RPs*

	Fast	Slow
A's RP	$100	$65
B's RP	$49	$30

To recap, if one sells only one type of printer, it should be the fast version at $100. If one now introduces the slow version as well, for a price of $30, it will appeal to the B segment as well as cannibalize sales from the fast version. Thus, to keep the A segment paying for a fast version, we must (in this example) lower the price of the fast version just enough that it will look more attractive than the slow version. The A segment will buy the fast version as long as the fast version delivers at least as much surplus to them as the slow one. The surplus of a buyer from the A segment on the slow version is currently $40 − $30 = $10. So, if we price the fast version at $90 (or just a hair beneath), the A segment will purchase the fast printer. The result is a revenue of $90 + $30 = $120. This is $20 more than selling the fast version only.   □

Example 15 shows that introducing a variant of a product produces two effects. On the positive side, the variant allows one to cater to a segment not previously being served. On the opposing side, the variant competes with the original product. This competition manifests itself in the cannibalization of sales from the original version, which may require lowering the price of the original version. In the preceding example, the positive effect outweighed the negative. But this is not always the case. The next example illustrates this possibility.

Example 16 *As in example 15 except the RPs of the segments are changed as in Table 6.4.*

As before, if one sells only the fast version, the revenue-maximizing price is $100, yielding a total revenue of $100. If one sells the slow version only, the revenue-maximizing price is $65, yielding a total revenue of $65. Can one do better by selling both versions?

If both versions are sold, then the slow version must be priced at $30. A buyer from the A segment receives a surplus of $35 from the purchase of the slow version. Thus, to ensure that the A buyer will buy the fast version, the fast version must be priced at $65. However, total revenues will be $95 only (buyer in segment A buys the fast version for $65 and buyer from segment B buys the slow are at $30). This is less than the revenues obtained from selling the fast version only.   □

The reason versioning provides no benefits in Example 16 is that the A segment perceives less of a difference between the two versions. This can be seen in the difference in the RPs. In Example 15, the difference in RPs for the A segment between fast and slow is $60. In Example 16 that difference is now $35. In other words, the added benefits of a fast version over a slow version have diminished, making them more alike in the buyer's mind. An instructive mathematical formulation of Example 15 appears in the Technical Aside at the end of the chapter.

Sellers can introduce versions of their base product or service simply by adding or subtracting features. Of course, the incremental costs of adding and subtracting features should be far smaller than the increased revenues generated. The student versions of some software programs, for example, are simply the professional versions with some features disabled. Different classes of service on airlines are also an example. The opportunity cost of selling a first class seat on an international flight is about twice the coach class fare. This is because a first class seat takes up the space that would have been occupied by two coach seats. However, the difference between first class and coach fares is substantially larger. Airlines that sell seats on the same flight both on their sites, as well as on priceline.com, are also engaging in versioning. Here the feature that is disabled is detailed information. On priceline.com, the buyer is not permitted to specify the exact arrival and departure time or the airport that will be used when there is a choice.

Hardback versus paperback books are another example of versioning. Here the versioning occurs along two dimensions. The first is that the hardback itself is viewed by many buyers to be a superior product to the paperback. Interestingly, the difference in production costs is only on the order of $2 a book. Second, the hardback version of a book is usually introduced first, whereas the paperback version is issued some time later. In this case, the versioning comes from the immediacy of consumption.

The channel through which the product itself is distributed is also a form of versioning. Think of the outlet mall in a location usually remote from the urban center versus a mall in the urban center.

Branding is also a way to version. Excedrin Extra Strength and Excedrin Migraine are the same product.[12] The Lexus ES car and the high end Toyota Camry share the same platform.

---

[12] Excedrin Extra Strength was introduced in 1960 by BristolMyers Squibb. It contains 250 mg acetaminophen, 250 mg aspirin, and 65 mg caffeine. In 1998, the FDA granted clearance to market Excedrin Migraine for the relief of migraine headache pain. It contains the same 250 mg acetaminophen, 250 mg aspirin, and 65 mg caffeine. Retail prices for the two brands, however, are not the same.

6.2.2 Bundling

A *bundle* is a collection of distinct products or services that are sold together as a package. A familiar example of bundling is a suite of software programs sold in one box. Season tickets to the theater, round-trip air tickets, and prix fixe menus and meal deals in restaurants are other examples.

The exact meaning of "distinct" requires clarification. Consider a hamburger. It consists of, among other things, a meat patty, special sauce, and a sesame seed bun. Because these are distinct products, a hamburger is a bundle. By this standard, though, everything under the sun, except the fundamental building blocks of nature, constitutes a bundle. This view is not particularly helpful. Instead, we suppose that what constitutes a bundle should be evaluated from the perspective of the buyer. For the buyer at McDonald's, the hamburger is not a bundle because there is no reasonable expectation that McDonalds will offer the ingredients of the burger for sale individually. On the other hand, for the buyer at home contemplating a meal, the hamburger is a bundle because this person can go to the supermarket to buy one or more of the individual components of the hamburger.

There are three kinds of bundling:

1. **Pure Bundling**
   The seller does not make the items in a bundle available for sale individually even though it could. For example, until 2010 the Windows operating system could not be purchased without Internet Explorer. Thus, one buys both or none at all.
2. **Mixed Bundling**
   The seller gives the buyer the option to buy the bundle or any subset thereof. Typically, the price of the bundle is less than the sum of the prices of the individual components. An example is a coupon for a discount on a Disney CD when one buys a Disney movie. A buyer can choose to purchase the CD only or the movie only, or use the coupon to get both for a price less than the sum of the individual prices.
3. **Tying**
   In this case, the sale of one good (the tying good) to the customer is conditional on the purchase of a second distinctive good (the tied good). The seller chooses to offer a bundle and only one of the components individually. For example, certain National Football League (NFL) programs are available only on DIRECTV. Thus, one can buy DIRECTV and not the programs, or both, but never the NFL programs by themselves.

Sellers bundle for reasons other than price discrimination, such as the following:

1. **Transaction Costs**

   A newspaper is a bundle of articles. Before the advent of the Internet, the transaction costs for an individual to put together his or her own newspaper each day would have been prohibitive. Thus, the buyer benefits when the seller offers a bundle. Houses are another example. A house can be bought ready-made (the bundle) or one can choose to build a house to one's particular specification. Buyers who buy the ready-made do so to avoid the transaction costs of building their own home.

2. **Complementarities/Synergies**

   If a collection of components complement each other, there is a clear benefit to bundling them. Printers and toner cartridges are an example.[13]

3. **Economies of Scale**

   Bundles are also offered because of economies of scale in manufacturing and distribution. The cost of packaging and selling an individual stick of chewing gum is prohibitive, so they are sold in bundles of ten at a minimum.

4. **Deter Entry**

   Bundling can also be used to deter entry, a subject we discuss later in this section.

5. **Overwhelming Choice**

   In the presence of too many choices, buyers may elect not to purchase at all. By bundling choices together, a seller can mitigate this effect.

6. **Variety**

   Sometimes a seller will bundle products that are substitutes for each other because buyers have a preference for variety. As an example, consider competing providers of television packages. In choosing among them, the customer will examine the channel options provided by each. The provider offering an extra channel will increase the chance that a customer will choose that provider. Once the customer chooses a provider, the different channels in the chosen package are substitutes.

---

[13] An extreme but vivid example of synergies is shoes. A left shoe by itself has no value. The same is true of a right shoe. However, the two together have a positive value. Thus, they are sold as a bundle. Interestingly, in 1950, the shipping magnate Achille Lauro attempted to win public office in Naples by offering right shoes to the people before the election, with the promise of a matching left shoe on winning the election.

Table 6.5. *Reservation Prices*

	Stones	John
A's RP	$80	$40
B's RP	$40	$80
C's RP	$90	$10
D's RP	$10	$90

In this section we show how bundling can be used to price-discriminate as well as to deter entry.

Example 17 *Our numerical example will consist of four buyers (A, B, C, and D) and two products: a ticket to a Rolling Stones concert and the other to an Elton John concert. Each buyer is interested in at most one ticket for each concert. Because most of the costs of putting on the concert are fixed, we will assume that the goal is to maximize revenue.*

The RP of each buyer for each product is shown in Table 6.5.

There are three ways in which tickets can be sold:

1. *Price and sell each ticket as an individual item.*
2. *Price and sell the tickets in a bundle of two only (pure bundling). The option of buying a ticket to a single concert is not available.*
3. *Price and sell a bundle as well as the tickets individually (mixed bundling).*

Which will generate the most revenue?

If we price and sell the Stones concert by itself, the revenue generated at each price point is shown in Table 6.6.

Thus, the revenue-maximizing price for the Stones concert is $80. A similar analysis applies to the pricing of the John concert, yielding the same price. This generates a total revenue of $320.

Table 6.6. *Price, Demand and Revenue for the Stones Concert*

Price	Demand	Revenue
$10	4	$40
$40	3	$120
$80	2	$160
$90	1	$90

Now, suppose we bundle the tickets together. There are three possibilities for how buyers may value the bundle. The first is that there are synergies – that is, the whole is greater than the sum of its parts. In this case, it is obvious that bundling will be beneficial. If one delivers more value, one can capture more of it with higher prices. The second is that bundling destroys value. For example, no buyer can attend more than one concert because of time constraints. Therefore, the RP of buyer A for the bundle will be $80. If one can attend only one concert, one would attend the one that is of most value. If bundling destroys value, then clearly selling a bundle makes no sense. The third possibility is that the the RP of a bundle will simply be the sum of the component RPs. Thus, A and B's RP for the bundle would be $120, whereas C and D's RP for the bundle would be $100. Pricing the bundle at $100 yields a revenue of $400, whereas setting the bundle price at $120 yields a revenue of $240. Thus, in the pure bundling case, pricing at $100 maximizes revenue. Notice that more revenue is generated in this case than in the first.

With mixed bundling, buyers have the option to buy a bundle or just one of the concert tickets. Here is a combination that generates more revenue than the pure bundling case. Price the bundle at $120 and each individual ticket at $90. Faced with these prices, the A and B maximize their surplus by purchasing the bundle, whereas C and D do so when they purchase one ticket each (C buys the Stones, D buys John). Total revenue is $420. □

Pure bundling generates higher revenues than selling individually in Example 17 because it increases demand. When the concert tickets are sold individually, a total of four tickets are sold. However, under pure bundling, eight tickets are sold. To see why this happened, compare the spread or variance in RPs for a single product versus the variance in RPs for the bundle. The variance for the bundle is lower. The reduction in variance helps the seller. With a single price, the seller loses in two ways. First, there are buyers who do not buy and second, there are buyers who pay much less than their RPs. The magnitude of these losses increases with the variance of the RPs.

Now consider the mixed bundling option in Example 17. The average price per unit paid by A and B is $60. The average price paid per unit by C and D is $90. Thus, the same product is sold to different buyers at different prices. Naturally, there must be an arbitrage possibility here: A can buy the bundle and then resell the components for $85 each to C and D. In practice, such arbitrage opportunities are forestalled by making resale illegal or designing the product to make resale difficult. For example, season ticket holders are given a ticket that cannot be split up into individual tickets or are required to present a valid ID when using the ticket.

Correlation and Bundling

The revenue benefits of bundling two products vary with the correlation between the RPs of the two products. Example 17 is not rich enough to illustrate this. The following example does. Furthermore, it allows for a graphical depiction of the effects of pure bundling on revenue.

Example 18 *Consider a monopoly supplier of two products, A and B, selling to a market of 1000 buyers. The cost of production for each product is zero. A buyer's RP for product A is a random number drawn uniformly between 0 and 10. A buyer's RP for product B is also a random number drawn uniformly between 0 and 10. Furthermore, these two RPs are independent of each other – that is, the correlation between RPs for different products is zero.*[14]

We first examine the case in which each product is priced individually. Focus to begin with on product A. At a price p, the expected demand for product A will be $1000 \times [1 - 0.1\,p]$ (see, for example, Section 4.7). To compute the revenue-maximizing price we must find the value of p that maximizes $p \times 1000 \times [1 - 0.1\,p]$. That value is $p = 5$, yielding an expected revenue of \$2,500. Notice that an identical analysis applies to product B. Thus, total revenue will be \$5,000.

An advantage of this more elaborate setup is that we can illustrate what is going on graphically. Each buyer has two numbers: the RP for A and the RP for B. This allows us to represent each buyer as a point in a 10-by-10 square because each product's RP is a number between 0 and 10. The RP for A will be plotted on the x-coordinate and the RP for B on the y-coordinate. See Figure 6.1.

Buyers with an RP for A that is at least \$5 will appear to the right of the vertical line through the 5 mark. See Figure 6.2. Similarly, buyers with an RP for B that is at least \$5 appear above the horizontal line through \$5. See Figure 6.3. Now let us overlay Figure 6.2 on top of Figure 6.3. The result is Figure 6.4.

The square in the upper right-hand corner of Figure 6.4 (cell III) contains all points that correspond to buyers whose RP for A is at least \$5 and whose RP for B is also at least \$5. The square in the lower left-hand corner of Figure 6.4 (cell IV) contains all points that correspond to buyers whose RP for A is at most \$5 and whose RP for B is also at most \$5.

The square in the lower right-hand corner of Figure 6.4 (cell II) contains all points that correspond to buyers whose RP for A is at least \$5 and whose RP for B is at most \$5. The square in the upper left-hand corner of Figure 6.4

---

[14] This example is based on McAfee, McMillan, and Whinston (1989).

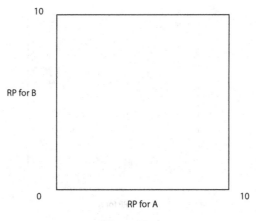

Figure 6.1.

(cell I) contains all points that correspond to buyers whose RP for A is at most $5 and whose RP for B is at least $5.

The assumption that RPs are uniformly distributed means that the number of buyers who have RPs that place them in the upper right-hand corner, for example, is proportional to the area of that segment. Thus, the fraction of buyers whose RP for each product is at least $5 is 1/4. Because there are 1000 buyers altogether, the number of buyers associated with the upper right-hand corner is 250.

Figure 6.4 also allows us to compute the revenue from pricing each product at $5. Observe that a quarter of the buyers will buy both products. These are the buyers in the upper right-hand corner (cell III). A quarter will buy A only (lower right-hand corner, cell II) and a quarter will buy B only (upper

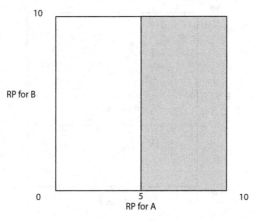

Figure 6.2.

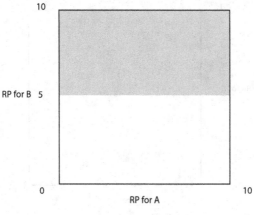

Figure 6.3.

left-hand corner, cell I). Thus, total revenue will be

$$2 \times 5 \times \frac{1}{4} \times 1000 + 5 \times \frac{1}{4} \times 1000 + 5 \times \frac{1}{4} \times 1000 = 5000.$$

Suppose, instead of selling each product individually for $5, we decide to sell a bundle of the two at, for no particular reason, $9. What will the revenue be? Only a buyer whose RP for A plus RP for B is at least $9 will buy the bundle. These buyers appear in Figure 6.5 above the diagonal line intersecting the vertical axis at 9 and the horizontal axis at 9. All points in the shaded area above this diagonal line in Figure 6.5 will thus have a RP for the bundle of at least 9.

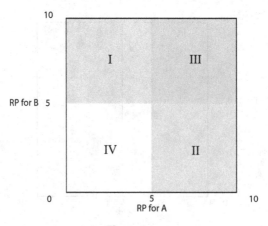

Figure 6.4.

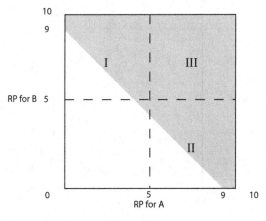

Figure 6.5.

The revenue from this is proportional to the area above the diagonal line. It is easy to see that this area is equal to $10 \times 10 - \frac{9 \times 9}{2}$ – in other words, the area of the square minus the area of the triangular region below the diagonal. Thus, revenue is

$$9 \times 1000 \times \frac{10 \times 10 - \frac{9 \times 9}{2}}{10 \times 10} = 5,335.$$

Bundling at \$9 generates more revenue than selling the items individually at \$5. Where does the extra revenue come from? First, buyers in unshaded portions of regions I and II of Figure 6.5 no longer buy anything, whereas before (when the products were sold individually) they were each buying one product. Thus, offering the bundle causes us to lose revenue from a portion of segments I and II. The segment marked region III now pay \$9 for both products, whereas before buyers in this segment were paying \$10 for both. Again we incur a loss. Where we gain is from buyers in the shaded portions of segments I and II. Before, these buyers were buying only one product for \$5; now they buy both products for \$9. That is an increase of \$4 per buyer in the shaded portions of I and II. In this case, the gain is more than enough to offset the loss from the unshaded portions of segments I and II.

In fact, we can compute the revenue-maximizing price for the bundle. If p is the price of the bundle and $p \leq 10$, the demand for the bundle is the area of shaded region shown in Figure 6.6.

The area of this shaded region is $10 \times 10 - \frac{p^2}{2}$. Hence revenue will be $1000 \times p \times \frac{10 \times 10 - \frac{p^2}{2}}{10 \times 10}$. The value of p that maximizes this is $p = 8.165$. □

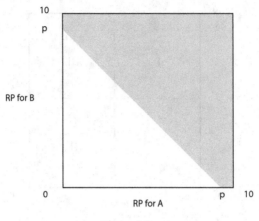

Figure 6.6.

The analysis of Example 18 was conducted under the assumption that the RPs of each product were independent of each other. In other words, there was zero correlation between the RP for A and the RP for B. Nevertheless, the analysis suggests what might happen in the case in which the correlation between RPs is not zero.

The idea is to divide up the buyers into four (not very precisely defined) segments as illustrated in Figure 6.7:

- Segment, I and II: Moderately high RP for one product and relatively low RP for the other
- Segment III: Relatively high RPs for both products

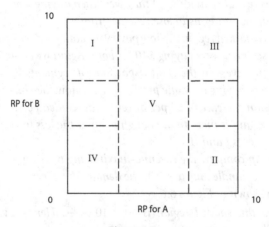

Figure 6.7.

Table 6.7. *Buyer RPs and Number*

Segment	III	II	I	IV
Number	81	9	9	1
RP for A	$10	$10	$1	$1
RP for B	$10	$1	$10	$1

- Segment IV: Relatively low RPs for both products
- Segment V: Relatively high RP for one product and moderately high RP for the other

If proportionally more buyers are in segments I, II, and V, then pure bundling is likely to increase revenues. If one introduces a bundle instead of selling individually, one would lose revenue from the buyers in segment III, because the bundle would be priced at less than the sum of the individual prices. On the other hand, the discount implied in the bundle may get buyers in segments I, II, and V to switch from buying just one of the products to buying two of them. If this group is large enough, this may generate sufficient revenue to offset the losses incurred on segment III through introduction of the bundle. This case would correspond to zero or negative correlation across RPs.

Going a step further, if there are sufficiently many buyers with a high RP for one product and a low RP for another, mixed bundling may warrant consideration. This situation would be consistent with a strong negative correlation between the RPs.

If most buyers are in segments III and IV, then pure bundling is unlikely to increase revenue over selling individually. The segment III buyers attach a high value to each product, so they would buy both products separately anyway. Introducing a bundle that presumably would be priced at less than the sum of the prices of the individual products would leave money on the table. To offset that by appealing to the segment IV buyers would require a steep drop in the price, because the segment IV buyers attach a low value to each product. This case would correspond to the RPs across products being positively correlated. An example of this appears next.

Example 19 *The number of buyers and their respective RPs are shown in Table 6.7.*

To see that the RPs are positively correlated, notice that if a buyer has a RP of $10 for one product there is a 81/90 probability that this buyer has a RP of $10 *for the other. The revenue-maximizing price for A alone is $10, similarly with B. Total revenue is $2 \times 90 \times 10 = \$1,800$. If we bundle, the best bundle price is $20 with revenue of $20 \times 81 = \$1,620$. There are very few buyers in segments I and II, so bundling is unlikely to be beneficial.* □

We conclude that pure bundling will probably increase revenues over pricing individually if the correlation between RPs is zero or negative. If the correlation is positive, then pure bundling is unlikely to increase revenues over pricing each product individually. The Technical Aside at the end of this chapter demonstrates how bundling changes the shape of the demand curve.

A Cable TV Interlude

An instance of bundling that perhaps every reader will be familiar with is the bundling of programming by cable television companies such as Comcast and Time Warner. All cable companies sell programming in the form of bundles with names such as Basic Service, Expanded Basic Services, and Premium Services. Although consumers may choose among bundles, they cannot pick and choose among individual networks. This absence of choice has raised the ire of some consumers. A recent *USA Today*/CNN/Gallup poll found that 54 percent of television viewers said they would prefer to buy channels individually, whereas only 43 percent said they would rather pay a flat fee for a fixed number of channels. This has pressured the Federal Communications Commission to consider forcing the cable companies to offer à la carte pricing. Cable industry executives argue that a majority of people still prefer buying the existing preordained packages of cable. One cable company notes that well under 10 percent of its subscribers bought pay-per-view or video-on-demand movies. However, 70 percent of them consume free video-on-demand programming, which is part of its digital package, once a month.

The first reason a cable company may bundle is costs. Unbundling requires the ability to prevent consumption by nonsubscribers. Early methods for doing so relied on electromechanical traps placed at the link between the household and the source. These were costly to install. However, if the costs of preventing consumption by nonsubscribers falls, the cost reason for bundling evaporates. At present many systems now offer "addressable" converters that control access via electronic communication with the source. Not all consumers opt for addressable converters, even when offered by their system. Nevertheless, uniform deployment of converters is likely in the long run.

A second possible reason is regulation. The 1992 Cable Act required the creation of a basic tier of service containing all offered broadcast and public-interest programming carried by the system, as well as cable programming networks (at the discretion of the system). In addition, it set different rules for bundled versus unbundled (à la carte) services. However, it is hard to believe that cost and regulation can be the reason for bundling. Direct broadcast satellite providers of multichannel programming that compete with cable systems face none of the same technological or regulatory constraints as cable companies. They also engage in widespread bundling.

A third reason for bunding is that the networks (MTV, CNN, ABC, TNT, and so on) benefit from bundling. The average cable network earns about 50 percent of its revenue from advertising.[15] Unbundling would reduce the set of consumers who would choose to watch a particular network. This would reduce advertising revenues to that network and require increases in license fees to compensate.[16] In addition, in the absence of bundling, networks with niche audiences would find it hard to identify and reach their intended audiences.

A fourth reason is that bundling is more profitable for the cable companies than selling channels individually. The argument for this resides in Example 17. Interestingly, consumers themselves benefit from bundling. The total surplus when tickets to each event are sold separately is $20.[17] When the tickets are bundled at $100, the total surplus is $40. When bundled, the price per ticket is $50. When unbundled, tickets are sold at $80 apiece. In fact, the example suggests that were cable companies to unbundle, prices for programming would rise. In the case of cable TV, an additional reason for an increase in prices would come from the networks themselves. ESPN, for example, currently charges the cable company $3 per subscriber per month. If the cable companies were to unbundle, suppose 25 percent of cable subscribers elect to subscribe to ESPN. Then, ESPN would have to collect $12 per subscriber per month from the cable company to maintain the same revenue. The cable company will pass along a portion of this

---

[15] Based on a 2003 U.S. General Accounting Office report.
[16] The typical cable network charges cable systems a fee ranging from nothing to $1 or more per subscriber per month. Some premium networks, such as ESPN, charge fees in excess of $1 per subscriber per month. On the revenue side, the average price of extended basic cable, the most popular type of channel package to which cable-watching households subscribe, is about $50 a month.
[17] Each ticket is sold for $80. A and C buy a Stones ticket generating a total surplus of $10. B and D buy the John ticket, generating a total surplus of $10.

increase to subscribers. At this point, less than 25 percent of subscribers may be interested.

Bundling and Entry Deterrence

In this section, we illustrate how bundling can be used to deter entry. We start with the classic case of IBM and its tabulating machines from the 1930s. IBM was the monopoly supplier of tabulating machines.[18] IBM also sold punch cards that worked on tabulating machines.[19] A tabulating machine required punch cards to operate, and a punch card's value lay only in the fact that it was used in tabulating machines. Thus, one product without the other was useless. Because of patent protection, only IBM could sell tabulating machines – but anyone could make punch cards. However, to buy a tabulating machine from IBM, one had to agree to buy IBM punch cards. (One was welcome to buy punch cards by themselves, of course, presumably to use as bookmarks.) Thus, the two products were sold as a bundle, an instance of tying. In this way, IBM used its monopoly power in one product to become a monopolist in another. The complementary nature of the products made it obvious that bundling the products would forestall competition in the punch card market. This sort of bundling is now considered illegal in the United States as well as a number of other countries.[20]

More interesting is the case in which the two products sold are unrelated, in the sense that one can be used without the other. Consider the same setup as in Example 18, except that the seller (whom we will call the incumbent) is a monopolist in product A only. In product B, our seller faces potential competition from an entrant selling an identical version of product B. Product A, for example, could be a medicine such as torcetrapib, with patent protection and no viable substitute. Product B, could be a medicine, such as Lipitor, that faces competition from a substitute, Zocor.[21] The entrant

---

[18] Invented by Herman Hollerith, these machines were first developed to process data for the 1890 U.S. Census. By the 1930s they were used for basic bookkeeping and accounting in large companies.

[19] The punch cards were inspired by a railway ticket. A hole punch was used to mark information, such as destination, on the ticket. Punch cards were chosen to be the same size as 1887 U.S. paper currency because containers of that size were available.

[20] Although bundling in this way will forestall competition in the punch card market, it is by no means clear that doing so is necessarily a good thing for IBM. We take up this issue in Section 7.4.3.

[21] Torcetrapib and Lipitor are owned by Pfizer. The first is supposed to increase "good" cholesterol, whereas the second reduces "bad" cholesterol. One product can be used without the other. Zocor is made by Merck and is now off patent. Thus, both Zocor and the generic version of Zocor compete with Lipitor.

offers its own version of B, which, for simplicity, we assume is identical in all respects. For both parties, production costs are zero.

Suppose the incumbent must decide on the price of A and its version of product B first. Furthermore, after choosing the prices, the prices cannot be changed. Then the entrant sets the price on its version of product B. The entrant cannot sell product A. This sequence of events stacks the deck against the incumbent. If bundling can benefit the incumbent in this situation, then it makes for a strong argument in favor of bundling.

We examine two cases: one in which the incumbent prices and sells each product individually and the other in which it sells them as a bundle. Consider the case in which the incumbent prices each product individually. Since the incumbent is the monopolist for product A, it should price product A at $5 a unit to maximize revenue. Now, what about product B? No matter what price the incumbent picks (as long as it is non-zero) for product B, the entrant will always set a price just below it. The result is that the incumbent will never make any sales of the B product. For example, if the incumbent prices B at $5, the entrant will price its version of B at just under $5, capturing slightly more than half the buyers.[22] If the incumbent prices B at $0, the entrant is forced to price its version of B at $0 as well, again capturing half the market (but with no revenue). Because the revenue-maximizing price for product B is $5, the best the entrant can hope for is that the incumbent will price B at $5, allowing the entrant to undercut and sell to slightly more than half the market for a price slightly under $5.[23] The incumbent's profits will be $2,500 from selling product A. The incumbent does not sell any units of B.

Now, suppose the incumbent, sells products A and B as a bundle for $10. Thus, a buyer must buy both products from the incumbent or none. What price should the entrant choose for product B? Let p be the price chosen by the entrant. Which buyers will consider the entrant's product? Clearly, any buyer whose RP for B is at least p will consider the entrant's offering. The shaded region in Figure 6.8 shows these buyers. The buyers in the cross-hatched region marked I of Figure 6.8 will definitely buy the entrant's product. Because they are below the diagonal, they are not willing to pay the bundle price of $10. However, they all have an RP for product B that is at least p.

---

[22] The entrant does not capture the entire market because the RPs of some buyers are less than the price charged by the entrant.

[23] Because product B is a substitute for a bundle of products A and B, the incumbent may have an incentive to maintain a relatively high price for product B.

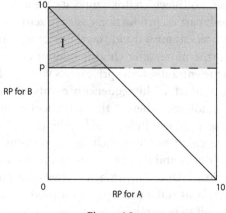

Figure 6.8.

Will some buyers who are prepared to buy the bundle at $10 switch to the entrant's offering? Yes, and we can guess who they are: the ones who assign low value to product A – that is, their RP for product A is relatively small. Just how small? Consider a buyer with an RP for A of x and an RP for B of y. This buyer will consider buying from the entrant only if $y \geq p$. The buyer would prefer to buy from the entrant only if the surplus from purchasing from the entrant exceeded the surplus from purchasing from the incumbent:

$$y - p \geq x + y - 10 \ \Rightarrow\ 10 - p \geq x.$$

Thus, the only buyers who would buy from the entrant have an RP for B that exceeds p and an RP for A that is below $10 - p$. These buyers are illustrated in the two shaded regions of Figure 6.9. From the uniformity assumption, the number of such buyers is proportional to the area of the shaded region. Hence, the demand the entrant sees with a price of p is given by $1000 \times \frac{(10 - p) \times (10 - p)}{100}$. Thus, the entrant chooses p to maximize

$$p \times 1000 \times \frac{(10 - p) \times (10 - p)}{100}.$$

This comes to $p = 3.33$ and translates into 44.4 percent of the total market. The incumbent's share is illustrated in Figure 6.10 and equals 27.78 percent. The entrant comes in at a lower price than before ($3.33 instead of slightly less than $5) and captures a smaller share. The incumbent's profits will be $2,778, which is larger than $2,500. Thus, the incumbent is better off and the entrant is worse off than when the incumbent sold each product

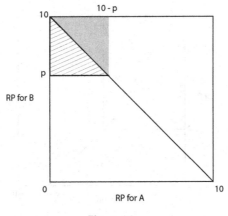

Figure 6.9.

individually. How can this be? By bundling, the incumbent forces its buyers to make a choice: buy the bundle or give up product A. The only buyers willing to do this are those who assign a relatively low RP or value to product A. Thus, the bundle reduces the size of the market that is available for the entrant. The entrant is limited to the buyers whose value for B is much higher than their value for A.

Recall from Example 18 that bundling at $10 is not the profit maximizing choice of a bundle price but $8.165 is. Suppose the incumbent chooses this price for its bundle. What price must the entrant choose? It is not hard to see that the entrant must enter with a price lower than before.

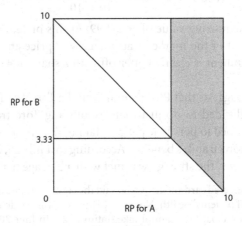

Figure 6.10.

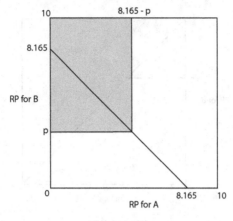

Figure 6.11.

Consider a buyer with an RP for A of x and an RP for B of y. This buyer will consider buying from the entrant only if $y \geq p$. The buyer will buy from the entrant if the surplus from purchasing from the entrant exceeded the surplus from purchasing from the incumbent:

$$y - p \geq x + y - 8.165 \Rightarrow 8.165 - p \geq x.$$

Thus, the only buyers who would buy from the entrant have an RP for B that exceeds p and an RP for A that is below $8.165 - p$. These buyers are illustrated in the shaded region of Figure 6.11. As in the previous case, the entrant will choose a price p to maximize

$$1000 \times p \times \frac{(10 - p) \times (8.165 - p)}{10 \times 10}.$$

The revenue-maximizing value of p is 2.99. At this price, the entrant captures 36.3 percent of the market – again, a lower price and much smaller share. The incumbent is clearly better off with a share of 43.8 percent and profit of \$3,576.

The analysis suggests that Pfizer should bundle Torcetrapib with Lipitor. Indeed, Pfizer decided to do just that. By offering Torcetrapib only in a bundle, Pfizer hoped to persuade patients taking Zocor, to switch to Lipitor if they wanted Torcetrapib's benefits. According to a July 26, 2006, report in the *New York Times*, the strategy was met with a barrage of criticisms.

But Pfizer's plan angered cardiologists, who said the company appeared to be putting its profits ahead of patients' health. Not all patients can easily switch from one statin to another, and some patients cannot take statins at all. In June 2005, an article in *The New England Journal of Medicine* sharply criticized Pfizer's strategy.

Besides complaints from doctors, Pfizer's plan faced commercial and legal challenges. Some lawyers questioned whether offering torcetrapib only with Lipitor might violate antitrust laws. Meanwhile, Lipitor, though still the top-selling drug in the United States with sales last year of $7.4 billion, is losing market share to Zocor, whose price has plunged since it lost patent protection last month. As a result, Pfizer risked damaging torcetrapib by tying it to Lipitor, said Richard T. Evans, an analyst at Sanford C. Bernstein & Company.

Pfizer subsequently abandoned plans to introduce the bundle. In December 2006, Pfizer, ended phase III trials of torcetrapib because of the increased mortality of patients using the drug.

Although our analysis assumed that the seller had monopoly power in product A, this is not essential. The idea carries through provided our seller's version of product A is considered to be superior to the competitior's version of product A. The trade-off for the buyer buying the bundle, though less dramatic, is still present: give up a superior version of product A for an inferior version of A.

Legality of Bundling

Bundling is usually considered illegal when it involves pure bundling, the seller has market power in one of the products being bundled, and the commercial impact is large.[24] The IBM case involving tabulating machines is the archetypal case. Xerox and its bundling of servicing with its copying machines (when it had a monopoly) is another example. In each case, the seller's dominance in one market allowed it, via bundling, to become dominant in another market. One might think that the sellers could circumvent the law by offering to sell individual products at inflated prices (mixed bundling). However, U.S. courts recognize that it is de facto pure bundling if prices are such as to limit the sales of individual products.

A seller that is accused of illegal bundling has two defenses. The first is that bundling does not give it dominance in the competitive market. Sandoz Pharmaceuticals, for example, had a patent on Clozaril, a drug for schizophrenia. The sale of Clozaril was bundled with a patient management system used to monitor the effect of the drug. Because this monitoring system was a fraction of the monitoring system market, this instance of bundling was not considered illegal. The second defense is that the bundling has offsetting benefits for consumers: either a substantial reduction in costs or an increase in value. Microsoft, in its now infamous battle with the U.S. Department of Justice over bundling, attempted such a defense. It argued

---

[24] To find out how large "large" is, consult a lawyer.

Table 6.8. *Incremental RPs*

Quantity	First Unit	Second Unit	Third Unit	Fourth Unit
A's RP	7	5	3	1

that the bundling of the Internet Explorer with the Windows operating system was necessary to provide consumers a seamless and trouble free experience. On this issue, Microsoft emerged victorious. In contrast, in Europe, with the same argument, Microsoft was found guilty of illegally bundling its operating system with its browser.

Bundling Multiple Units
The sale of multiple units of the product via quantity discounts is also a form of bundling. Our discussion will begin with the case of a single buyer who enjoys diminishing returns from consumption. As a vehicle for discussion, consider a SOMA-producing monopolist with unit cost of production of $1 each. There is only one customer, A, whose *incremental* RP for various amounts of SOMA are shown in Table 6.8.

You may assume that the RP for the fifth and higher units is zero. Notice that this buyer's RP for the fourth unit is less then the RP for the third unit, and so on. Buyer A exhibits diminishing marginal returns.

Table 6.9 shows how many units A will buy at various prices:

It is easy to see that the profit-maximizing unit price is $5, yielding a profit of $8. Can one do better than a profit of $8? Yes, because selling each unit at the same price leaves money on the table. At the $5-a-unit price, A buys two units. The surplus on this purchase is $7 + 5 - 2 \times 5 = 2$. Thus, $2 is left on the table. Here is one way to get (most of) the surplus: charge $7 for the first unit, $5 for the second unit, $3 for the third unit, and so on. This may not seem like bundling, but that is cosmetic. One could just as well have set a price of $7 for one unit, $12 for a pack of two units, $15 for a pack of three, and so on.

Announcing a price for each unit or a price for each possible bundle is impractical and, for that reason, one is interested in simpler price schemes

Table 6.9. *Price and Demand*

Price per unit	1	2	3	4	5	6	7
A's demand	4	3	3	2	2	1	1
Profit	0	3	6	6	8	5	6

Table 6.10. *Quantity and Surplus*

Quantity	1	2	3	4
A's surplus	< 0	< 0	0	0

that approximate what the ideal price looks like. Here is an illustration of one. Charge a fixed fee of $1.99 and sell every unit for $5. The fixed fee of $1.99 will not affect the quantity bought. It will determine whether the buyer chooses to accept the offer. Suppose the buyer does. Then the buyer can buy as many units as desired for $5 a unit. At this price, the buyer would maximize the surplus by acquiring two units. This will leave a surplus of $2. Because the fixed fee of $1.99 is less than that, by accepting this offer the buyer's surplus will exceed zero. Thus, given a choice between buying and not, the buyer will buy. Profit will now be $1.99 + $8 = $9.99. Such a pricing scheme is called a **two-part tariff**. It is composed of a fixed cost C and a per unit rate p. If one purchases q units, the cost will be $C + pq$. Such tariffs are ubiquitous. Take the cover charge in a night club, for example. You pay a fixed cost to enter and then more, depending on the number of drinks consumed. The two-part tariff can be disguised by how the fixed cost is framed. Razors and blades are an example. Pay a fixed price for the razor and, thereafter, a price per unit on the blades. Another example is energy (e.g., electricity). The fixed fee is tied to access and the per-unit fee to usage.

A two part tariff is an example of bundling. The buyer is offered one unit for $C + p$, a bundle of two units for $C + 2p$, and so on. The two-part tariff recognizes that A does not value all units the same. Ideally we should sell the first unit to A for $7, the second unit for $5, and so on. A two-part tariff attempts to do just this. Here is why: if the fixed cost is C and the per unit rate is p, A will spend $C + p \times Q$ to purchase Q units. The *average* price per unit buyer A pays will be

$$\frac{C}{Q} + p.$$

This quantity declines as Q, the amount A purchases, increases. Thus, the average price per unit decreases with the volume of purchase.

Can we do better than the two-part tariff just identified? Yes. Here is a two-part tariff that does better: $C = 12$ and $p = 1$. The surplus for various purchase quantities under this tariff are shown in Table 6.10.

Breaking ties in favor of the larger quantity, we see that A will buy four units, yielding a profit of $12 for us.

How does one determine the profit-maximizing two-part tariff? When selling to a single buyer (or multiple buyers with identical preferences), it is calculated using the following procedure:

1. First set the per-unit rate, p, at cost.
2. For this value of p determine how many units the consumer will purchase to maximize the surplus. Set C equal to this surplus.

The per-unit rate of the tariff is set to the seller's unit cost. Thus, the profits are made entirely from the fixed fee. Lowering p stimulates demand, thereby increasing the buyer's surplus. The seller can capture this increase in surplus by raising C.

The intuition that profits are made with the fixed fee rather than the per-unit fee is at variance with the well known razor and blade story: give away the razor and make it up on the blades. By the two-part tariff logic, the seller should first determine the buyer's lifetime value of shaving, say, $\$V$. Because the incremental value of a blade diminishes only on death, $\$V$ is uncertain. Assuming a long life, it might be some impossibly large number. If death were at the doorstep, then it would be vanishingly small. Thus, uncertainty on the part of the buyer about the number of blades he will consume reduces his incentive to pay a large sum (the fixed fee) up front. The uncertainty can come from many sources. A buyer may fear being locked into one kind of razor until death. He may decide at some later date that he looks better in a beard. Less trite, what is to prevent the seller from subsequently raising the price of blades or going out of business, or an innovation in shaving technology that would make the present razor obsolete? In short, the two-part tariff with a large fixed cost component imposes huge risks on the buyer when the buyer is uncertain about consumption, therefore making the buyer reluctant to accept such an offer. One can overcome this reluctance by lowering the fixed-cost component (C) and compensating for this by raising the per-unit price (p). This shifts the risk associated with the uncertainty in the volume of consumption onto the seller. In the case of razors and blades, the seller bears the cost of the razor, gambling that the buyer will spend enough on blades to recoup that cost and more. In other contexts, the seller may limit risk for both the seller and the buyer by placing time limits. For example, C could be an annual or monthly fee that entitles the buyer to unlimited consumption during the relevant period for a per-unit fee. Indeed, a seller can offer a menu of two-part tariffs, one with a large C but low p, and another with a low C and large p. Health clubs are an example: they may charge an annual membership (large C) in return for unlimited use of the facilities for a year ($p = 0$), or no membership fee

Table 6.11. *Incremental RPs of Heavy Users*

Unit	First	Second	Third	Fourth	Fifth	Sixth	Seventh	Eighth	Ninth
RP	$9	$8	$7	$6	$5	$4	$3	$2	$1

($C = 0$) but a daily use fee (high p). The first offering would be attractive to users confident that they will use the facilities with high frequency, and the second to those uncertain about how often they will use the facilities.

We now examine the case of buyers with different levels of consumption more closely. For this case, imagine a monopoly supplier of printers and the cartridges that go with them. Consumers receive utility from the use of the cartridges, but not the printer. However, no one can use a cartridge without a printer. The unit production cost of a printer is $5 and the unit production cost of a cartridge is $1.

There are two types of customers (assume one of each), heavy and light. Heavy users are prepared to pay more for each incremental cartridge than light users. The incremental reservation prices of the heavy users is shown in Table 6.11.

The incremental reservation price for the light users is shown in Table 6.12.

If the monopolist were selling only to the light user, what price would it charge for the printer and cartridge to maximize profit? This would just be the optimal two-part tariff. Sell the cartridge at cost – $1 a unit. At this price, the light user maximizes the surplus when buying 7 units (purchasing to the point at which the incremental RP is $1). At 7 units, the surplus of the light user is 21. Thus, the optimal two-part tariff is to charge $21 for the printer and $1 a unit for the cartridge. The profit is $21 − $5 = $16.

If the monopolist were selling only to the heavy user, a similar analysis suggests that the printer should be priced at $36 and each cartridge at $1. Profit is $36 − $5 = $31.

To summarize, when selling to light users, the seller would set $C = 21$ and $p = 1$. When selling to heavy users, $C = 36$ and $p = 1$. Such a scheme works provided the seller is in a position to distinguish between heavy and

Table 6.12. *Incremental RPs of Light Users*

Unit	First	Second	Third	Fourth	Fifth	Sixth	Seventh
RP	$7	$6	$5	$4	$3	$2	$1

light users. What happens if the seller is limited to imposing the same two part-tariff on all buyers?

At a printer price of $21 and cartridges at $1 a unit, both types of users would have interest in buying the printer and cartridges. However, this leaves money on the table with respect to the heavy users. On the other hand, a printer price of $36 and cartridges at $1 would make the products unattractive for the light user. Is there a combination of printer and cartridge prices that would be attractive to both heavy and light users and would also generate more profit than selling to one kind of buyer alone? A good starting point is the first pricing schedule: printer at $21 and cartridge $1 a unit. At these prices, both buyers make purchases, yielding a total profit of $42 − $10 = $32. Now, there is money left on the table with the heavy users. We can capture that in one of two ways: raise the price of the printer or price of the cartridges. In the first case, we would shut out the light users, which is unprofitable. Let us consider the second.

Increase the cartridge price to $2 a unit. At this price, the light users buy 6 cartridges and the heavy users buy 8. The surplus of the light users will be 15. The surplus of the heavy users will be higher. If we wish to serve both markets, the surplus of the light users will be the upper limit we can charge for the printer. So, set the printer price to $15 and each cartridge to $2 a unit. The total profit is $30 − 10 + 6(2 − 1) + 8(2 − 1) = $34. This is larger than before. Now, suppose a cartridge price of $3 a unit. Light users will buy 5 cartridges, and heavy users will buy 7. The surplus of the light users will be $10. Therefore, set the printer price to $10. At these prices, the profit will be $34. Profit is unchanged. In fact, it is easy to see that we can only lower profits by raising the cartridge price further.

Thus, with customers of various kinds, to maximize profits, we may have to increase the per-unit price and drop the fixed-cost component. As consumers become heterogeneous in their incremental RPs, we may be forced into taking our profits on the cartridges.

Next, assume a drop in the production cost of the cartridges. In this case, one would drop the per-unit price of cartridges and increase the price of the printer. Selling each cartridge for less gives the buyers more surplus and now the seller can rake it back with a higher printer price.

Finally, assume a competitor develops a low-cost substitute for the cartridges that sells for less than $1 a cartridge. How should that affect the price of the printer? Raise the price of the printer. In fact, if the numbers work out right, the monopolist might be better off by having a competitor come in to provide the cartridges at a low price. This encourages buyers to buy more cartridges, thereby increasing their surplus. This increase can be captured by raising the price of the printer.[25]

As an example, consider the popular iPhone and the applications that run on it. To access the benefit provided by the applications, a user must have an iPhone. Hence, Apple is in a position to capture the surplus generated by the applications through the price of the iPhone. In particular, Apple does not have to design the applications themselves, just encourage their design by others. In this sense, Apple has taken a leaf out of the Microsoft playbook.[26]

How Many Bundles?

When a seller offers a two-part tariff with a fixed cost of C and per-unit cost of p, the seller is allowing the buyer to choose the bundle size that best meets the buyer's needs. That is, the buyer is free to choose a bundle of size 1, size 2, size 3, and so on. Is that a good thing? In our printer example, the optimal two-part tariff when selling to both types of consumers was to set the price of the printer to $15 and sell each cartridge for $2. This leaves a lot of money on the table with the heavy users, though. Could we do better? Yes. Offer a bundle of size 4 (one printer and 4 cartridges) for $22 and another bundle of size 9 for $36. That's it. In other words, we limit the choice of the buyers to two different bundles. The light users get no benefit from the large bundle and so will buy the small bundle (because they value it at $22). The heavy users value the large bundle at $45 and the small bundle at $30. At the offered prices, their surplus is maximized on the large bundle. Total revenue will be $36 + 22 = 58$. Total cost will be $(2 \times 5) + (13 \times 1) = 23$. Thus, profits will be $58 - 23 = 35$.

Why has limiting the choice of the buyers made us better off? Because we have limited the arbitrage of consumption.

An Oncological Interlude

Until 2008, about 60 percent of Amgen's profits came from epoetin, sold in two versions: Epogen and Aranesp. The first is used to boost production of red blood cells (which carry oxygen) in dialysis patients suffering from

---

[25] It will be instructive for the reader to replay the story of the printer and the cartridges with the role of the printer replaced by IBM and that of the cartridges by the punch cards. It raises the question of why IBM chose to bundle its machines with the punch cards.

[26] Apple, however, has chosen to exercise more control over the distribution of these applications to ensure that they operate seamlessly with the Apple operating system and deliver an experience consistent with their brand. It does so by requiring applications to be approved and attempting to prevent an iPhone from running unapproved applications.

anemia. The second is used to do the same in cancer patients. In the cancer market, Amgen competes with J&J. J&J's version of epoetin for the cancer market is called Procrit.

Curiously, J&J makes Procrit under a license from Amgen. Amgen originally granted the license in 1985, to raise funds for clinical trials of Epogen. The license granted to J&J the right to use epoetin for all potential uses *except* the treatment of anemia in kidney-failure patients on dialysis.

Flush with profits from the dialysis market, Amgen decided to compete against J&J in the cancer market with a new version of epoetin named Aranesp. Patients on Aranesp can go two to three weeks between injections. Procrit patients need weekly injections. Aranesp was approved by the U.S. Food and Drug Administration in 2002. By 2004, Aranesp had a 45 percent market share to Procrit's 55 percent share.

Among the strategies employed by Amgen to increase its share of the cancer market was to offer hospitals discounts on Neulasta if they bought the bulk of their epoetin – that is, Aranesp, from Amgen. Neulasta (peg filgrastim) boosts white blood cells (infection fighters). Cancer patients undergoing chemotherapy need both kinds of blood boosters. Neulasta accounted for 98 percent of white blood cell booster sales to hospitals and cancer clinics.[27]

An example of such a discount is the following, made to *California Cancer Care*, one of the largest private oncology practices in the San Francisco area. If the oncology practice promised to give Amgen at least one-fourth of its epoetin business, they would get the highest-tier rebate (21 percent) on Neulasta. With a smaller commitment on Aranesp, the Neulasta rebate would be as low as 4 percent. These rebates on anemia drugs go straight into doctors' pockets. This is because oncologists buy the drugs and administer them in their offices. Thus, they can pocket the spread between the discounted price that Amgen billed them and the higher reimbursement Medicare paid them. Some doctors were receiving $2,500 from Medicare for a vial of Neulasta that cost them $2,100.[28]

That Amgen is bundling the sale of Aranesp with Neulasta is not a surprise, given the discussion earlier in this chapter. However, Amgen is not offering a pure bundle of Neulasta and Aranesp. So, why should such a discount scheme make sense? After all, what is the point of cutting the price of Neulasta to boost the demand for Aranesp? Why not just cut the

[27] To be precise, Neulasta and a variant, Neupogen, also owned by Amgen, account for 98 percent of white blood cell booster sales.
[28] This spread ended in 2005 when new legislation took effect.

price of Aranesp directly? Indeed, the federal court for the district of New Jersey asked just this question in 2008, when it dismissed a suit brought by the Sheet Metal Workers National Health Fund (SMW) against Amgen. The SMW sued Amgen for tying its products and engaging in a bundled pricing scheme in violation of state and federal antitrust law. The court rejected the suit on the grounds that in most tying arrangements, any increase in the tied product's price will be accompanied by a decrease in the tying product's price, resulting in no net economic harm to consumers.

On its face, the court's argument seems eminently sensible. However, if this form of tying had no effect on consumers, why did Amgen engage in it? The court's argument relies on an unstated assumption: consumption of Neulasta would not be altered by a change in Neulasta's price. To see why, we examine a numerical example. None of the data in this example are real; they are invented for demonstrative purposes only.

Suppose *California Cancer Care* is willing to pay at most $200 per unit of epoetin (whether Amgen's or J&J's) and is interested in buying at most 100 units of it. For this exercise we assume that the buyer sees no difference between Amegn's and J&J's version of epoetin. The unit cost of production of epoetin is $10 for Amgen as well as for J&J.

Assume that California Cancer Care's demand curve for Neulasta is $120 - p$, where p is the price per unit of Neulasta. The unit cost of production of Neulasta is, for convenience, $0 a unit.

In the base case, Amgen prices both Aranesp and Neulasta independently. The profit-maximizing price p of Neulasta will be chosen to maximize $p(120 - p)$. This results in a price of $60 a unit for Neulasta. At this price, *California Cancer Care* will purchase 60 units of Neulasta. The price of Aranesp, however, will depend on the intensity of competition between Aranesp and Procrit. Because the products are assumed identical in the eyes of buyers, let us make the extreme assumption that competition will force the price of Aranesp to cost – that is, $10 a unit.[29] Thus, in this example, Amgen makes a profit only on Neulasta, which comes to $3,600. *California Cancer Care* purchases 100 units of epoetin and 60 units of Neulasta and spends $4,600.

Now, suppose that Amgen offers *California Cancer Care* the following: buy all its epoetin from Amgen for $11 a unit, and in return get a discount of $10 off the $60 a unit price of Neulasta. If *California Cancer Care* accepts this offer, it will purchase 100 units of epoetin and spend $1,100. The unit price of Neulasta is now $50. At this price, *California Cancer Care* will purchase

---

[29] Assuming otherwise does not change the qualitative point of this example.

Table 6.13. *Price and Demand*

Price/demand	At least 1 unit	≥ 2 units	≥ 3 units	≥ 4 units	≥ 5 units
$2 per unit	90	75	55	30	5
$3 per unit	80	65	45	20	0
$4 per unit	65	50	30	5	0
$5 per unit	45	30	10	0	0

$120 - 50 = 70$ units of Neulasta. This will cost it $3,500. In total, *California Cancer Care* will spend $4,600. This is the same amount as in the base case. However, *California Cancer Care* has acquired strictly more Neulasta than in the base case. This means that the bundled offer from Amgen has increased the surplus to *California Cancer Care*. For the cynical, it means more units of Neulasta on which a rebate can be earned. This means that Amgen could actually increase the unit price of Neulasta and still have *California Cancer Care* purchase from it. In effect, Amgen is charging a two-part tariff. The fixed cost is associated with the epoetin and the per-unit cost is associated with Neulasta. To summarize, tying could actually benefit both Amgen and *California Cancer Care*.

The outcome of our example is at variance with the reasoning of the court. Why is that? In our example, the demand for at least one of the components was "elastic." That is, changing its price will change the volume consumed. The reasoning of the court applies if the quantities purchased are not influenced by a change in the unit price. Thus, the question of whether tying had an anticompetitive effect in this case should have turned on whether the buyers would have increased their purchases of Neulasta in response to a drop in the unit price of Neulasta.

Nonlinear Pricing
Nonlinear pricing represents the ultimate in pricing multiple units to absorb as much consumer surplus as possible. To illustrate the idea, we use a simple numerical example.[30] The starting point is information about how demand responds to price, but now one needs more information than a simple demand curve can provide. To implement a sophisticated nonlinear pricing scheme, one needs to break down the demand at each price into the number of people who bought only one unit at that price, two units at that price, and so forth. Table 6.13 is an example of just such a breakdown. The numbers in

[30] Based on page 76 of Wilson (1993).

the table record how many people bought at least that number of units for a particular price. For example, the 90 in the upper left means that 90 people bought at least one unit for $2 a unit. Manufacturing costs are $1 a unit. As we scan down a column, the numbers decrease. This is to be expected, because the demand drops as price increases. The numbers also decrease along the rows. Again, this is what one would expect from diminishing returns.

If we sold every unit at the same price, the profit-maximizing price would be $4 a unit, yielding a profit of $450.[31] We can do better by charging one price for the first unit purchased, a slightly lower price for the second unit and so on. Working out these prices is easy (in this case).

First, scan down the column of numbers corresponding to the purchase of at least 1 unit and ask what price would maximize profit on the first unit. It is easy to see that it is $4, with 65 people buying. Now, do the same for the next column (at least 2 units). The price here is also $4, with 50 people buying. For the remaining columns, the profit-maximizing prices are $3 (with 45 people buying), $3 (with 20 people buying), and $2 (with 5 people buying), respectively. So, charge $4 for one unit, $8 for 2 units, $11 for 3 units, and so on. The total profit will be

$$(4-1) \times 65 + (4-1) \times 50 + (3-1) \times 45 + (3-1) \times 20 + (2-1) \times 5,$$

which is equal to $480, more than before.

To see why this is correct, observe that at the $3 per-unit price, 65 people are willing to buy at least 2 units. Thus, for this group their incremental RP for the second unit is at least $3, based on diminishing incremental RP. Out of these 65, at $4 per unit, 50 are willing to buy at least 2 units. This means there are 15 people who would be interested in a two-unit bundle at $8. At the $3 unit price, there are 45 people who are willing to buy at least 3 units. This implies that their incremental RP for the third unit is at least $3. Out of these 45, at $4 per unit, 30 people are willing to buy at least 3 units. This means that there are 30 people who would be interested in a three-unit bundle for $11, which is lower than their valuation of $12. Finally, there are 20 people who are willing to buy at least 4 units at a price of $3 per unit, implying that their incremental RP for the fourth unit is at least $3. Out of these 20 people, 5 are willing to buy at least 4 units at a price of $4 per unit.

---

[31] At $4 a unit, five people will buy four units, $30 - 5 = 25$ will buy three units, $50 - 30 = 20$ will buy two units, and $65 - 50 = 15$ will buy one unit. Hence, $(5 \times 4) + (25 \times 3) + (20 \times 2) + (15 \times 1) = 150$ units will be purchased. This yields a profit of $150 \times (\$4 - \$1) = \$450$.

Table 6.14. *Modified Price and Demand*

Price/demand	At least 1 unit	≥ 2 units	≥ 3 units	≥ 4 units	≥ 5 units
$2 per unit	90	89	??	??	??
$3 per unit	80	40	??	??	??
$4 per unit	65	28	??	??	??
$5 per unit	45	20	??	??	??

It follows that 15 people would be interested in a 4-unit bundle at a price of $14 which is lower than their valuation of $16. From the table, no one is interested in buying 5 or more units. Accounted for this way, the profit equals $15 \times (\$8 - \$2) + 30 \times (\$11 - \$3) + 15 \times (\$14 - \$4) = \$90 + \$240 + \$150 = \$480$. In total, 60 people buy 180 units. When a flat rate of $4 per unit was charged, the profit was $450 and 65 people bought a total of 150 units. One objective of bundling is to get more people to buy (bundling is a way of reducing the price below the valuation), or, alternatively, more units to be sold. This happens here because we sell more units (180 vs. 150), although fewer people buy (60 vs. 65). The average bundled price is $3.67 per unit (revenue of $660 divided by 180 units), versus the flat rate price of $4 yielding revenue of $600 from the purchase of 150 units.

An important thing to check with this simple approach is that the number of people buying the first unit is *more* than the number buying the second, more than the number buying the third, and so on. In this case, the demands follow the expected patterns. Will this always be so? No. This is where the simple approach described previously breaks down. To see an example of where this might happen, suppose the number in the second row and third column of Table 6.13 changed from 75 to 89, and the number in the fourth row and third column changed from 50 to 28. To keep things consistent, the number in the third row and third column should also change to, say, 40, and the number in the fifth row and third column changes to 20. Table 6.14 shows the changes, with question marks for the other entries as they need to be adjusted as well. In this case, the profit-maximizing price for the second unit would be $2. But at this price, 89 people are expected to buy the second unit, whereas for the first unit, only 65 people are supposed to buy at a price of $4. What makes this example unusual is that it says that for the $2 price, buyers attach almost as much value to the second unit as they do to the first unit. Notice that 90 people buy at least one unit and 89 buy at least two at the $2 price. At higher prices, however, most buyers attach hardly any value to the second unit. In particular, because 65 people buy the first unit at the $4 price and less than half of them buy the second unit, there is a group of buyers who experience a sharp drop-off in value for the second unit.

When the simple-minded approach to nonlinear pricing breaks down, one must resort to more sophisticated techniques. Basically, one takes the prices from the simple-minded approach and adjusts them so they generate consistent demand patterns. A mathematical formulation of the nonlinear pricing problem appears in the Technical Aside.

6.3 Revenue Management

The biggest innovation in pricing in the past fifty years has been revenue management.[32] The full details could, and do, fill a book. Here we highlight, via stylized examples, just two aspects of revenue management.

In our first example, you sell widgets that cost $1 a unit to manufacture to two different customers for $2 a widget. Each customer has an RP per widget of $2. Widgets are a perishable product and last a day; thus, your customers place orders for widgets with you every day, but the sizes of these orders vary from day to day. You have guaranteed to fill 100 percent of each order when it arrives. What makes life difficult is that you must decide how many widgets to keep in stock *before* the orders for that day materialize. Widgets produced by you and subsequently never shipped cannot be reused.

Customer 1's average daily order is 50 widgets, whereas for customer 2, it is 100. Which customer is the most profitable for you? If you hesitate to answer because of insufficient information, we hope it is because you would like to know the variance in demand. Averages without variances are like Samson without his hair.

Customer 1 orders 50 widgets each day, with unerring regularity. Customer 2 is more volatile. On any given day, there is a 50 percent chance that he will order 200 widgets and a 50 percent chance that he will order nothing.

To fill customer 1's orders, it suffices to keep 50 widgets in stock each day. This yields a daily profit of $50. To ensure that customer 2's orders will be filled every time they arrive, one must keep 200 widgets in stock. But, half the time, customer 2 will order nothing, so you will be down $100, and the other half the time he will order all 200 and you will be up $100. On average, you make no profit from serving customer 2.

Customer 2's variability in ordering makes him a more expensive customer to serve because of the additional inventory or capacity one must reserve for him. This is capacity that you could have been allocated to

---

[32] The idea, however, is even older. One newspaper account observes that in the 1890s, the Coney Island amusement park deployed a simple version of it to price admissions.

other productive uses. To charge customer 2 the same price as customer 1 is therefore silly. Another way to look at this is to realize that you are selling customer 2 not just a widget, but also a bundle consisting of widgets and guaranteed availability (or flexibility). Given the huge variance in customer 2's demand, the guaranteed availability has a great deal of value to customer 2 and should be reflected in the price. Alternatively, the seller can ask for a quantity commitment contract to reduce the cost of excess inventory. The buyer commits in advance to purchase a certain minimum volume over the period of the contract. The buyer can choose when, and in what frequency, these units are to be delivered, but at the end of the contract period, the buyer must make up the difference if less than the minimum is ordered. There are variations on this, but the basic idea is that the seller is selling to the buyer something analogous to a call option.[33]

The advance purchase discount offered by airlines is a canonical example. One can buy at a low price if one forgoes the flexibility of being able to change the arrival and departure dates. One buys at a high price if he or she wants the flexibility of being able to change travel dates at will. Thus, low-variance customers are offered lower prices than high-variance customers. There is more, however. By purchasing well in advance of the departure date, one gets even more of a discount. Why is this? By promising to fly in advance of the departure date, one helps the airline reduce the variability in its forecasts, which allows it to make better capacity allocation decisions.[34] There is nothing special about the airlines that allows them to do this. Amazon.com, for example, does this, but in reverse. It offers a delayed purchase discount: pay less for later delivery.[35]

In our second example, the amount of inventory on hand is limited. You have a 100-room hotel. What price do you post for the rooms in advance of knowing what the demand for the rooms will be?

If, at the posted price, the realized demand exceeds supply, you leave money on the table. Some of those you turn away would have paid more than those you grant rooms to. On the other hand, if the realized demand

---

[33] A call option is the right to purchase a stock at some future date at a price specified now. If the price at the future date is higher than the price specified in the option, the buyer exercises the option and resells the stock at a profit. If the future price is less than the specified price, the option is never exercised. The option guards against the risk of owning a stock that will drop in value.

[34] Money today is also better than money tomorrow.

[35] One can imagine hotels doing the same: $250 a night for a room if one wishes to guarantee the reservation, and $175 a night if the hotel is allowed to cancel the reservation with 24 hours' notice. In this case, the hotel buys flexibility from the customer.

falls below 100, you may scare off some prepared to pay something less than the posted price but who would still be profitable.

Assume that future demand for hotel rooms will be in one of two states, high (H) or low (L), with equal probability. In H there will be 100 buyers looking for hotel rooms, each with an RP of $120. In L there will be 50 buyers for hotel rooms, each with an RP of $100.

If you could tell ahead of time which state will be realized, pricing is easy. If you do not, you might consider state-contingent pricing. That is, you announce not a single price but a schedule: if we are in state H, the price of a room is $120; otherwise rooms are priced at $100. This is not unheard of – think of pricing by seasons.[36]

State-contingent pricing requires two things: first, a knowledge of how relevant states are linked to the distribution of RPs; second, recognizing when one is in a particular state. To make life difficult in our example, suppose you cannot tell which state you will be in until after the fact. Let us start by supposing that you fix a single price for all rooms. There are just two choices, $100 and $120. If you choose the low price, your revenue in state L will be $100 × 50 = $5,000 and in state H will be $100 × 100 = $10,000. Thus, expected revenue will be ($5,000 + $10,000)/2 = $7,500.

If you choose the high price, you make no money in state L, but in state H your revenue is 100× $120 = $12,000. Thus, expected revenue with the high price is $6,000.

It appears that charging the low price is the best strategy. Can one do better? Yes: price 50 of the rooms at the low price ($100) and the other 50 at the high price ($120). In state L, one's revenue will be $ 100 × 50 = $5,000. In state H, revenue will be ($100 × 50) + ($120× 50) = $11,000, which means that expected revenues will be ($5,000 + $11,000)/2 = $8,000.

Revenue increases when you offer two prices for the same product and limit the quantity sold at the lower price. What drives this? It is how the uncertainty in value interacts with the uncertainty in volume. An increase in volume is correlated with an increase in RP, and vice versa. To benefit from this, the hotel must reserve some of its capacity for the case in which it might be in state H, high demand and high RP. This is consistent with

---

[36] A good example is ice-cold beer (but not in England). If the ambient temperature rises to a tropical 90 degrees Fahrenheit, one can expect two things: more people wanting cold beers, and willing to pay more for it than they otherwise would. In this fable, the uncertainty in value and volume is linked to the temperature. The easiest way, technology permitting, to respond to this uncertainty is to post temperature-contingent prices.

the conclusion of Chapter 5, in which we argued that with limited supply, a seller should sell by auction. Reserving a number of rooms at the low price is effectively an auction. The seller has announced that initially prices will be low, but as demand increases, the price rises.

In our example, state H consisted entirely of buyers with an RP of $120. What if we had a mixture of buyers, some with low RPs and others with high-RPs? If the high-RP buyers turn up first, we sell out of the low-priced rooms and leave money on the table. When the low-RP buyers turn up, the only rooms available are high-priced ones and the buyers walk away. Again, money is left on the table. In practice, the seller guards against this possibility by ensuring that the low-RP customers turn up first, followed by the high RP customers. How? Through the use of an advance purchase discount.

In the example of the hotel, two price levels were enough to increase profits over setting a single price. Could one do better with more price levels than just two? No, because there were only two possible future states, and RPs could take on only two possible values. In reality, there could be many more states and differences in RPs. Determining the number of price levels and the number of units to be set aside for each level (called *protection levels*) is a complex optimization problem. None of that, however, should take away from the qualitative point: a unit sold today at a low price could have been sold tomorrow at a higher price. Thus, one should weigh the profit to be made today with a low price against potential future higher profits. This trade-off is absent when supply is unlimited. Thus, when supply is restricted, this translates into limiting the number of units sold at the low price. The Technical Aside contains analysis of how to choose the protection levels in a simple case.

6.4 Gray Markets

The most visible instance of arbitrage associated with price discrimination are gray markets. Gray markets refer to the unauthorized transfer of goods from one distribution channel or market to another. Typically, goods in markets in which prices are lower are transferred to markets in which prices are higher. For example, during the Asian currency crisis of 1997–1998, the demand for heavy construction machinery from Asia evaporated. Prices in Asia fell. Because this equipment was in high demand in North America, profits were to be had by purchasing the machinery in Asia and selling it in North America. A fully equipped excavator could sell for $200,000 in North America. The same excavator was available on the gray market for

$130,000.[37] The range of products affected by gray markets is huge. Cars, cigarettes, tires, cameras, jewels, computers, liquor, prescription drugs, baby food, clothing, and perfumes are some examples. According to a 2001 study by the trade group Alliance for Gray Market and Counterfeit Abatement, about $40 billion of technology products are sold on the gray market each year.

The obvious beneficiaries of gray markets (other than buyers) are the arbitrageurs who buy low in one market and resell high in another. In some cases, these arbitrageurs can be authorized distributors because they get deeper discounts when ordering in large volumes. Tempted by the profits, they "overorder" and ship the excess to retailers in other markets. For years, Sa Sa Cosmetics in Hong Kong, a discount retailer, bought from such distributors located outside Hong Kong. Some arbitrageurs violate distribution agreements by selling overstocks of products that are near the end of their life rather than returning them to the supplier. Sales managers within the affected organization also benefit. The gray market allows them to meet sales quotas or annual sales goals.

A gray market poses four challenges to a seller:

1. It reduces the profits to be had from price discrimination.
2. Unchecked, it may damage channel relationships. Authorized distributors frequently shoulder expenses that a gray marketer does not. These expenses are associated with backup, spare parts, repairs, and promotional support to customers. This places them at a cost disadvantage with respect to the gray marketer. If they lose sales to the gray marketer, it reduces their incentives to incur the additional expenses.
3. It can damage the seller's reputation. For example, the image of luxury brands can be damaged if these products are readily available at lower prices.
4. It disrupts sales forecasts and inventory policies. The existence of a thriving gray market can distort the accuracy of sales forecasts because it cannibalizes sales that might otherwise have come through authorized channels. Second, a gray market can generate double bookings in the supply chain. This happens when the gray market is associated with an imbalance between supply and demand. Buyers in the region facing a shortage have an incentive to buy through the gray market. Such buyers will place one order through the authorized channel and a second order in the gray market.

---

[37] These numbers are from an article by Charles Yengst in the March 1998 issue of *Diesel Progress*.

The options a seller has for dealing with a gray market are obvious and not entirely palatable.

1. Reduce the degree of price discrimination. Apple, for example, has adopted a uniform price policy across the globe to prevent a gray market in its goods.
2. To reduce or prevent resale, the seller can limit the quantities sold to buyers. In the extreme, the seller can refuse to supply distributors and retailers that trade in gray-market goods. This presumes the ability to track gray-market sales. In addition to employing private detectives, some sellers do this by giving identical products different model numbers that identify the country for which the product is intended.[38] However, as in other matters, there is an arms race between gray marketers and sellers. For every technology used to track a product, there is eventually a technology to neutralize it.
3. The problem with authorized distributors selling into the gray market can be solved at the source with an appropriate qualification process for distributors. Agreements with distributors must carefully define the distributor's authorized territory as well as forbid gray-market participation.
4. To reduce arbitrage possibilities, the seller can engage in versioning. This may involve modifying, damaging, or enhancing the product for various markets. Porsche, for example, makes its cars for the U.S. market better equipped. In other cases, the seller will decline to honor the warranty of an item purchased on the gray market. Sony is an example. Nikon refuses to repair a gray-market camera even if a customer is willing to pay for the repairs. Other sellers rely on technology to make a product intended for one market unworkable in another market. DVD region codes are an example.[39]
5. In some circumstances legal action is possible to reduce the volume of trade in a gray market. Patents sometimes prohibit reimportation.[40] Trademark and copyright laws allow the seller to petition for the removal of advertisements that violate trademark or copyright

[38] Gray marketers will attempt to decode the product to avoid identification by the supplier. In the United States, courts have decided that this constitutes a material alteration, thereby infringing on the rights of the seller.

[39] Consumer groups are usually opposed to this, arguing that it is unjust and anticompetitive. For this reason, many governments decline to protect technologies such as DVD region-coding.

[40] These rights are limited by the first-sale doctrine in the United States and the doctrine of the exhaustion of rights in the European Union.

laws. Local laws that specify the content of labels and/or disclosure of nutritional content can also be invoked. Gray markets are not illegal in the United States and Canada. The European Union (EU) bans gray-market goods imported into the EU from non-EU countries; however, gray market goods imported from one EU member country into another are legal.

6. Educating customers about the dangers (real or hypothetical) of gray-market purchases is important. The message should be that gray-market products could be obsolete or worn-out models with ineffective warranties or models not designed to meet requirements for use in a specific country. In some cases, the gray-market retailers may modify the product to lower costs – for example, selling a digital camera without the battery and cables that normally come with it.

Before losing sleep over the existence of a gray market, it is useful to gauge the size and extent of the market. If it is relatively small and confined to a narrow market (defined either geographically, or by product line, for instance) and unlikely to grow, it may be worthwhile to do nothing. Second, a gray market is not merely a problem, but also a symptom. Its existence may be a sign that the relevant market is being commoditized, so price discrimination may simply not be viable anymore.

Third, it is possible that the gray market is reaching a segment that the seller is otherwise not reaching. In this sense, it is not so much a problem as an opportunity to be harvested. The gray market in Apple's iPhone is one example. The original iPhone was launched in the United States in June 2007, and was made available in the United Kingdom, France, and Germany in November 2007, and Ireland and Austria in the spring of 2008. In July 2008, the iPhone 3G was available in a total of 22 countries. In each country, Apple had signed an exclusive contract with a single carrier, and the device was expected to operate only on the networks of these carriers. Nevertheless, by 2008, about a million iPhones (about 25 percent of all iPhones) were sold (not by Apple) "unlocked."[41] That is, the device had been modified to run on networks not authorized by Apple. Apple could retard or even halt the trade in gray market iPhones by bundling the sale of the device with a service contract.[42] It does not. Many believe that the gray market in iPhones helps spread Apple's brand awareness.

[41] These figures are from a February 12, 2008 report in *Business Week* by Peter Burrows.
[42] It does limit the number of devices that may be purchased by any one individual; however, this is easy to get around: enlist friends or strangers, or pretend to be a small business.

6.5 Legal Aspects of Price Discrimination

Price discrimination of the variety discussed in this chapter is generally legal (at least in the United States). Although there is legislation (the Robinson-Patman Act) that prohibits price discrimination, it is very specific and motivated by a desire to mitigate the harm from "unfair" competition. The Robinson-Patman Act was passed in 1936 in response to complaints from independent retailers being driven out of business by chain stores. It was argued that the chain stores, because of volume discounts, enjoyed lower wholesale costs than did the independent retailers. This amounted to suppliers giving preferential treatment to one class of customers over others, thereby hindering competition.[43] Thus, the act is concerned primarily with manufacturers price-discriminating among distributors and retailers. Further, the discrimination must result in "competitive injury."[44]

The act applies only to tangible items such as appliances, handbags, and bicycles. It does not cover services or licenses to intellectual property, such as software. It is invoked when *all* of the following conditions are met:

1. Two or more sales during what could reasonably construed to be the same period;
2. Involving commodities of similar grade and quality;
3. Sold by the same seller at different prices to two or more different buyers;
4. The items sold must be for for use, consumption, or resale within the United States; and
5. The transactions may result in competitive injury.

The requirement that the sales be in the same period is a recognition that over longer periods of time, things can change. A product becomes obsolete and one would like to allow the seller to reduce the price of that product. The requirement that products be of similar grade and quality allows the seller to set different prices for different variations of the base product. For example, branded and non-branded condensed milk sold by the same seller are considered different products. The act also enumerates some possible defenses. For example, price differentials can be justified on cost grounds or

---

[43] Independent grocery stores lobbied Congress to do something about the large chains. The United States Wholesale Grocers Association drafted the original bill of what was to become the Robinson-Patman Act.

[44] Subsequent legislation recognizes that manufacturers may discriminate using promotional allowances, rather than just prices.

the need to meet the competition. If the two buyers are in different industries or at different levels of the distribution chain, then price discrimination may not result in competitive injury.

6.6 Key Points

1. Customers differ in their valuations. Therefore, matching the price charged to the RPs of the different customers will yield a greater profit than charging the same price to everyone. This practice is called price discrimination. From the seller's point of view, some changes to the product may be necessary. The cost incurred should be less than the price differences that can be charged. To protect the different prices, the possibility of arbitrage should be as low as possible.

2. There are three kinds of price discrimination. In first-degree price discrimination, each customer is charged a different price consistent with that customer's RP. In second-degree price discrimination, a number of versions of the item are offered and customers self-select the version consistent with their RP. In third-degree price discrimination, an observed signal (demographics, purchase history, place, type of application, and so on) is used to charge different prices. First-degree price discrimination is rare, whereas second- and third-degree price discrimination are quite common. Combinations of second- and third-degree are common as well.

3. A number of examples of third-degree price discrimination are provided. The signal used to charge different prices should be correlated with valuations, or equivalently, price sensitivity.

4. In second-degree price discrimination, different versions are presented with the objective of targeting the higher-priced versions to higher-valuation (less price-sensitive) customers and the lower priced versions to lower-valuation (more price-sensitive) customers. The goal is to sell the multiple versions to the appropriate segments. Two important observations are made in describing the application of second-degree price discrimination. First, if the prices are not carefully managed – for example, the higher priced version is priced too high – it is possible for the high-valuation customers to choose the lower-priced versions as well, leading to lower profits for the seller. Second, if the valuations for the different versions are not sufficiently different, versioning will typically not pay off in increased profits.

5. Three types of bundling – a pure bundle in which only the bundle is offered, a mixed bundle in which the bundle and à la carte are

offered, and tying, in which the bundle and one of the components is offered separately – are described. One reason to bundle is price discrimination. Bundling can be used for other reasons as well – for example, when transaction costs are high for the seller to provide the items individually, when there are complementarities among the units, to simplify decision making for the customer, and to satisfy customers' needs for variety. Several examples are provided to illustrate bundling.

6. Bundling is typically beneficial to the seller when there is considerable variance in the valuation of buyers for the different items. Bundling reduces the variance and helps the seller.

7. If the correlation between RPs for the different items among buyers is low or negative (for example, some buyers have high valuation for item 1 and low valuation for item 2, whereas other buyers have low valuation for item 1 and high valuation for item 2), bundling will typically yield more revenue to the seller than pricing items individually. On, the other hand if the correlation between RPs is positive, bundling is unlikely to increase revenues over individual item pricing.

8. In some cases, a seller selling multiple items could benefit by bundling against a seller selling fewer items. The logic is that bundling benefits the seller of multiple items by reducing competition on the common items.

9. A two-part tariff, charging a fixed fee and a variable fee, is also an example of bundling. Instead of setting a price for each bundle (consisting of different numbers of items) separately, the two-part tariff approximates the different bundle prices through a fixed fee and a per-unit fee. The fixed fee determines whether the buyer will accept the offer. An example is a fixed fee for a night club. The per-unit fee could be for the drinks.

10. When customers are homogeneous in their preferences, charging a higher fixed fee and a lower per-unit fee is optimal. When customers are heterogeneous, as is more likely to be the case, charging a lower fixed fee and a higher per-unit fee is better for the seller. This is what we see in the market with razors (priced low) and blades (priced high), with printers (priced low) and ink cartridges (priced high), and so forth.

11. Revenue management helps the seller to reduce variance or uncertainty in demand. The low price with restrictions clears the low-valuation customers, allowing the seller to charge a higher price to high-valuation customers.

12. Price discrimination could lead to the creation of gray markets, wherein goods destined for certain customers or certain markets are purchased and resold at lower prices to customers in other markets. Examples of gray markets and what actions the seller can take to minimize their impact are discussed.

6.7 Technical Aside

6.7.1 Formulation of Example 15

It is instructive to consider a mathematical formulation of Example 15. Let F be the price of the fast version and S the price of the slow version. Suppose also we wish to target the fast version to the As and the slow to the Bs. If we succeed in doing so, revenue will be $F + S$. However, to give the As the incentive to buy the fast version we need to ensure that their surplus on the fast version is no smaller than their surplus on the slow version:

$$100 - F \geq 40 - S.$$

Similarly, to ensure that the Bs buy the slow printer:

$$49 - F \leq 30 - S.$$

Therefore, we must find F and S that maximize $F + S$ yet satisfy:

$$100 - F \geq 40 - S$$

$$49 - F \leq 30 - S$$

These last two inequalities are examples of arbitrage constraints. They are absent if there is a single version, but appear when one has two or more versions to sell.

Is offering two versions always better than a single version? It would seem that it cannot be worse, because the underlying profit maximization problem has more control variables, giving the seller greater flexibility. However, selling two versions also imposes more constraints on the set of possible prices to prevent arbitrage of consumption. The end result is that it could go either way, depending on the numbers.

Unfortunately, the preceding mathematical formulation does not scale well with the number of segments and versions. In fact, its size grows exponentially with the number of segments and versions. This is because one must decide which versions should be targeted to which segments, and

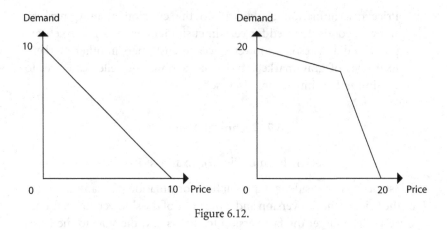

Figure 6.12.

the number of possibilities is large.[45] In these cases, one uses a reduced-form model that is tailored to the circumstances.

6.7.2 Analysis of Bundling

In Example 18, the RP for an individual product is uniformly distributed between 0 and 10. The RP for a bundle, however, has a triangular distribution between 0 and 20. This is because the RP for a two-item bundle is the sum of two independent uniformly distributed random variables. Figure 6.12 illustrates the demand curve for a single product, as well as the demand curve for a bundle of two products.

Figure 6.13 shows the demand curve for a bundle of twenty products.

Roughly speaking, the demand curve becomes less elastic as the size of the bundle increases. To formalize this, suppose the RP for each product i is a random number drawn from some well-behaved distribution (e.g., normal, log-normal, uniform, or exponential) with mean μ_i and standard deviation σ_i. Consider a bundle of n items. If r_i is the RP for product i, then the mean RP per item will be $\frac{\sum_{i=1}^{n} r_i}{n}$. The mean RP per item will be approximately normally distributed, with mean $\frac{\sum_{i=1}^{n} \mu_i}{n}$ for large n. More important, the standard deviation of the mean RP per item will be $\frac{\sum_{i=1}^{n} \sigma_i}{\sqrt{n}}$. Hence, for sufficiently large n, close to 99 percent of the population will have a value for the bundle that is very close to $\sum_{i=1}^{n} \mu_i$. The upshot is that the RP that each buyer attaches to a bundle is pretty much the same. In this

---

[45] One can reduce the size of the optimization problem by using a multidimensional demand curve in which the demand for version i is a function of the price of version i as well as the price of all other versions. However, there may be insufficient data to estimate such a curve.

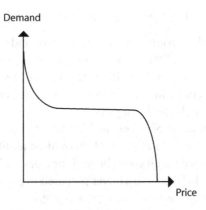

Figure 6.13.

case, we should expect the demand curve for a bundle of size n (where n is large) to be pretty close to flat. This is illustrated in Figure 6.13, which displays the demand curve for a bundle of twenty goods for the case in which the RP for the individual goods has a uniform distribution.

Suppose now that n is large. If item i is priced at μ_i, then only buyers with an RP that exceeds μ_i will purchase item i. Typically, the fraction of such buyers will be far less than 99 percent. The fraction that purchase all n items separately will be much smaller than that. However, if a bundle of n items is priced at $\sum_{i=1}^{n} \mu_i$, 99 percent of the population will buy the entire bundle.

6.7.3 Nonlinear Pricing

Here we show how the problem of finding the optimal schedule of non-linear prices can be formulated as a mathematical program. This mathematical program can be solved using software. For more on the underlying mathematics, see Wilson (1993). Let $D_k(p)$ be the number of people who purchased at least k units when the price per unit was p. Let c be the cost per unit and suppose that the largest number of units bought by anyone was n. In our example, $c = 1$ and $D_1(p)$ is just the first column of Table 6.13, $D_2(p)$ is the second column of Table 6.13, and so on. Let p_j be the price of the jth unit. The mathematical program to be solved is:

$$\max(p_1 - c)D_1(p_1) + (p_2 - c)D_2(p_2) + \cdots + (p_n - c)D_n(p_n)$$

$$\text{s.t. } p_1 \geq p_2 \geq p_3 \cdots \geq p_n \geq 0$$

$$D_1(p_1) \geq D_2(p_2) \geq \cdots \geq D_n(p_n).$$

6.7.4 Choosing a Protection Level

Assume a hotel with Q rooms. Buyers are of two kinds: one with an RP of H and the other with an RP of $L < H$. Suppose the number of buyers with an RP of H is a random number with distribution F. We will determine the optimal number, r, of rooms to set aside to be rented at a price of H. The remaining rooms will be sold at a price L.

Let N_H be the number of buyers with an RP of H and suppose r rooms have been set aside for sale at price H. Should an additional room be set aside on the off chance that it could be sold for a price H? This is an issue if that extra room could be sold to a buyer prepared to pay L. Setting aside the additional room makes sense if we expect $N_H \geq r + 1$. This happens with probability $1 - F(r)$. Thus, the expected revenue from setting aside the extra room is $(1 - F(r))H$. Hence, it is profitable to set aside the additional room if $(1 - F(r))H \geq L$. Conversely, given that r rooms have been set aside for sale at price H, an additional room does not need to be set aside if $(1 - F(r))H \leq L$. This suggests that the optimal choice of r should satisfy:

$$1 - F(r) = \frac{L}{H} \Rightarrow F(r) = \frac{H - L}{H}.$$

SEVEN

Pricing and Competition

The goal of this chapter is to convey the main principles of pricing in competitive environments. We approach them through a series of of of thought experiments. The advantage of these experiments is that every variable within them can be controlled. This allows one to precisely isolate how each aspect of the competitive environment affects prices. The result will be a clearer and deeper understanding of pricing in competitive environments than any collection of anecdotes or string of 'just so' stories is able to deliver. To apply the lessons of this chapter, one must know some basic facts about the industry one is in – specifically, entry costs, exit costs, structure of demand, number, concentration and the distribution of rivals' sizes.

7.1 The Pricing Dilemma

Imagine two firms selling identical widgets to a market of 100 individuals. Each buyer is interested in purchasing at most one widget, and the RP of each buyer is $3. Each buyer will buy from the seller that offers them the largest surplus. Because the products are identical (in the eyes of each buyer), each buyer will purchase from the lowest-priced seller. In the event that both firms set equal prices (and so yield the same surplus to all buyers), the buyers divide equally between the two firms.[1]

The production cost for each firm is $1 a widget. Production is instantaneous and defect-free, so neither firm needs to worry about inventory, returns, and the other complications of real life. Production capacity is unlimited for both firms.

---

[1] The situation just described is sometimes called the *Bertrand model of competition*. The name is in honor of the French mathematician, Joseph Bertrand (1822–1900).

Both firms and the 100 buyers exist for exactly one day. The firms must choose prices at which they will sell widgets simultaneously and independently of each other at the start of the day.[2] Once chosen, prices cannot be adjusted. They are communicated instantly to all 100 buyers, who then choose where to buy their one widget to maximize surplus.

We call the situation just described the "pricing dilemma" (PD). What prices would you expect each firm to post? What price would you (suppose you are firm 1) post?[3] The fundamental difficulty is that one's profit depends not just on one's own price, but on the rival's price as well.

You might argue that because all buyers have an RP of $3, one should price at $3. At this price, though you turn a profit only if your rival matches it.[4] If you were convinced that your rival would set a price of $3, then you could increase your profits by pricing at $2.99, say.

Suppose you pick a price of $2.99. What if the competitor undercuts you? Perhaps to guard against this possibility, one should pick a lower price, perhaps midway between $3 and cost – that is, $2. However, there is still a possibility that the competitor may undercut you. The only sure way to guard against this is to price at cost, which yields zero profit. This seems silly, because one should price at some palpable amount above cost to turn a profit. However, the higher you go, the greater the chance of your rival undercutting you.

You might reason that your rival will pick some price with equal probability between $1 and $3.[5] Given this, a price that would maximize expected profit will be $2. Should you pick $2? If you find this reasoning compelling, shouldn't your rival? If the rival does, then you know that it will price at $2. In that case, wouldn't you want to price at $1.99 instead?

To clarify matters, suppose both firms are limited to charging one of two prices: $3 a unit and $2.50 a unit. Table 7.1 (called a **payoff table**) summarizes the profit consequences of various price choices. The rows correspond to the price/strategy choices of firm 1 (you), and the columns represent the price/strategy choices of firm 2 (your opponent). The left-hand entry of each cell is the profit to firm 1, and the right-hand entry is the profit of firm 2.

---

[2] In particular, collusion is ruled out.

[3] To avoid spurious issues that arise because the smallest unit of currency is a penny, we will assume that a penny can be sliced as thinly as one likes. Thus, a price of $1.4242, for example, is possible.

[4] No one has an incentive to price above $3.

[5] Although this reasoning is common, it is fallacious. Merely because there are two options does not mean they will be chosen with equal probability.

Table 7.1. *Payoff Table*

Firm 1/Firm 2	Price = $3	Price = $2.50
Price = $3	$100, $100	$0, $150
Price = $2.50	$150, $0	$75, $75

What price would you pick? Suppose that you were told what price your rival will pick *before* you choose your price. Would such information be valuable? Let us see whether knowing what your opponent will do first makes a difference.

If you, firm 1, were told that firm 2 intended to choose the high price, $3, what would you do? Matching firm 2 on price yields a $100 profit. Undercutting (to $2.50) yields a $150 profit. Because more money is better than less, undercutting is the best option. Thus, you should choose the low price.

Suppose now you were told that firm 2 will choose the low price. If you respond with the high price, you gain $0. If you respond with the low price, your profit is $75, which is more. So, in this situation you still choose $2.50.

No matter which price firm 2 picks, you (firm 1) are always better off picking the low price. The same argument applies with equal force to firm 2. Thus, both firms would pick the low price and make $75 – which is odd, because if both firms had picked the high price, each would generate a profit of $100. They would both have been, better off. Recognizing this, why didn't firm 2 choose the high price? Why didn't you? Hence, the dilemma.

Would this conclusion change if the firms could choose any price? No. The argument is more elaborate, but the conclusion is the same. If one allows the firms to choose any price, no firm will choose a price that exceeds $3 because no buyer values a widget at more than $3. It is also obvious that no firm will choose a price below the variable cost of $1.

Now, is it sensible to predict, say, that firm 1 will price at $1.57 and firm 2 will price at $1.63? If this were your prediction, to check whether it is sensible, put yourself in the shoes of each firm in turn. As firm 1, you get the entire market, making a profit of $57. As firm 2, however, you make nothing. What's more, as firm 2, if you predicted that these would be the prices, it would not make sense for you to choose the $1.63 price. After all, if you, as firm 2, predicted that firm 1 would post a $1.57 price, then you should have priced just below that. Therefore, firm 1 pricing at $1.57 and firm 2 pricing at $1.63 is not plausible.

How about firm 1 at $1.89 and firm 2 at $1.76? Again, this is not sustainable. At these prices, firm 1 would rather undercut firm 2.

One could go on like this, but let's cut to the chase. The preceding analysis points out that the firms offering unequal prices is not plausible. The firm with the higher price would be better off dropping its price.

What if both firms offer *equal* prices – for example, $1.70 each? At these prices, firm 1 makes $35. Notice the following: if firm 1 drops its price by a penny to $1.69 and firm 2 does not, firm 1 can sell to the entire market and increase profits to $69. Therefore, even equal prices above cost is not a plausible outcome, because at least one firm could do better by dropping prices.

Where does that leave us? With each firm pricing at cost – $1. No firm can do better (profitwise) by undercutting the other. No firm can improve its profitability by unilaterally raising its price. This is the only plausible outcome.[6] Because pricing at cost yields zero profit, one could argue that one should price at $3 in the hopes of getting lucky. This may be true, but one could be even "luckier" by pricing at $2.99 and so on down the path already trod. The fundamental point is that the situation is constructed so all the incentives on price lead downward. The only argument in favor of "upping" price is a weak one based on luck.

Underlying the reasoning used to arrive at this conclusion is the notion of a Nash equilibrium,[7] which, as we shall see later is quite powerful. Formally, a collection of prices (not necessarily the same), one for each firm, form a **Nash equilibrium** (hereafter, just equilibrium) if no firm could unilaterally increase its own profits by changing its price from the equilibrium level, holding the prices of the other firms fixed.[8] In our present example, each firm pricing at $1 constitutes an equilibrium collection of prices. To verify that this pair of prices is indeed an equilibrium, consider firm 1. If both firms price at $1 then firm 1 makes zero profit. Let us see whether firm 1 can increase its profit by unilaterally changing its price. Dropping the price below $1 (cost) cannot increase profit. Raising the price above $1 also cannot increase firm 1's profit as long as firm 2 prices at $1. Thus, firm 1 cannot increase its profit by unilaterally changing its price from $1. A similar argument applies to firm 2. Thus, both firms pricing at $1 is an equilibrium.

Why should one find a prediction about prices based on the notion of equilibrium compelling? A combination of prices that does not form an equilibrium is unstable in that at least one firm could increase its profit

[6] You may think that a price of a penny above $1 is also correct. Yes, if we are limited to working with whole cents only. Recall that we are free to charge any fraction of a penny.
[7] Named in honor of John Forbes Nash, winner of the 1994 Nobel Prize in Economics.
[8] There can be situations in which in equilibrium, firms choose different prices and have different profits. Further, there can sometimes be multiple equilibria for the same situation.

Table 7.2. *Play vs. Don't Play*

Firm 1/Firm 2	Play	Don't Play
Play	$0, $0	$200, $0
Don't Play	$0, $200	$0, $0

by changing its price. Why wouldn't they? In what follows we use the equilibrium of a competitive situation as a prediction of what the relevant outcome will be. What matters is not the exact equilibrium price in a given situation, but how it changes with changes in the competitive environment. This is what the reader should focus on.

In general, determining the equilibrium prices is complicated. But this need not concern us, because we are interested in a simpler (and more interesting) question: Is it an equilibrium for all firms to price at cost?

The reader is now directed to the appendix on game theory (Chapter 9) before continuing.

7.1.1 Objections to the PD

If one takes the PD seriously, why would anyone choose to participate in a business that yields zero profit? If you were one of the sellers in the PD, would you choose not to "play"? To answer this, let us modify the PD. Suppose each player must first decide to play the game (before knowing what the other player has decided). After these decision are made, they become public. Then each player that decides to play chooses a price. Table 7.2 summarizes the profit consequences of the four possible scenarios. The payoffs in the upper left-hand corner come from the fact that if both firms decide to play, they would choose prices that are in equilibrium – that is $1 each. Therefore, they make zero profit. The payoffs in the lower left hand corner come from the fact that if firm 1 decides not to play and firm 2 does, firm 2 becomes a monopolist and will charge $3. As the reader can verify, the only equilibrium is for both firms to choose to play. The point is that both firms are attracted to the possibility of supplying a market with a total value of $3 × 100 = $300.

A more fruitful line of inquiry is to ask what are the features of the PD that force prices to be at cost. There are five:

1. The PD assumes just one chance to set prices.
2. Costs are the same.

3. There are no capacity constraints.
4. The products sold are undifferentiated.
5. Buyers and sellers have full information. That is, buyers are aware of each seller's offering and the price charged. Sellers are aware of each other's costs, offerings and prices.

These five features, in concert, remove any incentive whatsoever to price above cost. In this sense, the list is useful because it describes the characteristics of an industry in which one should expect prices to be close to cost. Here is the list reinterpreted:

1. Are managers focused on short-term gains? This can happen for two reasons. First, compensation is tied, for example, to quarterly targets. Second, the business may be one in which only a few deals are signed each year. The consequences of losing a couple of large orders in a row may result in layoffs. The jet engine industry is an example of this case.
2. Do sellers have similar cost structures?
3. Is there excess capacity?
4. How much differentiation exists between sellers in the market?
5. How much transparency is there?

If the answers to these questions are yes, yes, yes, none, and a great deal, respectively, then the industry resembles the PD and we should expect razor-thin margins.

Our analysis of the PD ignored the existence of fixed costs of doing business. Including them into the PD makes the outcome even more dismal. Industries with a high proportion of fixed-to-variable costs have an even greater incentive to cut price to gain volume.

As an illustration, consider the fabled bazaar of a hundred stalls selling essentially the same trinkets. Because the chance of a buyer returning to patronize the same seller is small, for all practical purposes each transaction is a "one off." In this sense, the situation is similar to "play once." Each vendor has paid the same cost to the supplier, and the fixed costs are similar. Thus, the cost structures of the suppliers are very similar. In the aggregate, their total supply exceeds the demand during any period. They sell the identical range of products. Sellers are fairly knowledgeable about one another's prices; they rely on their own spies as well the information from buyers who comparison shop. Because all the five features listed previously are present, we expect this to be a small-margin business; and, indeed, it is. Although this environment shares the essential features of the PD, it is not a perfect replica of it. For example, no buyer examines the price at *every* stall. This allows some small variation in prices among different sellers.

A bleaker example of the PD can be found in the system of artisanal mining prevalent in the Congo. Roughly two million people in the Congo make a living mining for copper and cobalt *by hand*. Three-man teams digging 60 feet below the surface can produce about 220 pounds of copper ore a day. After taxes, this generates about $4. By comparison, a loaf of bread costs $1.50.[9] Effectively, the miners make zero margin. First, anyone who can dig can mine. Because there are few alternative sources of income, the supply of miners, mainly ex-soldiers, is huge. Second, the costs of mining are essentially the same for all miners; sweat! Third, they are all selling the same thing, raw ore. Fourth, the miners are focused on short term gains: today's meal, which will fuel tomorrow's digging.

The second way in which the list is useful is that it provides a blueprint for organizing procurement. First, ensure that your suppliers are focused on winning your business today, rather than business they might or could obtain tomorrow. One way to do this is to consolidate orders so they form a substantial portion of a potential supplier's annual revenues. Second, identify and bring to the table as many qualified suppliers with similar cost structures as necessary to generate excess supply.[10] Some buyers invest in the capability to manufacture inhouse even when this is more expensive than outsourcing. They do so to put competitive pressure on suppliers. Where appropriate, some buyers threaten to go into the secondhand market.

The **request for quotes** (RFQ) that the buyer sends out should hold all suppliers to identical terms, to reduce differentiation.[11] Differentiation can be present even at the level of personal relationships between the supplier's sales force and the buyer's procurement staff. For this reason, some buyers limit the relationships and contacts that a member of the supplier's sales team can have with the buyer's organization. If a supplier has a distinguishing feature or function that the buyer may value, the buyer can make one of three responses:

---

[9] These figures were reported in an April 24, 2008 article in the *Washington Post*. That article summarizes the situation thus: "As world mineral prices soar, the former soldier makes less than $5 on a good day of toiling 20 yards underground, at the literal end of a chain of predatory middlemen, gold-wearing labor bosses and shadowy mineral traders stretching from here to China and India and places he only imagines."

[10] Little is gained by having suppliers with radically different costs. The high-cost supplier is not in a position to place competitive pressure on the low-cost supplier.

[11] The idea applies also to hiring employees. Design the tasks to be performed to increase the number of potential individuals who can perform the task – that is, reduce differentiation in skill sets.

1. Say thanks, but no thanks. In this case, the buyer is trading off something of value in return for a lower price.
2. Go to the other suppliers and ask for the same feature and function.
3. Concede that this feature is a must-have, but negotiate its price on the side. Recall that the seller benefits if it can bundle this feature along with the other features on which it has no competitive advantage.

Finally, insofar as promises of confidentiality allow, communicate what one supplier tells you to the others. In particular, use the cost reports of one supplier as a check on the costs reports of other, similar suppliers. In short, the goal is to replicate the PD as far as possible.

The procurement process described here imposes a substantial burden on the buyer. The buyer must explicitly identify his or her needs and precisely describe how they are to be met to be able to record them in an RFQ. An RFQ that is incomplete gives the winning supplier an opportunity to "hold up" the buyer at a later date.[12]

At no point have we urged the buyer to select the lowest-priced seller. Rather, the process we have described ensures that the prices submitted by these suppliers will be lower than they otherwise would be. To see why one must be careful about going with the lowest bidder, imagine a construction project being put up for bid. Typically, there is uncertainty around the cost of completing the project that will be resolved only after the project is completed. We are thus in the common values environment. As noted in Chapter 5, in these environments, there is a risk that the lowest-cost bidder may have underestimated the cost of servicing the buyer. (See the discussion on the winner's curse in Section 5.2. There, the winner overpaid. Here, the lowest-cost bidder may win the account, but still "lose.") The reason this should matter to the buyer is that the low bidder may renege or cut back on dimensions that are hard to monitor (such as quality).[13]

A perfect example of the procurement process we have described is the way Iberia airlines bargained Boeing and Airbus down on price. The story is told by Daniel Michaels in a March 2003 piece for the *Wall Street Journal* titled "Airbus and Boeing Duke It Out to Win Lucrative Iberia Deal." We summarize the essential facts of the tale here:

1. April 2002. Iberia starts to shop for new jetliners. Boeing and Airbus each send a model airplane as a calling card.

---

[12] The process described is used by companies such as Ariba on behalf of its clients (buyers) through a reverse auction.
[13] See also Baker, Marn, and Zawada (2001).

2. The jetliner market is projected to have sales of more than $1 trillion in the next 20 years.

3. The crisis in the air travel industry has produced excess capacity, making the two manufacturers desperate to nail down orders.

4. Enrique Dupuy de Lome, Iberia's CFO, led the search for wide-body jets. He described his procurement strategy thus: "Everything has been structured to maintain tension up to the last 15 minutes."

5. The Spanish carrier was looking to replace six Boeing 747-200 jumbo jets that were more than 20 years old. It wanted as many as 12 new planes to complete a 10-year modernization program for Iberia's long-haul fleet. Based on list prices, the 12-plane order was valued at more than $2 billion.

6. Airbus had sold Iberia more than 100 planes since 1997. In June 2002, Iberia had closed a separate deal with Airbus for three new Airbus A340 widebodies.

7. Dupuy first needed to induce Boeing to bid, as Boeing viewed Iberia as locked into Airbus. The last time Boeing had sold to Iberia was in 1995.

8. July 2002. Dupuy meets Toby Bright, Boeing's top salesman for jets. Dupuy tells Bright that Iberia wants two suppliers.

9. Replacing Iberia's old 747s with new 777s would be Boeing's last chance for years to win back Iberia.

10. November 2002. Airbus and Boeing present initial bids on their latest planes. The four-engine Airbus A340-600 is the longest plane ever built. Boeing's 777-300ER is the biggest twin-engine plane. The new A340 can fly a bit farther and has more lifting power than the 777. The new Boeing plane is lighter, holds more seats, and burns less fuel. The Boeing plane, with a catalog price around $215 million, lists for some $25 million more than the A340.

11. Dupuy sets his own tough terms on price and performance issues, including fuel consumption, reliability, and resale value. Rumors say that he demanded discounts exceeding 40 percent.

12. Dupuy tells both companies, "Whoever hits its target wins the order."

13. Dupuy announces he will go shopping for secondhand airplanes. These are spilling onto the market at cut-rate prices as the airline industry's problems force carriers to ground older jets with their higher operating costs.

14. January 2003. The 777 is now less than 3 percent above Mr. Dupuy's target.

15. The rivals' offers are so close that on the final day of haggling, Iberia stands ready with multiple press releases and extracts last-minute

concessions in a phone call between the airline's chairman and the winning bidder (Airbus).

7.1.2 A Silver Lining

When faced with a procurement process as just described, what can a seller do? There is a silver lining, but a rather thin one. To see it, return to the PD, but this time suppose a single buyer is interested in buying up to 100 widgets and prepared to pay up to $3 a widget. Imagine that you are one of the sellers.

If you and the other seller agree to participate in the procurement process, then by the preceding equilibrium analysis, both of you will price at cost, making zero profit. The buyer would purchase 100 widgets at $1 apiece. Suppose now that you were to decline to participate. What then? The remaining seller would simply price each widget at $3 and make $200 in profit. In both cases, the buyer acquires 100 widgets. However, the price paid for them differs by $2 per unit. Thus, your decision to participate or not makes a difference in terms of the price paid by the buyer. Therefore you provide a benefit to the buyer that has nothing whatsoever to do with widgets. That benefit is competition. Competition results in lower prices for the buyer. The challenge then, for the seller, is to figure out how to capture some of this benefit. That is the silver lining. Some sellers do this by asking for bid preparation expenses to be paid up front. Others agree to bid for business provided they obtain a volume commitment or a last-look provision.[14] The basic point is that agreeing to compete for a buyer's business provides a benefit to the buyer in terms of lower prices. Before agreeing to compete, the seller should ask for something in return. An example is the pharmaceutical supplier McKesson, whose main customers are retail and hospital pharmacies. They are under significant pressure to cut price, so they pressure their suppliers, such as McKesson, to offer them bigger discounts. McKesson's response has been to encourage the retailers to buy all their generic drugs from it (a volume commitment) and redeploy their purchasing teams to other projects. This way both sides come out ahead.[15]

Why is the silver lining thin? Imagine, instead, that there are three sellers, each with sufficient capacity to supply all the buyer's needs. If you withdraw,

[14] Such a provision is a promise from the buyer to the seller. If the buyer gets a better offer elsewhere, it is obliged to give the existing supplier a chance to match it. If matched, the buyer continues with the existing supplier.

[15] From a January 8, 2009 article in Fortune magazine by Geoff Colvin, titled "Ten Ways to Weather the Storm."

it makes not a whit of difference to the price paid by the buyer. The lesson here is that only a small number of sellers is sufficient for the buyers to reap the benefits of competition. In our example, two suffice, because each seller has enough capacity to serve the buyer. The actual number will depend on the demands of the buyer and the distribution of capacity among sellers. Nevertheless, the point remains; for buyers to benefit from competition, a small number of suppliers suffices. Farsighted buyers recognize this and engage in dual sourcing to keep competition going. Thus, there is a dominant supplier from whom the buyer purchases most, but not all, of its needs. The remainder is purchased from secondary suppliers. The buyer keeps the secondary suppliers around to put competitive pressure on the dominant supplier.

7.2 Repetition

Would the outcome to the PD be different if there were more than one round of play? One might hope to use the multiple rounds to signal one's rival, through one's prices, that prices should be kept high.

More than one round of play is not sufficient. To see why, suppose you had to play the PD for exactly ten rounds. For simplicity, let us focus on the version of the PD in which the sellers are limited to just two possible prices; recall Table 7.1. On the last round, round 10, the logic of the one-round game applies and you should choose the low price of $2.50. On round 9, both you and your rival know that on round 10 each of you will choose the $2.50 price. Hence, there is nothing one can do in round 9 to influence what happens in round 10. Therefore, one can treat round 9 in isolation to round 10, and the argument of the one-round case applies again. Round 9 is like a one-round game, and again logic dictates that one should price at $2.50. Now to round 8, and so on. In each round one chooses the low price. The existence of a definite last round is what drives the conclusion.

With no definite end, things can be different. What one does on the current round can influence a rival's behavior in a future round. Why? Because there is always a "future." Notice we say "can" and not "will." You and your rival could end up charging low prices in every round (perpetual price war), high prices in every round, or something in between.

In repeated play of the PD, a strategy is no longer what price you pick in each round but rather a *rule* used to select a price in each round. This rule could (but need not) depend on what has happened in the previous rounds. Here are three examples of such rules:

1. Choose the low price in each round. This rule ignores entirely what goes on in the game from one round to the next.
2. Choose a high price in the first round. In subsequent rounds, choose a high price if the rival chose a high price in the previous round. If the rival chose a low price in the previous round, then choose the low price in every round thereafter. This particular rule is called the *grim trigger*.
3. Choose a high price in the first round. In subsequent rounds, choose the price that the rival chose in the previous round. This rule is known as *tit for tat* (TFT).

Suppose you were convinced that your rival was guided by the first rule. Then, the best you could do against the rival is to choose the low price in each period. If you could convince your rival that you would play by the first rule, the best your rival could do is choose the low price in each period. Thus, in the repeated version of the PD, both sellers playing by the first rule is an equilibrium.

Now, suppose you believe that your rival will play by the second rule. How should you respond? If you pick the high price in each period, you enjoy an income stream of $100 in each period. Suppose you decide to undercut your rival in the first period. This gives you $150 in the first period. However, in all subsequent periods you know that your rival will choose the low price and your profit is maximized if you match it. In this case, your profit will be $75. Thus, the extra $50 gained in the first period is paid for by an income stream of $75 in all subsequent periods. Clearly, an income stream of $100 in every period is better than one that yields $150 in the first period followed by $75 in all subsequent periods. If you adopt a rule that will choose a low price at some other time (it does not matter when), then from that time on the best you can do is garner a profit of $75 in all following periods. If the game goes on long enough, average per-period profits will be close to $75. On the other hand, if you play by the rule that chooses the high price in each round, average per-period profits will be $100. Therefore, against the second rule, your best option is to choose the high price in each round. Thus, both firms adopting the second rule is an equilibrium of the repeated version of the PD.

The third rule has an intuitive appeal that combines sticks and carrots. If you follow this rule and your rival undercuts you, it dictates that you respond in kind: the stick. If your rival subsequently raise its price, then you follow: the carrot. In other words, you reward a move to higher prices by your rival by doing the same and punishing it when it does not by cutting the price. The reader may verify that the rival's best response to a TFT on your part is to choose the high price in each round.

So far we have two possibilities: one in which the sellers average $75 per period and the other in which they average $100 per period. It turns out that for any number between $75 and $100, there is an equilibrium that gives each player that much per period (on average). This is what we mean by saying that anything can happen.

Just because anything *can* happen does not mean that it *will*. It seems more plausible to believe that firms will be thinking and doing things that lead them to the equilibria with high per-period payoffs. In particular, the firms will use the repeated interactions to signal each other and effectively collude on higher prices. Nevertheless, there are obstacles.

First, the signaling hypothesis relies crucially on the ability of firms to monitor each other's prices. In many cases, this may be difficult to do. Price cuts can be disguised in myriad ways – for example, rebates, changes in payment terms, warranties, changing product serial numbers, or adding features. Indirect observations of prices, such as changes in demand and profit, are also imperfect. For example, the fact that the volume of business one does with a client is steady is not a sign that one's rival has not cut its price. Imagine that the client's business is growing but it is sending a larger share of it to one's rival. Where there is evidence of signaling succeeding, it has usually been the case that sellers have sold a standardized offering and prices are easily monitored. Airlines are an example. In 1992, the U.S. Justice Department filed suit against the then eight largest American airlines because they were using the common computerized reservation system to fix airfares. Using the common reservation system, an airline could, for example, signal that starting on January 1 it would increase its unrestricted economy fare by $75 between Washington, D.C. and Boston. In some cases, airline A, for example, would signal its intention to reduce a fare on a profitable route for airline B. Airline B would respond by signaling its intention to reduce a fare on a route that was lucrative for airline A (i.e., TFT). Subsequently, both fare reductions would be abandoned. United and US Air agreed to end the practice of using the reservation system to "feel out" rivals about price increases. The other six eventually settled in 2000.

Second, the period between price changes may be quite large, on the order of months or years. This could be because purchases are infrequent (think aircraft) or because buyers sign long-term contracts. Thus, profits made on the tenth round are not the same as profits made on the second round – that is, discounting matters. If the discount factor is high enough, then in the eyes of the firms, round 5 and higher, say, do not matter anymore and we are back to charging low prices every round.

Price Matching Guarantees

Promises to match a competitor's price – price matching guarantees – are common in a variety of retailing contexts ranging from electronics (e.g., Best Buy) to automotive tires (e.g., Sears) to toys (Toys RUs). They serve two purposes.

The first is that, under certain conditions, guarantees help to soften price competition. One way to see this is to recognize such guarantees as an implementation of the TFT strategy described earlier. Suppose that in the PD, firm 1 sells its output for $3 a unit along with the following guarantee: should the buyer get the same product elsewhere for a lower price, firm 1 will refund the buyer the difference in price. Assuming the guarantee to be credible, what effect, if any, does it have? Because the guarantee is public knowledge, firm 2 is aware of it. What price should firm 2 charge? If it charges $3, it gets $100. If it decides to undercut firm 1 by charging $2.50, it gets only $75. This is because the guarantee has the effect of automatically reducing firm 1's price the moment firm 2 lowers its price.

The guarantee is actually a threat: "If you don't keep prices high, I will immediately punish you by dropping prices." Rapid retaliation is important. Otherwise, firm 2 might make a killing before firm 1 realizes that firm 2 has lowered its prices. The nature of the guarantee is such that firm 2's price drop cannot be kept secret from firm 1. The guarantee causes the customers to police firm 2. Last, the entire scheme depends on firm 1's ability to follow through on the guarantee. If there is any doubt about this, the guarantee may have no effect. Thus, it is not sufficient to give such a guarantee. It must be credible.

In practice, the guarantee by itself is not sufficient to soften price competition. If the buyer must incur a transaction cost to invoke the guarantee, it reduces the effect of the guarantee. A buyer may prefer to buy the item from the store with the lowest price rather than incur the hassle cost of obtaining the lower price at the store that offers the guarantee but whose price is higher. For this reason some sellers promise to take on the burden of searching for a lower price and promising the buyer they will refund the difference (if any) within a defined period (e.g., within thirty days of purchase). An example of this was the specialty consumer electronics retailer, Tweeter.[16]

---

[16] This company shut down in December 2008.

In B2B settings, price matching guarantees take the form of a "last look provision" or right of first refusal in a contract. Here, the buyer promises to the supplier that if it receives an offer from another, it must allow the incumbent supplier to match it, and if matched, the buyer is obliged to remain with the incumbent supplier. Such a guarantee allows the incumbent supplier to decide which customers to keep and which to relinquish to a competitor. Thus, its existence deters potential competitors.

Instances of price matching guarantees used to soften price competition in retail settings appear to be rare. This is because many retailers that offer such guarantees do so on products or services not offered by their competitors. In these cases, a price matching guarantee is a signal to consumers that the seller has low prices and helps the store increase traffic. This signal is easier for consumers to observe, whereas gathering information on prices is more difficult. It is a credible signal because a high-priced firm offering the guarantee will be forced to lower price in the face of knowledgeable consumers.

7.2.1 Collusion and Signaling

One response to the ravages of price competition is agreements between rivals to fix prices or quantities. Such agreements, however, are illegal in most countries.[17] In the United States, the statute that outlaws such collusion is the Sherman Act of 1890, frequently referred to as the Magna Carta of free enterprise.[18] Section 1 of the act reads:

---

[17] Firms rarely fix prices. Instead, they fix shares or volumes. Typically, these agreements divide up the market either geographically or customer by customer. A particularly vivid case comes from South Australia, involving two newspapers: the *Murray Valley Standard* and the *River News*. Traditionally, the *Standard* was available in the towns of Murray Bridge and Mannum. The *News* was available in the town of Waikerie and along the Murray River in South Australia. One day, the *News* broached the traditional divide and solicited for advertisers in Mannum. The publisher of the *Standard* responded with the following missive:

I wanted to formally record my desire to reach an understanding with your family in terms of where each of us focuses our publishing efforts. If you continue to attack in Mannum, a prime readership area of the *Murray Valley Standard*, it may be we will have to look at expanding our operations into areas that we have not traditionally serviced. I thought I would write to you so there could be no misunderstanding our position.

[18] To recognize what an innovation this was, it is enough to consider a judgment handed down by the English Court of Appeal in the 1892 *Mogul Steamship Company* case. A cabal of Far Eastern shipping companies combined to eliminate competitors through low rates for freight and threats to dismiss shipping agents if they loaded competitors' ships. The Court of Appeal ruled that it was no business of the courts to prevent a combination

Every contract, combination in the form of trust or otherwise, or conspiracy, in restraint of trade or commerce among the several States, or with foreign nations, is declared to be illegal.

Section 2 reads:

Every person who shall monopolize, or attempt to monopolize, or combine or conspire with any other person or persons to monopolize, any part of the trade or commerce of the several states, or with foreign nations, shall be guilty of a felony.

The act makes agreements to fix prices or quantities per se illegal. This makes the action itself illegal. There is no defense to be found by arguing that price fixing was necessary to preserve the health of the industry. One cannot defend against the charge by arguing that the agreement to fix prices or volume did not not succeed or harm consumers. Furthermore, the act applies to foreign sellers who sell into the United States. Many other countries have legislation of a similar nature.[19]

The penalties for violation of the Sherman Act are severe. In October 2005, Samsung was fined \$300 million for participating in a conspiracy to fix the price of dynamic random access memory (DRAM). This represents the second largest antitrust penalty in U.S. history. (The largest penalty in U.S. history was set in 2007 when Visa agreed to pay American Express \$2.25 billion to settle a price-fixing suit.[20]) Penalties for the executives involved in price fixing are not unheard of. In the DRAM case, the following individuals employed by Samsung were each fined \$250,000 in addition to jail time:[21]

1. Sun Woo Lee, Samsung's senior manager of DRAM sales (8 months)
2. Yeongho Kang, associate director of DRAM marketing for Samsung's subsidiary in the United States (7 months)
3. Young Woo Lee, sales director for Samsung's subsidiary in Germany (7 months)

---

of traders from driving a mutual rival out of business by reducing the price of goods and services. It was not the role of government, the tribunal argued, to succor merchants from the hazards of severe competition when such competition was unaccompanied by menaces, violence, or fraud.

[19] See Chapter 9 of Tybout and Calder (2010).

[20] Actually, American Express sued both Visa and Mastercard. Visa and Mastercard settled. In Mastercard's case, it was for \$1.8 billion over three years.

[21] Condign punishments for the executives involved are inspired by Baron Thurlow's remark that "corporations have neither bodies to be punished, nor souls to be condemned; they therefore do as they like."

Agreements to fix prices shift competition from the marketplace to haggling in hotel rooms. Participants spend their time bargaining over how to split the profits from collusion among themselves. Over the longer term, they must coordinate capacity expansions and decide whether to include new entrants into the cartel. In some cases, this can result in a falling out among thieves.[22]

Tacit or unspoken agreements to fix price, say, by signaling, are illegal under certain circumstances. In U.S. law, this is known as *conscious parallelism*. Evidence of prices moving in unison is not by itself illegal. Additional evidence, called *plus factors*, is required to establish a violation of the Sherman Act. Such factors include evidence of secret meetings between principal rivals, invitation to common action by others, price increases in times of excess capacity, or price increases coupled with increased standardization.

7.2.2 Predation

If firms have budget constraints, having an unlimited number of rounds gives you a chance to wear the other down and force them out of the market. Specifically, set your price low for a sustained period. The rival is eventually driven out of business and you are left as the monopolist in the market. The hope is that the period in which one is the monopolist allows one to recoup sufficient profits to cover the costs of driving the rival out. The practice is called **predatory pricing**.

The strategy is a risky one. First, it is rarely clear how deep an adversary's pockets are, and this can cause problems.[23] A clean way to think about the issues is via an **all pay auction**. Imagine you and a rival are to bid on an envelope containing an unknown amount of money. Suppose the bidding takes place in rounds and bidding continues as long as the second highest bidder is willing to top the current high bid. The highest bidder wins, but *each* bidder must pay its highest bid; hence, the term all pay auction. The envelope can be thought of as the market for which the firms are competing. The bidders are the firms. Their bids in each round represent the investments

---

[22] In some cases, the participants really are thieves. The notorious price-fixing case involving Archer Daniels Midland is a case in point. One of the principals in the case, Mark Whitacre, president of its bioproducts division, was stealing from his employers. This last claim is disputed by some observers. Readers can watch the movie, *The Informant*, with Matt Damon and decide for themselves.

[23] In some cases, buyers may be willing to aid the adversary to ensure sufficient competition. In other cases, the government will do so.

they must make each day to stay in business. These investments must be paid for whether or not the market is "won."

How should you bid? One obvious thing to worry about is the winner's curse: you win with a bid that exceeds the contents of the envelope. Let us put this issue to rest by supposing that the amount of money in the envelope is known to you and your rival, say $50. At this point, the only issue is how much money each of you must bid. Suppose you have $10, your rival has $5, and this is known to each of you. Then it is clear (why?) that your rival will simply not bid and let you walk away with the $50 for a nominal bid. Thus, in the case in which budgets are common knowledge, the bidder with the larger budget wins for a nominal bid.[24] However, budgets are seldom common knowledge. When budgets are secret, life is more complicated. From our first observation, you would like to convince the other bidder that your budget is larger. The only credible way to do so is to put your money where your mouth is and bid aggressively. But your rival may suspect you of bluffing and respond by being aggressive as well. Before you know it, you've reached your budget or bids exceed $50. How can this be? Well, consider two bidders, Avi and Ravi. Suppose Avi has the current high bid of $49 and Ravi the second highest bid of $48. Suppose it is Ravi's turn to bid or drop out. If Ravi drops out, by the rules of the auction he will be out $48. On the other hand, he could top the current high bid, say, with a bid of $50. If Avi drops out, then Ravi is out only zero. Thus, it makes sense for Ravi to top the current high bid. Now let us switch to Avi. He now faces a high bid of $50. If he drops out now, he is out $49. If he tops the high bid with a bid of $51 and wins, he is out only a dollar. Which is better? Clearly, bidding above $50.

Thus, to make your initial claim about your budget credible, you must be prepared to spend it. If you are not careful, or your rival is skeptical, you will be forced to expend it all. You win the envelope, but pay exactly what it is worth; a Pyrrhic victory.

Second, even if you succeed in driving out your rival, what happens to the rival's capacity? It may not disappear. As long as it remains, it poses a competitive threat to you.[25] Third, after you have driven out your rival, presumably you will raise your prices to recoup the losses incurred. When that happens, what is there to prevent another rival from coming in?

---

[24] Some clerical details arise when the budgets differ by very small amounts relative to the bid increments that we ignore so as not to obscure the big picture.

[25] When the *Washington Post* went bankrupt in 1933, neither plant, personnel, or name evaporated. Eugene Meyer acquired all three for a fraction of an earlier rebuffed offer.

Fourth, predatory pricing is illegal under U.S. law. The standard of proof, however, is very high. First, one must show that the predator was pricing below some measure of marginal or average cost. Second, one must prove that the predator is in a position to recoup the losses incurred while driving out the prey. The first involves tedious evidence about how costs are to be allocated and accounted for. The second involves a discussion of what might, could, and should have been. Other countries have different standards. In Germany, for example, Lufthansa was convicted of predatory pricing on the Frankfurt–Berlin route in 2001–2002 even though it had a price higher than that of the supposed prey. On November 12, 2001, Germania, a low-cost airline, began service from Frankfurt to Berlin with a one-way fare of 99 euros. Prior to Germania's entry, Lufthansa was the monopoly carrier on this route. The lowest round-trip economy fare was about 485 euros. After Germania's entry, Lufthansa introduced a one-way 100-euro fare with the same restrictions as Germania's. The German antitrust authority (the Bundeskartellamt) argued that Lufthansa provided a higher-value offering.[26] An equal price for a product with higher value, it was argued, was tantamount to undercutting. Furthermore, Lufthansa introduced the lower fare on just this one route. Finally, the Bundeskartellamt estimated that Lufthansa's price did not cover average cost.

Interestingly, there have been no successful prosecutions of predatory pricing in the United States in the last 50 years. As noted earlier, strong arguments suggest that it is irrational to engage in it.[27] Nevertheless, history records examples of successful cases of predatory pricing, which we pass over.

The history of commerce also records tales of failed attempts at predation, which receive less attention. An engaging one involves Dow Chemical versus a German cartel, called Bromkonvention. In 1904, Dow, under the leadership of its founder Herbert Dow, entered the bromine market with a lower cost way of producing bromine. This allowed Dow to sell bromine in Germany at 36 cents a pound. At this time, Bromkonvention was selling bromine in Germany for 49 cents a pound. Bromkonvention responded by pricing below cost in the United States. It priced bromine in the United States at 15 cents a pounds. Herbert Dow instructed his agents to buy Bromkonvention's bromine, repackage it, and resell it in Germany for 29

---

[26] The higher value was ascribed to the fact that Lufthansa passengers received a newspaper, a soft drink, and 500 frequent flier miles, and enjoyed a higher frequency of flights.

[27] In fact, the U.S. Supreme Court declared predatory pricing, to be "inherently uncertain," and noted its "general implausibility."

Table 7.3. *Each Has 20 Units*

Firm 1/Firm 2	Price = $3	Price = $2.50
Price = $3	$40, $40	$40, $30
Price = $2.50	$30, $40	$30, $30

cents a pound. Bromkonvention drove the price of bromine in the United States to 10 cents a pound before it caught on to what Dow was doing.

7.3 Capacity

In this section we will examine the impact of capacity on prices. Return again to the version of the PD with two possible prices. However, now suppose that each seller has the capacity to supply only 20 widgets each. In this case, total industry capacity is 40 widgets, whereas the number of potential buyers is still 100. Because demand exceeds capacity, intuition suggests that prices should be high. This is correct. The possible outcomes are summarized in Table 7.3. To confirm intuition and gain practice at using the equilibrium idea, let us check to see that both firms pricing at $2.50 is *not* an equilibrium. Suppose both firms price at $2.50. Now look at each firm in turn and ask whether it could do better by unilaterally switching to a different price. Starting with firm 1, we see that if it switches to the $3 price (and firm 2 remains with the $2.50 price) firm 1 increases its profits from $30 to $40. Thus, both firms pricing at $2.50 cannot be an equilibrium. The reader should check that each firm pricing at $3 is an equilibrium.

Now let us see what happens when capacity is increased. Suppose each firm has 60 units of capacity. Industry capacity is now 120, which exceeds the total number of buyers. Would the equilibrium price fall? To answer this consider Table 7.4.

You should check that both firms pricing at $2.50 is *not* an equilibrium. In fact, the equilibrium is both firms choosing to price at $3. How can that be? Partly it is that firms were limited to one of two prices: $3 and $2.50.

Table 7.4. *Each Has 60 Units*

Firm 1/Firm 2	Price = $3	Price = $2.50
Price = $3	$100, $100	$80, $90
Price = $2.50	$90, $80	$75, $75

Hence, dropping the price by 50 cents a unit to increase the number of buyers to be served by 10 is not worth it. Although cutting the price will bring the entire market to one's door, one does not have the capacity to serve this additional demand. In the case of firm 1, for example, cutting the price brings in an additional 50 customers. However, it can serve only 10 of them. The 10 additional customers bring in $15 (= [$2.50 − $1] × 10) in additional profit. But this does not offset the revenue loss of $25 (= $0.5 × 50) from the lower prices to the initial 50 customers. Thus, cutting price is a bad idea for firm 1. The same logic applies to firm 2.

If the firms were free to choose any price, the equilibrium price would indeed fall.[28] However – and this is the important part – the equilibrium price will not fall to cost. Why is this? Suppose both firms were to price at cost – that is, $1 a widget. At these prices, the market divides evenly between the two sellers – each sells 50 units. Consider firm 1. If it raises its price, how many buyers can it lose? Because its rival has only 60 units of capacity, there will still be 40 units of demand unserved. Firm 1 will find it more profitable to charge $3 and sell to these 40 units. Thus, both firms pricing at cost is *not* an equilibrium.

Therefore, what determines price is not just the balance between capacity and demand, but how the capacity is allocated among the firms. The reader interested in a full analysis of the capacity game should consult the Technical Aside at the end of this chapter.

The lesson of these examples is simple: if firms could limit their capacities, prices would be higher. Why don't firms do this? Greed. To make this point, return to the case in which each firm has 20 units of capacity. Suppose that, for a fee of $75, each firm could increase its capacity by 80 units. This is an increase of 80 units all at once. Capacity is "lumpy," so it is either the whole 80 units or nothing. The rules of engagement are this: first each firm decides (simultaneously and independently) whether to expand. Then, prices are chosen.

To see what happens, put yourself in the shoes of firm 1. Suppose first that firm 2 does *not* increase capacity. Should you, as firm 1, increase capacity? If you don't, we know that both firms will price at $3, yielding a profit of $40 for you. Now let us examine what would happen if you expanded. In that case, you would have 100 units of capacity, whereas your rival would have

---

[28] We can see this by establishing that both firms pricing at $3 is *not* an equilibrium. If both firms price at $3, profits for each are $100. Suppose, firm 1, say, drops its price to $2.99. This will attract more buyers. In particular, firm 1 will be able to sell 60 units rather than 50. Its profit will now be ($2.99 − 1) × 60 = $119.40, more than $100.

Table 7.5. *Firm 1 Expands*

Firm 1/Firm 2	Price = $3	Price = $2.50
Price = $3	$160, $40	$160, $30
Price = $2.50	$150, $0	$120, $30

20 units of capacity. The payoff table (ignoring the cost of expansion) for the case in which firm 1 has 100 units of capacity and firm 2 only 20 units is shown in Table 7.5. To obtain the profit numbers in the upper left and lower right cells we have assumed that firm 2 will fill to capacity. Recall that when prices are equal, buyers flip an unbiased coin to decide where to go. Thus, 50 buyers head to firm 2, but only 20 can be served, so the remaining 30 go to firm 1.[29] It is easy to see that at equilibrium both firms price at $3. Notice that firm 1 makes a profit of $160. This is $120 more than when its capacity is 20 units. This is more than enough to pay for the $75 cost of expansion. Hence, it is in firm 1's interest to expand, assuming that firm 2 does not.

What happens when both firms increase capacity? Now both have the capacity to serve the entire market. We are back in the benchmark case. Both firms choose the low price of $2.50 and have profits of $75 − $75=0. Table 7.6 summarizes the four possibilities: The lower right entry is simply the profits made at equilibrium when both firms have 20 units of capacity. The upper left is the profit made at equilibrium when both firms have 100 units of capacity each (less the cost of expansion). The upper right is the equilibrium profit when firm 1 has 100 units of capacity and firm 2 has 20 (less the cost of expansion for firm 1); similarly for the lower left.

We can eliminate one possibility: neither firm boosting capacity (lower right cell). This cannot be an equilibrium. If I think you will not increase capacity, I am better off boosting capacity. The same is true for you.

Both firms increasing capacity (upper left) is not an equilibrium either. What is left is firm 1 expanding and firm 2 not, or vice versa. Both of these are equilibria. Which one should we use in making a prediction about this capacity expansion game? Each firm would rather the other does not expand. Who gets to expand? One cannot say exactly. The game now is like a game of chicken. I want you to flinch (not expand) and you want me to flinch. Sometimes we underestimate each other and both expand, driving profits down. Sometimes we both flinch and neither expands.

---

[29] You can also think of this as being the worst-case outcome for firm 1.

Table 7.6. *Capacity Choice*

Firm 1/Firm 2	Capacity = 100	Capacity = 20
Capacity = 100	$0, $0	$85, $40
Capacity = 20	$40, $85	$40, $40

The upshot is this. Faced with limited capacity, each firm has an incentive to expand capacity. However, if they do not coordinate their capacity expansions, they both expand, resulting in excess capacity and lower prices.

7.3.1 Capacity Preemption

Now we introduce a change. Suppose that we offered to sell you (firm 1), for $20, the option to expand first. That is, you will be allowed to decide first whether to expand. After you have made your decision, the decision will be relayed to firm 2. Then firm 2 gets to decide what to do. Is this option valuable?

To decide, ask what you would do with the option. Notice that if you expand first, firm 2's most profitable response is to not expand. This yields a certain profit of $160 − 75 − 20 = $65 for you. If you decide not to expand, firm 2 will, and will force your profits to $40. Therefore, the option is worth it.

Thus, in the capacity expansion, game you want to move first. By so doing you deter the opposition from expansion, boosting profitability. The difficulty, of course, is that the right to move first is not handed out, but must be seized. Some sellers attempt just this with announcements about plant expansions. However, unless such announcements are credible, they do little to deter rivals.

One setting in which a seller has the ability to move first is in pharmaceuticals. When the patent on a particular drug expires, it is subject to competition from generic versions of the drug. Some patent holders choose to introduce their own generic before expiration of the patent. This has the obvious negative effect of cannibalizing sales of the patented product, but this is offset by the preemption effect. Expanding first in the generic category will reduce the scale at which other generic products will enter the market. Upjohn, for example, succeeded in controlling 90 percent of the generic market for its patented drug Xanax by introducing its own generic substitute one month before expiration of the Xanax patent. *Syntex* introduced its own generic version of its patented drug Naproysn two months before patent expiration with similar success.

Table 7.7. *Cost and Capacity Information*

Plant	Per-Unit Cost	Capacity
York 1	$5	100
York 2	$3	150
Lancaster	$2	75
Stuart 1	$4	60
Stuart 2	$6	70
Stuart 3	$9	80

The capacity preemption idea is a by-product of the Cournot model, which is discussed in the Technical Aside to this chapter.

7.3.2 Pricing Using the Supply Curve

One of the standard constructs of economics is the supply curve that shows how much output the sellers in an industry can produce for a given cost per unit. Often overlooked, it is in fact a useful device for thinking about where prices should be in a capacity-constrained industry. We illustrate with an example.

Suppose that there are three producers of widgets – York, Lancaster, and Stuart. The plants they own, their respective capacities, and unit costs of production are shown in Table 7.7.

From Table 7.7 we see that the York company has two plants, the Lancaster company has one plant, and the Stuart company has three plants. The first step in constructing a supply curve is to sort the plants by increasing unit cost as shown in Table 7.8.

Next we plot the data in Table 7.8 in Figure 7.1. Cost is displayed on the vertical axes and capacity on the horizontal axes. Each plant will appear as a

Table 7.8. *Ordered Cost and Capacity Information*

Plant	Per-Unit Cost	Capacity
Lancaster	$2	75
York 2	$3	150
Stuart 1	$4	60
York 1	$5	100
Stuart 2	$6	70
Stuart 3	$9	80

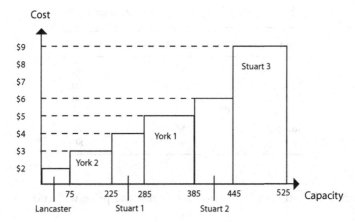

Figure 7.1. Widget supply curve.

rectangle. The width of the rectangle will correspond to the capacity of the plant and the height to the cost.

Now suppose that on the demand side there are 400 buyers, each interested in buying at most one widget and prepared to pay up to $7. How should each seller price its widgets? Widgets should be priced at no less than $6 a unit. To see why, put yourselves in the shoes of the York company. York's number 2 plant can be underpriced by Lancaster and York's number 1 plant can be underpriced by Lancaster and Stuart's number 1 plant. Even if the latter were to underprice York, the total capacity of Lancaster and Stuart's number 1 plant is only 135 units. Thus, there would still be 275 units of demand still to be filled. That means that York could, at the very least, price its widgets at $5 and be guaranteed to sell 250 units. If York were to price higher than $6 a widget, Stuart's number 2 plant would be able to undercut it. Thus, York could comfortably set the price at $6 a widget and be guaranteed to sell 250 units.

In general, to determine the floor on the price, we assume that buyers first approach the lowest-cost provider to meet their needs. When this provider's capacity is exhausted, the remaining buyers go to the next lowest-cost provider, and so on. In our case, we had 400 buyers, each willing to pay up to $7 a widget. Starting with the lowest-cost (i.e., most efficient) plant first, we see that to fill the 400 units of demand, Stuart's number 2 plant must be used. Thus, the unit cost of the number 2 Stuart plant sets the floor on the price. Now, Stuart should recognize that there are buyers who will be forced to buy from it because its competitors with lower costs cannot serve all the demand. Therefore, Stuart will price widgets at

Table 7.9. *Modified Cost and Capacity Information*

Plant	Per-Unit Cost	Capacity
Lancaster	$2	90
York 2	$3	150
Stuart 1	$4	50
York 1	$5	100
Stuart 2	$6	70
Stuart 3	$9	80

$7 a unit. The others will follow suit. Thus, the price will end up at $7 a unit.

Suppose now that Lancaster considers expanding its capacity from 75 to 90 units. How does this change things? First, Lancaster, York 2, Stuart 1, and York 1 will have sufficient capacity to serve the entire market. In this case, York 1 will be the last plant called up. Thus, the floor on the price will be $5 a unit. York knows that if it prices higher than $6, it would become profitable for Stuart to sell out of its number 2 plant. Thus, York is constrained by the presence of Stuart's number 2 plant to price below $6 a unit. Therefore, we expect the price to be $6 a unit. Notice that the increase in Lancaster's capacity results in a lower price.

What happens if Stuart reports a decline in the capacity of its number 1 plant of 10 units, after Lancaster's expansion?[30] The capacities are now as shown in Table 7.9. Now, to serve the market, Stuart's number 2 plant will be called up. This will set a floor on the price of $6 a unit. Clearly, Stuart could price at $7 a unit. At this price, Stuart would sell 50 units out of its number 1 plant and 10 units out of its number 2 plant. This yields a profit of $(7 - 4) \times 50 + (7 - 6) \times 10 = \$160$, after the reduction. Before this reduction, Stuart's profit was $(6 - 4) \times 60 = \$120$. Thus, this strategic reduction would result in an increase in the profits for Stuart. This is a short-term benefit only, however. If the price of widgets stays at $7 a unit, that may give an incentive to the other sellers to expand their capacity, so lowering the price.

We illustrated the usefulness of the supply curve with a particularly simple form for the demand side of the market; every buyer had the same RP for widgets. Now let us consider a more sophisticated setup.

---

[30] In fact, during the height of the California power crisis, some power providers would strategically reduce the capacity of some of their plants for "maintenance."

Table 7.10. *Demand for Widgets*

Price	Demand	Supply
$2	400	75
$3	370	225
$4	325	285
$5	300	385
$6	275	455
$7	200	455
$8	150	455
$9	100	535

We now use Table 7.8 to determine the available supply at each price. This information is recorded side by side with the demand at each price and displayed in Table 7.10. For any price of $4 or less, demand exceeds supply. Therefore, no seller will price at $4. At a price of $5 or more, supply exceeds demand. Hence, no seller will price below $5. The last seller called up, is York 1. York 1 can afford to price just below $6 before losing business to Stuart 2. Thus, prices should be set in the $4 to $6 range.

7.4 Differentiation

Everyone and his mother knows that differentiation is a good idea, as it softens price competition. Less well known are the precise conditions under which this is true. In this section we examine carefully how differentiation softens price competition. Typically, differentiation involves offerings that are imperfect substitutes for each other. It is this form of differentiation that we examine.

7.4.1 Differentiation and Substitutes

There are two kinds of differentiation, vertical and horizontal. Vertical differentiation means that your product or service is superior to your competitor's product or service in the eyes of *all* buyers. In other words, every buyer assigns a higher RP to your offering than to the competitor's. This superiority allows one to extract a premium in price. In horizontal differentiation, one segment of buyers rates your offering superior to the competition and is prepared to pay a premium over the competitor's offering. Another segment rates your rival's offering superior to yours and will pay a premium over your price for its offering. For example, your widgets are colored blue and

Table 7.11. *Distribution of RPs*

Buyer Type	RP for Blue	RP for Red	Number
Blue Lover	$5	$3	50
Red Lover	$3	$5	50

the rival's product is painted red. Some customers value the blue color more than the red color, and vice versa. This manifests itself in a higher RP for the blue widget or for the red widget. This differentiation allows firms, in some cases, to sell at prices above cost.

The model we analyze is a variation of the PD.[31] Firm 1 decides to paint its widgets blue (Blue firm) and firm 2 paints its widgets red (Red firm). Manufacturing costs for both firms remain at $1 a unit. Of the 100 buyers, 50 prefer blue widgets to red widgets (blue lovers). These 50 value blue widgets at $5 and red widgets at $3. The other 50 prefer red widgets to blue ones (red lovers). These 50 value red widgets at $5 and blue ones at $3. This is summarized in Table 7.11. Further, assume that firms are free to charge any price they like. Note that in this case just because a buyer prefers, say, blue to red widgets does not mean that the buyer will buy only blue widgets. If the price on red widgets is low enough, the buyer might switch to buying red widgets. To illustrate this, suppose that the price of blue widgets was $3.50 and the price of red widgets was $1.00. Consider someone with a preference for blue widgets. If this person buys blue, the surplus is $5 − $3.50 = $1.50. If the person buys red instead, the surplus will be $3 − $1 = $2. Because the surplus on a red widget is higher, this person buys a red widget, even though he or she prefers blue widgets. In other words, the red widget is an imperfect substitute for the blue widget, and vice versa.[32]

Let us check that pricing at cost is *not* an equilibrium. Suppose both firms charge $1 for their widgets. Now ask: could any one firm do better by raising its price? If it could, then pricing at cost is not an equilibrium.

Consider the Blue firm, for example. At a $1 price, it makes 0 profit. Now suppose it raises its price by 1 penny. Does it lose all its customers to the

---

[31] Although simple to describe, it is limited in what can be done with it. A more sophisticated model, the Bertrand-Hotelling model, is described in the Technical Aside at the end of this chapter.

[32] In the event that prices lead to the same surplus for a buyer, we assume the buyer will buy the color he or she prefers.

Table 7.12. *Modified Distribution of RPs*

Buyer Type	RP for Blue	RP for Red	Number
Blue Lover	$5	$3	99
Red Lover	$3	$5	1

competition? No. The surplus for a blue lover from a blue widget at the new price is $5 − 1.01. The surplus from a red widget would be $3 − 1. Notice that $5 − 1.01 > 3 − 1$, so the blue lovers continue to buy from the Blue firm. At this new price the Blue firm makes a penny profit on each sale. Therefore, it is better off. Thus, pricing at cost is not an equilibrium.

Let us check that charging a high price (of $5) is an equilibrium. As always, it suffices to determine whether any one firm has an incentive to undercut. Consider the Blue firm. When blue and red both charge $5, the Blue firm makes $(5 − 1) \times 50 = \$200$. Could the Blue firm make more by dropping its price? The only reason to drop the price is to get new customers. These new customers have to be red lovers. To induce them (the reds) to buy a blue widget, the Blue firm must drop its price to something slightly below $3 – that is $3 − \epsilon$ (why?). But this means that its profits will be $100 \times (3 − \epsilon − 1) < 200$, less than before. So the Blue firm has no incentive to cut its price. Similarly, the Red firm has no incentive to cut its price.

Differentiation, as this example shows, softens price competition. Why? There are two ways to think of differentiation. The first is that differentiation imposes switching costs (of the psychological kind, in this case) on buyers. A blue lover gives up $2 in value to consume a red widget. Because it is costly for the blue lovers to switch to red widgets, the Blue firm can afford to raise prices above marginal cost.

The second way is to recognize that differentiation naturally divides the market into segments. From the point of view of the Blue firm, the market consists of a **strong market** (of customers who prefer blue) and a **weak market** (those who prefer red). When Blue thinks about cutting the price, it must balance the profit gain from the weak market against the revenue loss from the strong market. If the strong market is sizable enough relative to the rest of the market, the incentive to cut prices is reduced. To see why, consider the modification summarized in Table 7.12. The products of the two firms are still differentiated. Can a price of $5 each be sustained? No. Suppose both firms post prices of $5 each. This cannot be an equilibrium. Consider the firm selling red widgets. At the $5 price, it makes $5 − 1 = \$4$ in profit. If it drops its price to $2, for example, it captures the whole market and makes $(2 - 1) \times 100 = \$100$ – that is, more profit. Even though the Red firm is differentiated from its rival, it is along a dimension, color, that hardly anyone cares about.

The obvious lesson of the last example is that one should differentiate in a way that leads to a sizable strong market. The less obvious lesson is that one should differentiate in a way that leaves a sizable (relative to the market) strong market for one's rival. If the rival has no strong market, it has nothing to lose by cutting its price. Dropping its price makes its product more attractive to your strong market. More generally, to determine a rival's incentive to cut price, one should compare the size of its strong market with the incremental volume it will attract from a price cut.

Return to the case summarized in Table 7.11. Suppose you, as the Red firm, could offer two prices: a high price to red lovers and a lower price, for the same red widgets, to the blue lovers.[33] For example, red lovers pay $5 for red widgets but blue lovers pay $2.50. Would you want to engage in this kind of price discrimination?

Let us see what happens if you did. A $2.50 price for red widgets would give blue lovers a surplus of $0.50. This is more than the surplus they receive on the blue widgets priced at $5. Therefore, for the Blue firm to keep its buyers, it must drop its price. In the market consisting of just blue lovers, what would the price of a red widget and the price of a blue widget be in equilibrium? The Red firm would price its red widgets to blue lovers at cost – that is, $1 – and the Blue firm would price its blue widgets at $3. All blue lovers would buy blue widgets. Thus, the Red firm gains no additional revenue but ends up lowering the price that the Blue firm charges. However, the market is more than just blue lovers. The Blue firm faces the following choice: price its widgets at $3 and sell only to blue lovers, or drop the price slightly below $3. Why contemplate a further price drop? If red lovers are paying $5 for red widgets, they would switch to blue widgets priced below $3 because it gives them more surplus. It is easy to see that dropping price below $3 is more profitable for Blue. This in turn forces Red to drop the price of its red widgets to red lovers to keep them. The net effect is that *both* firms end up lowering prices on their strong markets without necessarily gaining share from the other.

This kind of price discrimination destroys the benefits of differentiation. By going after your rival's customers, you force it to lower the price on its

---

[33] And suppose also that you could prevent resale of red widgets bought at the lower price to red lovers.

product. This makes your rival's product more attractive to your strong market. To keep your strong market, you are forced to lower the price to the strong market, so prices spiral downward. The preceding example is an extreme one to make the point. In this example, lower prices lead to lower profits. This is not always so, however, because there are two effects of this kind of price discrimination. One is positive and is the one that most sellers identify right away. It allows you to sell to a segment to which you were not previously selling, and this brings additional profit. The other is negative and is often overlooked. Doing this forces your competitor to lower its prices and thereby forces you to lower prices to your strong segment. This lowers profits. In the preceding example, the negative effect outweighs the positive one. It can go the other way as well.

Apple has carved out a strong market that is about 10 percent of the market for personal computers in the United States. Because Apple's strong market is small relative to the rest of the market, wouldn't Apple gain by making its computers compatible with the Windows Operating System (OS)?

If Apple targets the PC market, one would expect the PC firms to cut prices to make PCs more attractive. To compete, Apple would have to cut prices to attract PC customers. However, this will reduce profits in its strong market. Unless the number of customers it attracts from the PC market compensates for the margin loss in its strong market, it is not profitable for Apple to venture into the PC market. PC firms have no incentive to invade Apple's market, because it is not large enough. In fact, Apple has only made modest attempts to target the PC market with an emulation OS software.

7.4.2 Loyalty Programs

A popular response to the vicissitudes of competition is loyalty programs.[34] Loyalty programs have five possible objectives:

1. Attract new customers. The promise of future rewards is an imperfect substitute for a price cut that may attract new customers. The advantage of future rewards over a straight price cut is that rewards may be cheaper to deliver.
2. Prevent current customers from defecting. Rewards that must be forgone to switch suppliers act as switching costs.

---

[34] Loyalty, here, does not refer to the *pro patriae mori* variety.

Table 7.13. *Reward Types*

	Internal	External
Tangible	Discounts on future purchases, product upgrades	iPod if open an account
Intangible	Personalized greeting, service priority	Dinner with celebrity chef

3. Increase the share of a customer's wallet and create incremental demand. This is done by linking the magnitude and/or the speed at which the reward is received to the amount spent. In addition, the reward can be an opportunity to encourage consumption of other parts of the seller's portfolio of offerings.
4. Increase differentiation by creating a sense of emotional attachment to the seller. This is done through the choice of rewards.
5. Obtain information about customers.

The design of a rewards program requires decisions about the kinds of rewards offered and the buyer activity that will trigger them. Rewards can be categorized along two dimensions. One is whether the reward is tangible or intangible. The other is whether the reward is "internal" – that is, a product or service provided by the seller; or external – an object or service provided by a third party. Examples of rewards that fall into each of these categories are displayed in Table 7.13.

Internal rewards may be less costly to deliver, and their quality is easier to manage. External rewards, on the other hand, can have more "sex appeal." Intangible rewards emphasize differentiation, as they may be hard to compare across sellers.

The biggest challenges in a loyalty program are designing the formulae that link rewards to activities. The first challenge is to decide on the activity that the seller wishes to encourage. Is it volume of purchase or profitability, for example? Second, how high should the thresholds be for the various reward levels? Low reward thresholds are helpful in attracting new customers. However, they reduce the lock-in effect. Third, how is the seller to generate momentum? The farther along a buyer is in the program, the greater the lock-in. But how does one get the buyer to take the first step? What is the inducement to sign on?

Gigliano, Georgiadas, Pleasance, and Whaley (2000) report that 53 percent of grocery customers are enrolled in loyalty programs. Of those who join them, 48 percent spend more than they otherwise do.[35] Nevertheless, many loyalty programs are not profitable. There are two reasons:

1. They are expensive. The Gigliano, Georgiadas, Pleasance, and Whaley (2000) study reports that 16 major European retailers have $1.2 billion per year tied up in loyalty programs. They are usually not structured to discourage free-riding. Second, they don't provide enough value to make a difference to customer purchasing behavior. Even if they did, the margins are probably too small to make it profitable to do so. Also, many retailers fail to track the expenses of such programs accurately. Maintenance, program support, and order fulfillment can eat up large chunks of cash.
2. Once started, the terms of the programs are difficult to change. Buyers react negatively to a move that reduces the benefits of participation.[36]

The Logic

Here we examine the logic underlying the argument that loyalty programs increase retention and profitability. As a vehicle for analysis we consider the PD with a twist. Firm 1 paints its widgets blue and firm 2 paints its widgets red. The color scheme does not change the unit manufacturing costs. Manufacturing costs for both firms remain at $1 a unit.

On the demand side, buyers behave a little differently than they do in the PD. When the prices quoted for widgets by the two firms are **unequal**, all 100 buyers buy from the lowest-priced seller. When prices are equal, 50 of these buyers always buy from firm 1. Call them **blue bloods**. The other 50 always buy from firm 2; call them **red bloods**. Both firms know which customers are blue bloods and which are red bloods. All buyers are willing to pay up to $3 for a widget of any color. In all other respects, the setup is the same as the PD. In particular, each seller has enough capacity to serve the entire market and it has one chance to set the price.

Suppose you are firm 1. If you are to charge any price between 0 and $3 per widget, what price would you charge? Equilibrium analysis dictates that the price will be $1 per widget. This should be clear because if you charge any price greater than cost, the other firm can undercut you and gain 100 percent of the market.

---

[35] For casual apparel retailers, the numbers are 21 percent and 18 percent, respectively.
[36] Starting in about 2006, U.S. airlines have significantly increased the miles required for upgrades and benefits, angering customers.

Now suppose you, and you alone, issue a coupon good for $1 off the price of a blue widget, but distribute them **only** to blue bloods. What price would you charge? The obvious response is: how can the coupon make a difference? It adds no value to the buyers, so how can the firms do more than price at cost? Nevertheless, the coupon does make a difference. To see why, let us see whether pricing at cost is an equilibrium. Pricing at cost would mean that firm 2 (the red one) posts a price of $1. Firm 1 (the blue one), if it is to price at cost, must price at $2. Anything less generates negative profits, given the coupons in circulation. Thus, firm 1 (blue) is at $2 and firm 2 (red) is at $1. At these prices, they split the market. The blue-bloods buy from firm 1. Why? With the coupon, the effective price of a blue widget is $1. The red bloods buy from firm 2.

Could this combination of prices (firm 1 at $2 and firm 2 at $1) be an equilibrium? No. Firm 2 could do better by unilaterally raising its price. In fact, it should raise its price from $1 to $2. Will firm 2 lose its customers from a unilateral price increase? No. The red bloods can buy their favorite widget from firm 2 for $2. Their alternative is to buy blue widgets from firm 1 for $2, as red bloods do not have a coupon for blue widgets. Because prices from their viewpoint are equal, they buy the color they prefer – that is, they stay with firm 2. Thus, firm 2 has raised its price and kept its buyers; therefore, its profits must go up.

Could firm 1 pricing at $2 and firm 2 at $2 be an equilibrium? Again, no. Firm 1 has an incentive to raise the price. Suppose firm 1 prices at $3 while firm 2 is at $2. To see that firm 1's profits must increase, it is enough to check that it does not lose any customers. Observe that blue bloods will pay $2 for blue widgets because they have the coupon. If they go to firm 2 instead, they must pay $2 for red widgets. Because the prices from their viewpoint are equal, they buy the color they prefer – in other words, they stay with firm 1.

Could firm 1 pricing at $3 and firm 2 pricing at $2 be an equilibrium? Again, no. In fact, as the reader can verify, there is no pure strategy equilibrium. It does not matter what the mixed strategy equilibrium is.[37] What matters is that pricing at cost is no longer an equilibrium. This is remarkable because in the absence of the coupon, equilibrium profits were zero. In other words, there is now an upward incentive on price, whereas before there was none. The availability of this coupon, which has no effect on either costs or how customers value the product, introduces an incentive to raise prices. Why? When firm 1 issues a coupon to blue bloods only, it

---

[37] One can show that expected profits are positive for each firm.

is effectively announcing two prices: one for blue bloods and one for red bloods. Furthermore, the price to red bloods is *higher* than the price to blue bloods. Firm 2, recognizing this, knows that it can raise its price without losing customers. Because firm 2 is going to raise prices, this gives firm 1 room to raise its own price above $2 and turn a profit.

A provocative way of summarizing the insight is this: raising my customers' switching costs is good and so is raising my rival's customers' switching costs. If it is expensive for my rival's customers to switch to me, the rival can raise its price. If it raises its price, it makes it more expensive for my customers to switch to the rival and so allows me to raise my price.

The coupon does just that. By issuing the coupon **only to** your customers and raising price (to compensate for the coupon), you make your offering more expensive for your rival's customers. This gives your rival the room to raise its price. Simply announcing a price increase is not enough. Your rival will be concerned that you might rescind it. Issuing the coupon forces you to raise your price and makes it expensive to drop it.

Does it matter if firm 2 also issues coupons to its customers only? No; equilibrium profits will still be positive. In fact, they will be higher, because the coupons mutually reinforce the incentive to raise prices.[38] What if you, firm 1, issues coupons to everyone? In this case, the equilibrium profits will be zero. Why? If all buyers have the coupon, they don't care from whom they buy. This intensifies price competition.

The coupon story illustrates one benefit of loyalty programs. By locking in customers, one can raise industry prices. In effect, a loyalty program acts as a no-poaching agreement on customers. There is a downside, however. The initial cost of signing people up, if not managed, may wipe out the subsequent benefits from higher prices.

Is the coupon story real? Yes. Consider frequent flyer miles. The airlines solve the problem of who should get which coupon by allowing customers to self-select (we shall come back to this). What is to prevent someone signing up with every program? Nothing, only that the rewards are doled out in such a way that spreading oneself among different programs delays the date at which one can cash in the miles for the reward, thus reducing the value of the reward. But is the program not just a glorified quantity discount? Yes, in the sense that those who make many trips get more rewards, but the discount is linked to the *cumulative* volume of purchases. This is what encourages buyers to concentrate their purchases.

---

[38] For example, each firm will make $100 in profit if both firms charge $4 with a $1-off coupon.

Now let us return to the sign-up phase. For the scheme to be beneficial to the firm, one needs to sign up a sizable number of customers. Thus, competition shifts to this phase. There is another wrinkle. Suppose one succeeds in signing up the lion's share of customers. This leaves your rival with a small strong market in the second phase. This reduces its incentives to raise prices in the second phase.

What happens when customers cash in their miles? Now they are indifferent between the different airlines. How can the airlines prevent this? By allowing them some rewards, even though their current balance is zero.

7.4.3 Competing with Complements

Here we consider what happens when firms that compete do so with products and services that complement each other. Our discussion will begin with the case of the IBM punch cards introduced in Section 6.2.2. Suppose, initially, that IBM sells computers only and another, separate company, say, C, sells punch cards. For arithmetical convenience only, suppose that the unit cost of computers and punch cards is zero. Customers assign zero value to a computer by itself. They also assign zero value to punch cards by themselves. Each customer, however, has an RP of $10 for a combination of one computer and one punch card.[39]

Suppose IBM and C announce prices simultaneously. Let p_{IBM} be the price that IBM charges and p_C be the price that C sets. It is easy to see that any pair (p_{IBM}, p_C) that satisfies

$$p_{IBM} + p_C = 10$$

forms an equilibrium. If IBM, for example, were to raise its price, then the total price of a computer and punch card system would exceed $10 and no one would purchase it. If IBM lowers its price, demand stays fixed, and IBM's revenue falls. In words, IBM and C jointly produce $10 in value and must figure out how to divide it between themselves. In the absence of any other information, we cannot say whether IBM will capture the lion's share or whether it will be C. If, before setting prices, IBM were to announce that it was committed to charging a price of $9.99 and C believed this, then C would be forced to charge $0.01. On the other hand, if C thought that IBM was bluffing, it might choose a price larger than $0.01, resulting in

---

[39] Once again, the assumption that one punch card suffices to work a computer is for convenience only and plays no important role in the analysis.

Table 7.14. *Table of RPs*

Buyer Segment	AG, AM	BG, BM	AG, BM	AM, BG	Number
AA	$10	$5	$5	$5	100
BB	$5	$10	$5	$5	100
AB	$5	$5	$10	$0	100

a total price for a computer and punch card that exceeded $10. Thus, in this particular case there might be an argument for IBM to enter the punch card market to ensure that the price of punch cards is low enough.[40] More generally, if there was competition in the punch card market but it was not sufficiently intense, IBM would have an incentive to enter the punch card market. In doing so, it could lower punch card prices, raise prices for the computer, and so capture a larger share of the $10 value that is generated per customer.[41] If competition in the punch card segment were sufficiently intense to force prices for punch cards down to cost, then, IBM would have no incentive to enter the punch card business (unless it can produce punch cards at even lower cost).

Now we examine what happens when competing sellers have offerings that complement each other. It will be useful to have a concrete example in mind. Suppose there are two firms, A and B. Each makes a graphics card and a monitor. Label the graphics card and monitor made by A as AG and AM, respectively. Label the graphics card and monitor made by firm B as BG and BM, respectively. For simplicity, manufacturing costs of all products are zero.[42]

Buyers are interested in purchasing a system, rather than individual components. That is, they want to purchase a graphics card and a monitor. We can divide buyers into three equally sized groups, labeled AA, BB, and AB. They differ in the value they place on different graphics card and monitor combinations. These valuations are summarized in Table 7.14.

The AAs prefer a system that is made up entirely of A components and the BBs prefer one that is made up of B components only. The ABs have a preference for a system that combines a particular component from each

---

[40] Readers should recognize echoes of double marginalization in this example.

[41] If demand for a computer and punch card system was elastic, then dropping the price in the punch card market could stimulate demand for computers and punch cards. This would be an added benefit that our story does not account for. See, for example, the discussion at the end of Section 6.2.2.

[42] This discussion is inspired by Mattutes and Regibeau (1988).

firm. In particular, they have value for combining a graphics card from A and a monitor from B, but not a graphics card from B and a monitor from A. If the ABs did not exist, the systems would be imperfect substitutes for each other. It is the ABs that see value in combining a component from one seller with a component from another seller.

Given the price of a system, buyers will buy the system that generates the largest surplus. For example if the price of an A system is $8 and that of a B system is $2, the AAs will buy the B system because their surplus is $2 for the A system but $3 for the B system.

There are two scenarios to consider. In scenario 1, the graphics card of A is incompatible with the monitor of B and the graphics card of B is incompatible with the monitor of A. In this scenario, firms set prices on systems and sell only whole systems.

In scenario 2, each firm's products are compatible with the other firm's products. In this scenario, firms set prices on individual components and sell individual components.

As one of the sellers, is there a reason to prefer one scenario to the other? Making the components incompatible increases differentiation and presumably supports higher prices.

Observe first that the largest revenue that any firm can achieve is when it is a monopolist. In this case it is revenue maximizing to price a system at $5 and sell to all three segments. This yields a revenue of $5 × 300 = $1,500. Is there an equilibrium in scenario 1 that supports this outcome, or even comes close? No. For example, suppose each firm were to price its (incompatible) systems at $10. Firm A will sell its system to the AAs only and firm B will sell its system to the BBs only. Each will generate a revenue of $1000. Let us see whether firm A has an incentive to unilaterally cut the price. From firm A's point of view, its strong market consists of the 100 AAs. Its weak market is the 100 BBs and the 100 ABs. For a price cut to be worthwhile, firm A must cut sufficiently to attract buyers from its weak market. If firm A drops the price of its system to $5, it will attract the ABs but not the BBs.[43] Such a drop does not increase profit, as it results in a $5 loss in revenue from each AA buyer and a $5 increase for each AB buyer. Because these segments are of equal size, the loss is exactly balanced by the gain. If firm A drops the price of its system below $5 – say, to $4.99 – this will attract the BBs as well. This price will capture all three segments, yielding a revenue of $4.99 × 300, which exceeds $1000. Furthermore, it will give firm A profit

---

[43] The surplus for the BB segment is zero for B's system as well as A's system. In this case, the BBs choose the B system.

close to the monopoly profit. However, firm A at $4.99 and firm B at $10 cannot be an equilibrium. This is because firm B will have an incentive to undercut A. High prices in scenario 1 are hard to sustain because of the ABs. Their number makes the size of the weak market dwarf the size of each seller's strong market, putting downward price pressure on each seller.

Consider scenario 2 now. In this case, each firm pricing each of its components at $5 is an equilibrium. At these prices, firm A sells two components to the AAs and one to the ABs. Firm B sells two components to the BBs and one to the ABs. Revenues for each firm are $5 × 300 = $1,500, equal to the monopoly profits. To check that it is an equilibrium, examine firm A's choices (a similar analysis will hold for firm B).

Suppose A raises the prices of any one of its components. Then it will lose the AAs because the price of A's system will exceed their RPs. Suppose A drops the price of any one of its components. The only reason to drop is to attract the BBs and get the ABs to switch to buying two components. This can work only if A drops the price enough to hand them at least $5 of surplus. However, any surplus given to attract the BBs means a corresponding revenue loss on the AAs. Any surplus given to the ABs means zero revenue on them. The last possibility is to raise the price of one component and drop the other. Whether this increases profits depends on whether this changes the surplus enjoyed by the BBs and the ABs. From the previous reasoning, this will not happen.

Scenario 2, then, benefits both firms. Why is this? The first reason is that by switching to compatible systems, they have reduced the intensity of price competition. This can be seen from the fact that the gains from cutting the price of a component in terms of volume are not sufficient to compensate for the drop in price. A second reason is that compatibility increases value in the sense that ABs are catered to, and this may permit higher profits for both firms.

Now let us put flesh on this example. Suppose there are two sellers, each offering cellular phones and applications that run on them. For the moment, we are making the unrealistic assumption that the seller produces both the phone and the applications.[44] Buyers have no interest in a phone by itself or the applications by themselves. They do however, care about a package of the two. Should each seller design its applications to operate on its rival's phone?

---

[44] As well as the fact that the phone provider does not have to go through a service provider such as Verizon.

The earlier analysis highlights the justification for doing so. There is also an argument, however, for making their systems incompatible. If the goal of one of the sellers is to drive out the other, making the systems incompatible will do that. It forces buyers to make a choice. If the seller can get enough buyers to commit to its system (by pricing aggressively), it kills interest in the competing system. Thus, the choice facing the seller is whether it is better off sharing the market or incurring the cost of securing the market for itself.

Now, let us consider what happens when applications are produced not by the phone producer, but by third parties. There is now, unsurprisingly, a conflict of interest between application providers and phone manufacturers. A popular application that runs on one phone, but not the other, increases differentiation in the phone market. This benefits the phone manufacturer that runs the application. For the application provider, the phones provide access to customers. Interoperability increases the size of the market the application provider can reach.

7.5 Tale of the Inferior Entrant

Can an entrant with higher costs and an inferior product enter one's market? To think clearly about this question, it is useful to have a particular setup in mind. Here is the one we will use:

1. There are 100 buyers.
2. The entrant moves first by building a facility to serve upto N buyers.
3. Then the entrant announces a price p per unit for its output.
4. The incumbent responds by announcing its price (the same price to all buyers).
5. Buyers choose the offer that gives them the largest surplus.
6. The game ends.

Suppose the incumbent's production costs are $100 a unit and all 100 buyers value the incumbent's product at $200. The entrant's production costs are $120 a unit, and all buyers value the entrant's product at $160. Thus, the entrant has the inferior product and is at a cost disadvantage relative to the incumbent. Can the entrant gain a toehold in the market?

Suppose the entrant chooses $p = 140$ and $N = 19$. In words, the entrant offers a low price and targets 19 percent of the market. How should the incumbent respond?

The incumbent has two choices. The first is to accommodate the entrant, by giving up on the market targeted by the entrant. In this case, the incumbent should charge $200 a unit and sell to the 81 percent of the market that the entrant cannot serve. This yields $(200 - 100) \times 81 = \$8100$ in profit.

The second choice is to fight the entrant. If the incumbent wishes to displace the entrant, it has to cut the price from $200. The incumbent does not have to match the entrant on price since it has the superior product, but it does have to match (at least) the surplus offered. Because the entrant is offering $20 in surplus, the incumbent must price at $180 a unit at most. At this price, even if the incumbent captures the entire market, its profit is $(180 - 100) \times 100 = \$8000$.

Thus, the incumbent is better off accommodating. The entrant gets in. At first glance, this seems surprising. After all, the deck appears stacked against the entrant. It has higher costs, delivers less value, and must commit first to capacity and price. Further, if an entrant inferior on both dimensions can gain a toehold, how much easier must it be for an entrant that is superior to the incumbent on at least one dimension (e.g., higher value but higher cost or lower value but lower cost). Therefore, it becomes important to understand what it is about the setup that makes the incumbent vulnerable.

First, the combination of the incumbent's size and the fact that it must charge the same price to everyone makes it weak. Why? By coming in small, the entrant forces the incumbent to make a trade-off between high price on the segment not targeted by the entrant and low price on the entire market. It is cheaper for the incumbent to accommodate the entrant if the market targeted by the entrant is small enough. This is just the strong/weak market story all again. The entrant arrives and divides the market but leaves a sufficiently large share for the incumbent, which reduces the incentive for the incumbent to undercut the entrant. Competition in the retail petroleum market in the United Kingdom in the late 1980s and early 1990s illustrates nicely how being forced to charge the same price to everyone weakens the incumbent. In the late 1980s, the three main sellers of petrol at the retail level were Shell, BP, and Esso (now called Exxon Mobil). There was little price competition between the three and the margin on a liter of petrol was 6 pence. In the early 1990s, supermarkets began selling petrol. In the late 1980s their share of the retail petroleum market was less than 1 percent. By 1991, their share had grown to at least 6 percent. A good portion of these supermarket outlets were in direct competition with Esso outlets. In 1991, Esso had 21 percent of the market and it forecasted that its share would fall below 18 percent if it did nothing. Thus, Esso decided to respond by cutting prices, but selectively – only at outlets facing direct competition from supermarket locations. To match supermarket prices, Esso reduced margins to 4 pence a liter. Shell and BP, however, interpreted these moves by Esso as the start of a price war and responded by cutting prices at every outlet. Esso was forced to follow suit by cutting prices at all its locations. Margins fell to 2 pence a liter. Eventually, Shell, BP, and Esso backed off. By 1995, supermarkets had gained 20 percent of the market and Esso's share had fallen to 16 percent.

The second reason that the incumbent is vulnerable is that the "game ends." If we extend the game by more than one period, then the incumbent may have incentive to fight if it feels that entrant may encroach again. Suppose that the entrant takes a nibble in the first period, then a nibble in the second period, and so on. Or suppose a series of entrants, each arriving one after the other and taking a nibble. Thus, the incumbent must balance the loss in profits from fighting today against the profits to be made when the entrant is out of the market.

The lesson for the entrant is this: come in small and, most important, credibly convince the incumbent that it intends to stay small. In our numerical example, "small" refers to size, but it should be interpreted more broadly to mean targeting segments not of primary importance to the incumbent.[45] In 1992, for example, Kiwi Airlines entered the Atlanta–Newark market with flights offering gourmet meals and expanded legroom. It undercut Delta and Continental prices by as much as 75 percent. At entry, Kiwi represented less than 7 percent of that route's capacity, which made it expensive for Delta and Continental to respond.[46] Another example is Vans in athletic footwear. It targets niche markets, such as skating, snowboarding and skiing, and avoids direct competition with giants such as Nike and Adidas. Schweppes in the beverage market leaves the cola market alone and avoids direct competition with Coca Cola and Pepsi.[47]

Our setup involved an entrant that was inferior to the incumbent in both cost and value. However, the lessons we draw from it apply more generally.

---

[45] The entrant could develop an entirely new segment, one not yet identified or cultivated by the incumbent. In this way, the entrant grows, but not at the expense of the incumbent. Because entrant and incumbent are not in direct competition, this situation is uninteresting from our point of view.

[46] Within a year Kiwi had 1200 employees and $116 million in revenues. By 1995, it collapsed because of internal management problems.

[47] Cadbury Schweppes has since been broken up and both brands were sold; the Schweppes brand is marketed and sold around the world now by a number of companies.

For example, the entrant may have lower costs and an inferior product, Or higher costs and a superior offering. The point is the same: do not rouse the incumbent by taking away too much of its market. There are three approaches to targeting a segment that may not be of primary importance to the incumbent:

1. Low price with lower functionality, lower quality, less convenience, smaller assortment, and so forth. Here the customer is willing to give up on a number of features to get the lower price. Examples are dollar stores, discount airlines, and the way Toyota, Honda, and Hyundai entered the U.S. car market. In these cases, the entrant offers lower value (relative to the incumbent) but probably has lower costs as well.
2. High price supported by image of high quality or exclusivity. Luxury goods are an example. In this case, the entrant probably has higher costs, but delivers more value.
3. High price supported by specialized functionality. In the consumer space, Herman Miller with the Aeron chair is an example, as is Alienware with gaming computers that sell for a few thousand dollars.

How can the incumbent fend off the entrant? By using selective discounts: cutting price only to the segments and volume at risk of going over to the entrant – in other words, engaging in price discrimination. The difficulty is identifying the segments at risk and preventing arbitrage between buyers and possible erosion of brand image. Recognizing that the incumbent will fend it off in this way, the entrant must work to encourage the arbitrage possibilities associated with price discrimination. This forces the incumbent to charge the same price to everyone, making it expensive for the incumbent to retaliate. A direct way to do this is to become the arbitrageur: buy up the incumbent's low-priced offering and resell to customers facing a higher price from the incumbent. One example of this is Dow versus Bromkonvention in bromine, recounted in Section 7.2.2. An indirect way is to approach the incumbent's customers facing the high price and point out that other customers of the incumbent benefit from lower prices. The incumbent, in response, must distinguish its low-price offering from the high-price one by versioning – for example, introducing a fighting or flanking brand. An example of this can be seen in the competition between national brands and private-label brands.[48] The private-label brands are cheaper than the

---

[48] Private-label brands are offered by the same retailers that carry the national brands. Retailers use their private labels to pressure national-brand players into offering them better wholesale prices.

national brands, and typically of inferior quality. Some sellers of national brands have responded by issuing secondary brands to compete with the private labels. P&G, for example, sells two diaper brands, Pampers and the lower priced Luvs brand. Pampers averages about $10 a package, and Luvs is about $8. Target sells two store brands, one similar to Pampers and the other similar to Huggies, made by Kimberley-Clark. The Target brands are priced below Luvs. Walmart's own diaper brand, White Cloud, goes for about $6 a package. In addition, P &G spends heavily on R&D and uses differentiation to position its products at a price premium. Evaluation of the P&G brands indicate that they are considered superior to the store brands.

7.5.1 An Airline Interlude

As a first illustration of the ideas just presented, we describe the 1985 entry of PEOPLExpress Airlines (PE) into the Southeast, which at that time was dominated by Piedmont Airlines.[49]

When U.S. airlines were deregulated, the first new airline to enter the airline market was PE. It launched in 1981 with service from Newark to Buffalo; New York; Columbus, Ohio; and Norfolk, Virginia. PE's strategy was to offer a no-frills, two-tier price (peak–off peak), high-frequency regionwide service to 13 peripheral Middle Atlantic cities, with Newark as a hub. PE's costs, by almost any measure, were lower than those of the incumbent airlines.[50] PE targeted customers who saw regional air travel as a commodity. These were customers who would occasionally fly at low enough fares rather than drive 350 to 500 miles. For example, PE flew from Newark to Pittsburgh for $39 (weekday) and $19 (weekend), whereas the competing lowest-cost flight was $128. Thus, PE was offering an inferior product at a lower cost.

To prevent retaliation by incumbents, PE decided to provide very high-frequency service on only 13 peripheral routes in its Middle Atlantic hub-and-spoke network out of Newark. High-frequency service on the chosen routes was deemed essential. Otherwise, incumbents would respond with increased flight frequency, more convenient departures, and additional services. Thus, PE chose routes not of primary importance for incumbents,

---

[49] The details presented here are based on Harris (2007).

[50] It achieved this cost through 15 to 20-minute turnaround times, longer crew shifts, and converting all first-class and galley space into additional coach-class seats. Like a bus, fares were paid on the flight. Passengers were permitted to bring one carry-on bag for free, and each checked bag was charged a fee of $3.00. On-board snacks and drinks cost extra.

but it entered at large scale on these routes. The strategy succeeded because PE created a new segment not previously served by the more expensive and infrequent Mohawk, Allegheny, and U.S. Air flights. It was this segment that filled PE's seats.

In 1984, PE was offered the chance to buy 38 used 737s at very attractive prices. Against the advice of senior management, founder and CEO Donald Burr bought the planes. PE began flying from Newark to Chicago and Minneapolis, the hubs of United and Northwest, respectively. These routes were extremely lucrative feeder spokes for United, Northwest, and American. They immediately matched PE's price rather than accommodate its entry. Failure on the Chicago and Minneapolis routes caused PE to turn its attention to Greensboro, North Carolina, a major hub for Piedmont. PE felt that there was an untapped market of flyers who would welcome low fares.

Piedmont was the second-fastest-growing and among the most profitable airlines at that time. In anticipation of PE's entry into the Greensboro market, Piedmont dropped its $139 fare to Newark to $79 (peak) and $49 (off-peak). The $49 figure represented Piedmont's estimate of PE's fully loaded costs for the similar Columbus–Newark route and 300 percent of Piedmont's incremental costs per passenger. Thereafter, Piedmont waited for PE's prices and then matched them. From $79/$49 in December 1984, prices went down to $29/$19 in April 1985. By September 1986, PE was forced to shut down its operations in the Southeast.

Why did the strategy that PE pursued in the Middle Atlantic fail in the Southeast? There were two reasons. The first has to do with customer characteristics. Piedmont managers studied every passenger on and off every flight that PE flew into Piedmont cities. They discovered that all customers preferred the low-priced seller when there were substantial price differences. However, loyalty to the incumbent prevailed when prices were equal. Thus, a low-priced large-capacity entry by PE was likely to capture a large portion of Piedmont's share. Furthermore, if Piedmont matched PE's low prices, it was likely to keep existing customers as well as attract new customers because of the low prices. This combination of circumstances gave Piedmont the incentive to fight PE's entry. It did so in two ways:

1. It encouraged loyalty through scheduling convenience, reliability, amenities, and responsiveness to changes in travel plans. Some of these enhancements are, of course, substitutes for a price cut. However, many of them were focused on business travelers – for example,

ensuring, when possible, that one was seated next to an empty seat. Thus, Piedmont was cutting price selectively. AT&T, for example, a large corporate travel customer from the Greensboro regional office to Newark headquarters, offered Piedmont a price of $79 near the start of the price war to secure high-delivery reliability.

2. Piedmont lowered prices in cities within driving distance of Greensboro. This was to prevent customers in those cities from flying out of Greensboro, thus reducing the available market for PE.

7.5.2 A TV Interlude

As a second illustration, we discuss the entry of Vizio into the flat-panel TV segment. Founded by William Wang in 2003, Vizio started by selling a 46-inch plasma TV for $2,799, which was about half what other brands then charged. The product was not of good quality and sales were poor. Since then, however, the company has made a concerted effort to improve quality as well as keep prices down. Even so, based on *Consumer Reports* ratings, Vizio scores lower than top brands such as Sony and Samsung.

Vizio outsources procurement of components and assembly. Design and manufacturing are handled by Amtran Technology of Taiwan and Hon Hai Precision Industry (the parent of Foxconn) of Taiwan. Both companies are also shareholders of Vizio. Vizio optimizes the supply chain, holding minimal inventory through continuous monitoring of retailer sales. Because component prices fall rapidly, it is expensive to hold inventory. Also, unlike other big-name players, Vizio has only one product in each set size. In addition to keeping inventory low, the company has a very small number of employees; in 2007, it had fewer than 100 employees. The company spends very little on marketing and advertising. Only in 2007, four years after entry, did Vizio launch a TV advertising campaign featuring San Diego Chargers running back, LaDainian Tomlinson. Vizio's big break came in 2004, when Costco agreed to carry the brand, providing the company access to millions of shoppers. Now, Vizio is the best-selling TV brand for Costco. It is also available through Walmart, Sam's Club, BJ Wholesale, and other discount stores.

How have the better-known brands, such as Sony and Samsung, competed with Vizio? For the first three years, they largely ignored Vizio. This is consistent with the lessons from the tale of the inferior entrant. The entrant has targeted a segment not of primary importance to the main

Table 7.15. *Table of Sony Prices at BestBuy.com*

Size	Low	Medium	High
32″	$685	$899	$1199
37″	$949	$1199	$1499
40″	$1499	$1899	$2299
46″	$1599	$2399	$2799

incumbents. Vizio accomplished this by offering an inferior product and using retail channels that did not overlap significantly with the incumbents. The incumbents, such as Sony and Samsung, have chosen to distinguish themselves from Vizio by incorporating several advanced features in the TVs and have kept their prices relatively high. Sony, in particular, stayed at the high end, with prices typically 80 percent to 100 percent higher than Vizio's for the same set size.

Eventually, Vizio started to gain traction and increase sales dramatically. Sales increased from $142 million in 2005 to $700 million in 2006 to about $2 billion in 2007. This growth came from the fact that Vizio started to sell through Sears, Circuit City, and the Dell web site. Sony and every other major player are now threatened by Vizio. Philips licensed its brand name to Funai and exited the U.S. market. Pioneer, which sold a high-end plasma product discontinued sales in the United States. Prices have fallen significantly, both because component prices have been reduced and because of competition from Vizio and other lower-priced entrants.[51]

Sony has countered with three price ranges in each set size. Tables 7.15 and 7.16 provide a sample of prices on August 3, 2008 for Sony and Vizio HDTVs. In Costco, Vizio only has one version of each size.

Sony's lowest prices are still higher than Vizio's prices, with the highest price being about double Vizio's prices. Has Sony been able to keep Vizio at bay? Sales results favor Vizio. In the fourth quarter of 2007, Vizio shipped 12.4 percent of North America's liquid-crystal display (LCD) TVs, just behind Sony's 12.5 percent share and Samsung's 14.2 percent, according to research firm iSuppli Corp. Despite the higher-quality reputation of Sony and the higher ratings in *Consumer Reports*, the significantly lower price of

---

[51] Vizio's success has attracted copycat low-price players such as Westinghouse and Olevia. Both have followed Vizio's strategy of outsourcing for design and manufacturing.

Table 7.16. *Table of Vizio Prices at Costco*

Size	Price
32″	$599
37″	$749
42″	$999
47″	$1299

Vizio has been very attractive to consumers. The lowest-priced Sony Bravia is an attempt by Sony to more aggressively target Vizio.[52]

7.5.3 Loyalty Discounts

We return to the setup of the inferior entrant, but with two modifications.

1. There is one buyer, interested in purchasing up to 100 units.
2. The entrant, with the capacity to produce up to 19 units, moves first by announcing a price of p per unit for its output.
3. The incumbent responds by announcing its unit price.
4. The buyer chooses how much to buy from each supplier to maximize surplus.
5. The game ends.

Suppose the incumbent's production costs are $100 a unit and the buyer values the incumbent's product at $200 a unit. The entrant's production costs are $120 a unit and the buyer values the entrant's product at $160 a unit.

The first difference is that 100 buyers are replaced by a single buyer interested in acquiring 100 units. The second is that the capacity of the entrant is fixed a priori. Thus, we are analyzing a situation in which a large incumbent must compete against a small entrant.

As before, if the entrant chooses $p = 140$, the incumbent is better off pricing at $200 a unit, yielding a profit of $8,100, and letting the buyer purchase some of its supply from the entrant. In fact, a price of $140 a unit will maximize the entrant's profit. We now show that the incumbent with a different pricing scheme can reduce the incentives for the entrant to enter the market.

---

[52] Since 2007, Vizio has grown rapidly and ended 2010 as the number one seller of HDTVs in the U.S. market. Vizio now has multiple offerings at each screen size as well.

Recall that the incumbent is made weak by the fact that it must charge the same price for every unit. As we noted earlier, the incumbent would be better off if it could price-discriminate. Here there is a single customer, so the price discrimination cannot take place by customer. Instead it will take place by the "unit" – that is, through a loyalty discount. Loyalty discounts are a form of nonlinear pricing in which the unit price of the good drops when the fraction of a buyer's needs purchased from the supplier exceeds a certain threshold. Linking the discount to the share, rather than the volume, purchased is what distinguishes loyalty discounts from traditional quantity discounts.

Suppose the incumbent offered the buyer the following deal. If the buyer purchases 81 percent or less of its requirements from the incumbent, the buyer will be charged $200 a unit. However, if the buyer purchases more than 81 percent of its requirements from the incumbent, the buyer needs to pay only $182 for each unit.

If the buyer purchases 81 units from the incumbent and 19 units from the entrant, its surplus will be $81 \times (200 - 200) + 19 \times (160 - 140) = \$380$. On the other hand, if the buyer purchases all 100 units from the incumbent, it pays $182 a unit and realizes a surplus of $(200 - 182) \times 100 = \$1,800$, which is larger. Because the buyer purchases all 100 units from the incumbent, the incumbent realizes a profit of $(182-100) \times 100 = \$8,200$. Thus, the incumbent's profits are larger.

In fact, faced with the pricing scheme announced by the incumbent, the entrant would have to choose p so that

$$(200 - 200) \times 81 + (160 - p) \times 19 \geq 1800$$

to encourage the buyer to purchase from it. The left-hand side of this inequality is the surplus from buying 81 units from the incumbent at $200 a unit and 19 units from the entrant at p a unit. The right-hand side is the surplus the buyer enjoys from purchasing all 100 units from the incumbent. Solving this inequality for p, we discover that $p \leq 65.26$. In other words, the entrant would have to price below its cost.[53]

The loyalty discount turns the tables on the entrant by making its small size a weakness. When the buyer purchases less than the threshold amount from the incumbent, it gives up a discount offered by the incumbent on

---

[53] In this example, the incumbent can price higher than $182. At a price of $192.40, the surplus the buyer receives from purchasing all 100 units from the incumbent would exactly equal the surplus from splitting the purchase between incumbent and entrant (81 units from incumbent at $200 each and 19 units from the entrant at $120 each; that is, the entrant's unit cost).

those units. In order to induce the buyer to do this, the entrant must discount the price on the units it sells. Because it sells only a small number of units, it must discount deeply – in this case, so deeply as to be unprofitable.

An example of the use of a loyalty discount to fend off an entrant can be found in how Pacific, a manufacturer of mechanical snubbers used in building pipe systems for nuclear power plants, priced to one of its large customers, Grinnell.[54] Given the volume of Grinnell's business, it received a 20 percent discount off the list price. At the time (the late 1970s), Pacific had no viable competitors, so Grinnell decided to pay the Barry Wright corporation to develop a full line of mechanical snubbers. Grinnell agreed to subsidize Barry Wright's development costs, and use it as its exclusive source for two years. In the interim, Grinnell purchased snubbers from Pacific at 20 percent off the list price.

Once Pacific became aware of the deal with Barry Wright, it offered Grinnell a 30 percent discount off the list price for small snubbers and 25 percent off the list price for large snubbers. However, to secure these discounts, Grinnell had to commit to spend $5.7 million on snubbers. This amounted to more than a year's worth of Grinnell's needs. If Grinnell declined, it would continue to be charged 80 percent of the list price. Notice that the loyalty discount here is pegged not to a share of the number of units but to a dollar volume, but as is easy to see, this is cosmetic, as one can back out a volume share from the unit prices.

Grinnell, anticipating that the Barry Wright corporation would make up the difference, declined and placed a $1 million order at the standard 20 percent off list price. When the Barry Wright corporation came up short, Grinnell entered into a contract to purchase $4.3 million worth of snubbers from Pacific, enough to fill that year's demand. The contract price specified the higher 30/25 percent discount off list, and gave Grinnell the option to buy the following year's requirements at these prices. Soon afterward, Grinnell ended the connection with Barry Wright.

Although the advantages of loyalty discounts for a large incumbent are clear, their legal status is murky. Some forms have been found to be illegal in North America, and others legal. For example, the Barry Wright corporation unsuccessfully sued Pacific on the grounds that the discount amounted to a form of predatory pricing. On the other hand, when Nutrasweet (large incumbent) employed a similar tactic in Canada against HSC (small entrant), the Canadian authorities found it to be illegal. In 2008, Amgen discontinued the use of such loyalty discounts on the sale of anemia drug

---

[54] Snubbers are devices that limit pressure or velocity surges in measurement devices.

Aranesp.[55] In Europe, however, rebates granted by dominant firms to customers provided the customer achieves a certain individualized volume target are viewed with suspicion. Indeed, it is just such behavior that led to Intel being charged in May 2009 with anticompetitive behavior by the European Union and fined $1.45 billion.

7.5.4 Retreating Brands

When Timex watches entered the Indian market, it did so via a joint venture with Titan, another watch company. Under the terms of the joint venture, Titan would handle the marketing and distribution of Timex watches. Further, a noncompete clause in the agreement prevented Titan from selling watches priced at less than Rs 1,000.

Initially, Timex sold watches in two distinct ranges. The high end was about Rs 3,000 and the low-end prices were in the range of Rs 450 to 1,200. Eventually, Titan broke the agreement by introducing two watches priced under Rs 400 (called the Sonata and the Dash). Timex responded by introducing its own offering (called Timex Basics) at under Rs 350. In other words, Timex introduced a fighting brand. Thus far the story is consistent with our earlier analysis of how an incumbent should respond to an entrant. However, in this case, Timex eventually chose to withdraw the fighting brand. Why?

The Timex example described here differs from the setup of the inferior entrant described earlier, because in that case the incumbent had only one version. Because all buyers had the same RP for the incumbent's offering, there was no reason for the incumbent to engage in versioning in the absence of competition. To understand why Timex was forced to withdraw its fighting brand, it is useful to revisit Example 15 from Chapter 6.

Suppose that an incumbent can produce two kinds of printers (fast and slow) at zero cost to a market consisting of two equal-sized segments. For convenience, we reproduce the RPs of each segment for each kind of printer in Table 7.17. Recall that in the absence of competition the incumbent should offer a fast printer priced at $90 and a slow printer at $30.

Now consider an entrant that can produce an identical slow printer at zero cost. If the entrant offers its slow printer at a price below $30, to keep any portion of that market, the incumbent will have to drop the price of its slow printer. However, if it does so, it will encourage the A segment to purchase a

---

[55] Amgen claimed that it did so in response to criticisms that such loyalty discounts encouraged the "overconsumption" of Aranesp; see the Oncological Interlude for more details.

Table 7.17. *RPs for Printers*

	Fast	Slow
A's RP	$100	$40
B's RP	$49	$30

slow printer rather than a fast printer. Thus, to keep the A segment buying the fast printer, the incumbent must lower the price of the fast printer as well. In particular, for every $1 drop in the price of the slow printer, the incumbent must drop the price of the fast printer by $1 as well. Therefore, competition in the slow printer market is a liability for fast printer sales. If the price in the slow printer market becomes low enough, it will be better to give up that segment to the entrant. This will allow the entrant to raise the price of its slow printers and reduce pressure on the fast printer.

Suppose the incumbent exits the slow printer market. What is to prevent the entrant from pricing its slow printer to go after segment A as well? Nothing. Suppose it does. The incumbent can respond by dropping the price of the fast printer to $60. This gives each buyer in segment A a surplus of $40. To match that surplus with a slow printer, the entrant would have to price at zero! Thus, it would be better for the entrant to just price at $30 and sell to the B segment only.

7.6 Key Points

1. The pricing dilemma identifies the four conditions necessary to drive prices to unit costs: sellers focussed on short-term gains, excess capacity, absence of differentiation, and transparency.
2. The procurement process should mimic, insofar as possible, the environment of the pricing dilemma.
3. Even if total capacity exceeds demand but each firm does not have sufficient capacity to serve the entire market, the market price will be above marginal cost.
4. Competition benefits only the buyer. A seller, by agreeing to participate, benefits the buyer, so the seller should try to capture some of this benefit up front.
5. The incentive for a seller to cut price is inversely related to the size of its strong market. The smaller the strong market relative to the entire market, the greater the incentive to cut price.
6. Differentiation along dimensions that matter serve to divide up customers among sellers. This gives each seller a sufficiently strong market to discourage price cutting. However, the benefits of differentiation are

destroyed if any seller engages in selective price cuts targeted toward competitors' strong markets.

7. Loyalty programs can be used to lock in customers. They do so by raising switching costs for customers and can lead to higher prices.

8. By entering small with a differentiated product, the entrant can avoid direct confrontation with the incumbent. The incumbent may be better off accommodating the entrant rather than trying to drive out the entrant. The entrant, however, may not continue to stay small, which poses a greater threat to the incumbent. In such a case, the incumbent could resort to selective price cuts to pressure the entrant.

7.7 Technical Aside

7.7.1 Analysis of the Capacity Game

Here we consider the situation in which the capacities of the firms are fixed and they must choose prices. Consider a situation in which there are Q buyers, each with an RP of \$$u$ for a single unit of the product. Firm 1 has a capacity of q_1 and firm 2 a capacity of q_2. We'll suppose that $q_1 \geq q_2$; that is, firm 1 is the larger firm. For simplicity, there are no manufacturing costs.

One issue that must be resolved is what happens when the combined capacity ($q_1 + q_2$) of the firms exceeds the total demand (Q) and the two firms charge equal prices. How do the buyers decide which firm to patronize? We resolve this by assuming that buyers break ties at random. Another issue to be resolved is what buyers do if they are turned away empty-handed by a seller because the seller's capacity is exhausted. We will assume that they go to the other firm, which serves as many of these as possible. This is called **efficient rationing**.

In this setup, what prices would we expect to see the firms charge in equilibrium? In particular, will the larger firm charge the higher prices?

A rigorous derivation of the equilibrium prices is quite involved and will not be reproduced here.[56] Instead the main findings are summarized as follows:

1. $Q \leq q_2$
   Because each firm has the capacity to supply the entire market, at equilibrium both firms would quote a price of 0.

2. $q_2 < Q < q_1$
   In this case, there is no equilibrium in pure strategies. Firm 1 would pick a price p_1 at random from within the range: $u\frac{Q-q_2}{Q} < p_1 \leq u$.

[56] The derivation may be found in Ghemawat (1986).

Firm 2 would pick a price p_2 at random from the range: $u\frac{Q-q_2}{Q} < p_2 \leq u$. In fact, the expected price of firm 1 will be higher than the expected price of firm 2.

The expected revenue for firm 1 will be $u(Q - q_2)$, whereas the expected revenue for firm 2 will be $u(Q - q_2)\frac{q_2}{Q}$. The expected revenue of the larger firm will exceed that of the smaller firm.

3. $q_1 \leq Q < q_1 + q_2$

   In this case, also, there is no equilibrium in pure strategies. Firm 1 would pick a price p_1 at random in the range: $u\frac{Q-q_2}{q_1} < p_1 \leq u$. Firm 2 would pick a price p_2 at random in the range: $u\frac{Q-q_2}{q_1} < p_2 \leq u$. The expected revenue for firm 1 will be $u(Q - q_2)\min\{\frac{q_1}{q_2}, 1\}$, whereas for firm 2 it will be $u(Q - q_2)\min\{\frac{q_2}{q_1}, 1\}$.

4. $Q \geq q_1 + q_2$

   In equilibrium, both firms would charge a price of u and their revenues would be uq_1 and uq_2, respectively.

The first and last cases are easy, so we focus on the middle two cases. The important point of these two cases is that, on average, the larger firm will quote the higher price. Why is this? To understand what is going on, suppose we are in the case in which $q_2 < Q < q_1$ and both firms happen to have announced the same price. Which firm has more to lose if its rival undercuts it in price?

If firm 1 undercuts firm 2, firm 1 gets the entire market and has the capacity to serve the entire market. Firm 2 gets nothing. If firm 2 undercuts firm 1, then firm 2 can only serve q_2 of the market, which leaves firm 1 to serve the remaining $Q - q_2$ buyers. Thus, firm 2, if it is not selling at the lowest price, loses everything. This gives it a strong incentive to press for a low price. Firm 1 has a choice. It can race firm 2 to the bottom, or it can charge a high price to the customers not served by firm 2. At some point, it can make more money by not trying to undercut firm 2 and charging a higher price.[57] Thus, the larger firm ends up holding a price umbrella over the smaller one.

7.7.2 Cournot Model

The traditional microeconomics textbook models competition in capacities using the Cournot game.[58] In this game, strategies consist of simultaneous

---

[57] If you carry this reasoning one step further, you will see why there can be no equilibrium in pure strategies.

[58] Named in honor of Antoine Augustin Cournot (1801–1877), French mathematician and economist. Ignored by the French academicians of the day, he was celebrated by the

quantity choices.[59] In terms of information, each knows as much as the other. Collusion is ruled out.

If firm 1 chooses q_1 units of, say, SOMA, and firm 2 chooses q_2 units of the same, the market price for each unit will be $\max\{1 - q_1 - q_2, 0\}$. Both firms have a constant unit cost of production of $c < 1$. The model is predicated on the idea that in the long run, the price of a product is determined by the balance between supply and demand. Thus, when firm 1 chooses q_1 and firm 2 chooses q_2, the price that will emerge in the market is the one that clears the market. The essential feature of such a price is that it declines as $q_1 + q_2$ increases. The particular functional form of the relationship between the price and $q_1 + q_2$ is for convenience only, and does not affect the main qualitative insights.

Suppose firm 1 chooses a quantity q_1 and firm 2 chooses a quantity q_2 with $q_1 + q_2 \leq 1$. Then, firm 1's profit will be

$$q_1 \max\{0, 1 - q_1 - q_2\} - cq_1,$$

whereas firm 2's profit will be

$$q_2 \max\{0, 1 - q_1 - q_2\} - cq_2.$$

Each firm's profits depends not only on its own quantity choice, but on its opponent's choice as well.

It is obvious that no firm will choose a quantity exceeding 1. Thus, each player has as many strategies as there are numbers between 0 and 1. Therefore, writing down a payoff matrix is out of the question. Instead, we will determine the profit-maximizing output level a firm should choose given that its opponent has fixed on a quantity choice. Let us do this for firm 1. Suppose that firm 1 believes that firm 2 will choose a quantity $q_2 = 1/4$, say. The profit that firm 1 makes by choosing a quantity q_1 will be:

$$q_1 \max\{0, 1 - q_1 - 1/4\} - cq_1.$$

Because firm 1 will never choose $q_1 > 3/4$, we know that $1 - q_1 - 1/4$ will always be larger than or equal to zero. Hence we can write Firm 1's profit as

$$q_1(1 - q_1 - 1/4) - cq_1.$$

English, who complained loudly of his neglect. The first review of his work, in French, was penned many years after his death by Joseph Bertrand. The review was critical not of the mathematics, but of the model.

[59] If you are bothered by the fact that firms choose quantities, imagine that they choose capacities instead.

Firm 1 must now choose q_1 to maximize its profit. In this case, the optimal choice for q_1 is $3/8 - c/2$.[60] Thus, if firm 1 believes that firm 2 will choose $1/4$, firm 1 should choose $3/8 - c/2$.

We seek the optimal response of firm 1 not for a specific choice of firm 2's capacity, but as a function of all of firm 2's possible capacity choices. That is, we want firm 1's **reaction function**. This is the rule that specifies firm 1's optimal quantity choice for each of the rival's quantity choices. If firm 2 chooses q_2, it is clear that firm 1 will choose q_1 so that $q_1 + q_2 \leq 1$. In this case, firm 1's profit as a function of q_1 and q_2 will be

$$q_1(1 - q_1 - q_2) - cq_1.$$

We need the revenue-maximizing choice of q_1, given fixed q_2. This profit-maximizing choice must depend on q_2. To determine it, differentiate the profit function with respect to q_1 and set to zero:

$$1 - 2q_1 - q_2 - c = 0 \implies q_1 = \frac{1 - q_2 - c}{2}.$$

If $q_2 = \frac{1}{4}$, then $q_1 = \frac{3}{8} - \frac{c}{2}$, as mentioned earlier. In addition, q_1 declines as c increases, as one would expect. If unit costs rise, we expect the quantity produced to decline.

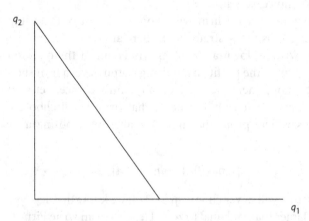

Figure 7.2. Firm 2's reaction function

Figure 7.2 shows graphically how q_1 varies with q_2. Here, q_1 is on the vertical axis and q_2 is on the horizontal.

---

[60] Which you should verify.

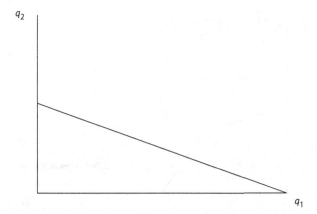

Figure 7.3. Firm 1's reaction function

By symmetry, firm 2 should choose q_2 according to the following equation, assuming that firm 1 has chosen q_1. Firm 2's reaction function is

$$q_2 = \frac{1 - q_1 - c}{2}.$$

A graphical representation can be found in Figure 7.3.

A pair of quantity choices (q_1, q_2) form a Nash equilibrium if q_1 is an optimal response to q_2 and vice versa. Hence (q_1, q_2) must satisfy the following two equations *at the same time*:

$$q_1 = \frac{1 - q_2 - c}{2},$$

$$q_2 = \frac{1 - q_1 - c}{2}.$$

Solving these equations, we deduce that $q_1 = (1 - c)/3 = q_2$. Graphically, this is where the two reaction functions cross. This is shown in Figure 7.4.

Firm 1's profits will be

$$\frac{1 - c}{3} \left(1 - \frac{2(1 - c)}{3} \right) - c \left(\frac{1 - c}{3} \right) = \frac{(1 - c)^2}{9};$$

similarly for firm 2.

In general, at the equilibrium, firms make profits that are less than monopoly profits but more than in the perfectly competitive situation. This is so because there is less of an incentive to steal business from one's competitors. The price is set so the amount demanded exactly equals the

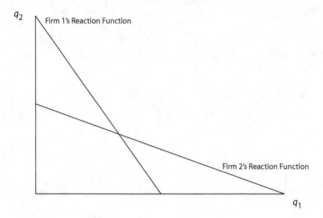

Figure 7.4. Both reaction functions

capacities they have chosen. Either firm could choose to sell below the market price, but neither has the capacity to meet the added demand. Thus, there is no incentive to decrease prices further.

Now we make a change. Firm 1 moves first. Once it chooses a quantity, this decision is irrevocable. Then firm 2 chooses a quantity.[61] What happens in this case?

Let firm 1 choose the quantity q_1. From the preceding analysis, firm 1 knows that firm 2's best response is to choose a quantity q_2 such that

$$q_2 = \frac{1 - q_1 - c}{2}.$$

Thus, the market price will be

$$1 - q_1 - q_2 = 1 - q_1 - \frac{1 - q_1 - c}{2} = \frac{1 - q_1 + c}{2}.$$

Firm 1's profit will be

$$q_1 \frac{1 - q_1 + c}{2} - cq_1.$$

The value of q_1 that maximizes this profit is $q_1 = (1 - c)/2$. Thus, $q_2 = (1 - c)/4$. Some algebra shows that firm 1's profits will be

$$\frac{1 - c}{2}\left(1 - \frac{3(1 - c)}{4}\right) - c\frac{(1 - c)}{2} = \frac{(1 - c)^2}{8}.$$

[61] This variation is by Heinrich Freiherr von Stackelberg (1905–1946).

In this scenario, firm 1 makes more profit than it did before, because

$$\frac{(1-c)^2}{9} < \frac{(1-c)^2}{8}$$

as long as $c < 1$. Therefore, when competing in quantities or capacities, the first mover has an advantage.

7.7.3 Bertrand–Hotelling Model

The basic model of competition between differentiated firms (equivalently firms offering imperfect substitutes) is the Bertrand–Hotelling model.[62] Between 0 and 1 are 1,000 customers, evenly distributed.[63] Each of these customers wants exactly one unit of SOMA. Travel cost for both sellers (called Left and Right) and buyers is \$1 per mile. The cost to a customer at distance d from 0 of going to Left to purchase a unit of SOMA is d. The cost of going to Right is $1 - d$. Given the prices charged by Left and Right, customers base their purchase decisions on the relative delivered cost of the product. The delivered cost is the travel cost plus price of the item. For example, the delivered cost of the customer at distance d from Left is $d + p_L$, where p_L is the price per unit of SOMA being charged by Left. If p_R were the selling price of SOMA at Right, this customer would buy from Left if and only if

$$d + p_L < 1 - d + p_R. \tag{7.1}$$

If the inequality were reversed, the customer would buy from Right. We will ignore the case of a tie.

The strategies of the two firms consist of choosing a price for their product. Suppose Left chooses the price p_L and Right chooses p_R. The customers that will buy from Left must be at a distance d from Left that satisfies inequality (7.1). Simplifying:

$$2d < 1 + p_R - p_L.$$

Thus a total of $\frac{(1+p_R-p_L)\times 1000}{2}$ customers will go to Left. Similarly, $\frac{(1+p_L-p_R)\times 1000}{2}$ customers will go to Right.

---

[62] Harold Hotelling (1895–1973) was an American mathematician and economist. He took Bertrand's model and introduced differentiation.

[63] This means the number of customers in any segment between 0 and 1 is proportional to the length of that segment. For example, the number of customers between 0 and 0.25 will be 250.

In effect, Left's demand curve is $\frac{(1+p_R-p_L)\times 1000}{2}$. It is of the kind one might obtain from performing a linear regression in which demand is the dependent variable and one's own price, as well as the competitor's price, are the independent variables.

Next, we determine each player's reaction function. Assume that the marginal cost of production for each firms is c. Focus on Left. Assume that Right has chosen its price, p_R, and will not change it. What is the revenue-maximizing choice of p_L (as a function of p_R) for Left? This would be Left's reaction function.

We know that when Left charges a price p_L, the demand for its product will be

$$\frac{(1 + p_R - p_L) \times 1000}{2}.$$

Using the formula for elasticity of demand, we deduce that the elasticity of demand will be[64]

$$\frac{p_L}{1 + p_R - p_L}.$$

Using the markup formula, we know that the profit-maximizing price for LEFT must satisfy

$$\frac{p_L - c}{p_L} = \frac{1 + p_R - p_L}{p_L}.$$

If we solve for p_L, we get

$$p_L = \frac{1 + p_R + c}{2},$$

which is the reaction function we seek.

An exactly symmetrical argument establishes that Right's reaction function is

$$p_R = \frac{1 + p_L + c}{2}.$$

Where the two reaction functions cross is the equilibrium price. To work this out, we need to solve the pair of equations for p_L and p_R, which gives:

$$p_L = p_R = 1 + c.$$

Thus, in equilibrium, the firms charge $1 above unit cost. The reason for the 1 is that the distance between the two firms is 1 mile and travel costs are

---

[64] Recall that if $D = a - bp$, then the elasticity of demand is $\frac{bp}{a-bp}$.

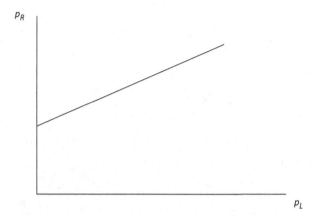

Figure 7.5. Right's reaction function

$1 per mile. Had travel costs been $2 per mile, equilibrium price would have been $2 + c$. Had travel costs been $1 per mile and the distance between the firms been 0.5 miles, equilibrium prices would be $0.5 + c$. Thus, the premium above unit cost that both firms can charge depends on just how separated they are in monetary terms. In other words, increased differentiation, other things held fixed, increases prices.

A second observation, which follows from the reaction functions, is that each firm's price increases with the other's price. Thus, if my competitor raises its price, it is my incentive to raise mine.

Had we done the analysis with different costs for each seller (say, c_L for Left and c_R for Right), the equilibrium prices would be:

$$p_L = 1 + \frac{2c_L + c_R}{3}$$

and

$$p_R = 1 + \frac{2c_R + c_L}{3}.$$

From these two expressions, we would conclude that the firm with the higher cost would have the higher price, which is no surprise. It would also mean that, in some circumstances, a customer closer to Left may choose to buy from Right if Left's costs, and thus its price, are high enough.

We can summarize the lessons of the numerical example above in a series of graphs. In Figure 7.5 we have a graph with p_L on the horizontal and p_R on the vertical.

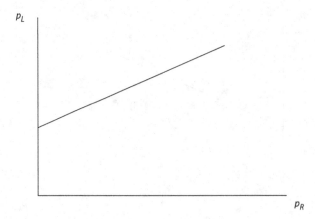

Figure 7.6. Left's reaction function

The line shown relates the profit maximizing price that Right should charge as a function of Left's price. For example, if we want to know what price Right will charge given what Left has charged, say, $2, we look for the $2 on the p_L axis and then zoom vertically up to the line and make a left to the p_R axis. Where we hit the p_R axis is the price we seek. This line is called a reaction function; what matters about it is not that it is a line, but that it is upward sloping. This means that if Left raises (lowers) its price, the best thing for Right to do is raise (lower) its own price.

Figure 7.6 exhibits a similar response with the roles of Left and Right reversed. This line is Left's reaction function. It indicates Left's profit maximizing price as a function of Right's price.

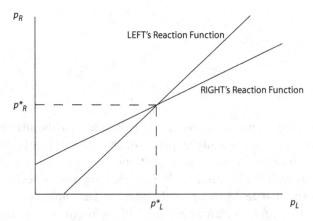

Figure 7.7. Both reaction functions

In Figure 7.7, both reaction functions are displayed on the same graph. Where these two lines cross is the equilibrium price. To see why, assume that Left picks the price p_L^*. Then Right's best response is to pick the price p_R^*. Observe now that Left's best response to the price p_R^* is p_L^*. Thus, the pair (p_L^*, p_R^*) is the mutual best response, thereby forming an equilibrium.

EIGHT

Bringing It All Together

To price effectively, one must account for the specifics of the industry, such as regulation and supply and demand; specific aspects of the product market, such as competition, customer value, costs and channel issues; and, finally transaction-specific elements, such as discounts, allowances, payment terms, rebates, and the like. In other words, one needs sound industry knowledge, sound product market knowledge, and sound transaction-specific knowledge to price effectively. As Sherlock Holmes notes: "Data, data, data. I cannot make bricks without clay."

Each chapter in this book provides key information that helps in pricing effectively. Two important principles underlie effective pricing. First, one must have some knowledge of price response or the demand curve for the product (or service). From the demand curve, one can obtain an estimate of price elasticity. Chapter 3 discusses several ways of getting at price response, ranging from managerial judgment to use of analogous products, benchmarking, focus groups, surveys, experimentation, using regression analysis on historical data, and EVC to conjoint analysis. The bottom line is that you cannot price with confidence if you do not know how your customers will respond to price.

The second important principle is to understand the value that customers place on your product. Value is connected implicitly to price elasticity because the demand curve is a representation of customer willingness to pay. However, you should be trying to influence customer valuation and, thus, customer response to price. Chapter 3 also provides a step-by-step approach to assess customer value, as well as how to influence value upward.

These two principles underlie the rest of the book. Chapter 4 discusses different demand curves, shows how to determine profit, introduces the markup formula that relates optimal price to cost and elasticity, illustrates break-even and the link between costs and volume and profit, and ends with a short discussion of McKinsey's price waterfall, which has an important effect on transaction pricing.

Although selling via posted price is popular, it is not always the best selling mechanism. Auctions are an alternative. Chapter 5 discusses when it makes sense to use auctions to sell a product or service. It also discusses the advantages and disadvantages of various popular auction formats.

Because customers are heterogeneous in their valuations, charging a single price is never optimal. High-valuation customers should be charged more than low-valuation customers. Chapter 6 provides a number of ways of charging different prices to different customers. These range from second-degree price discrimination mechanisms, such as versioning and bundling, to third-degree price discrimination mechanisms, such as using demographic variables and usage. In particular, this chapter demonstrates how to use bundling to enhance revenue, when to use pure bundling versus mixed bundling, and how to use bundling to deter entry.

Finally, Chapter 7 deals with the important topic of competition. This chapter provides some important lessons. First, when there is little differentiation among products, when sellers have similar cost structures, when there is excess capacity, when prices are transparent, and when decisions are focused on the short term, it is very difficult for one seller to charge more than another. If one finds differences in prices, it must be because of differentiation that customers value, lack of availability of some products, lack of full information on the part of consumers, and so forth. The second lesson is the role of capacity in price setting. It is received wisdom that overcapacity will depress prices, but that is somewhat misleading. If no player in the market by itself can supply the full market demand, then prices in the market will be higher than the pricing dilemma case, in which all players have capacity to serve the market by themselves. The third lesson is the role of differentiation in price setting. Differentiation can lead to higher prices, but if you attract too many of the competitor's customers, the competitor has an incentive to cut price, which could lead to your cutting price as well, reducing the role of differentiation.

Here is a step-by-step approach to effective pricing based on the material covered in the book.

1. **Assemble data on the market.**
   Gather volume, price, and cost data on the product market as a whole, as well as data on specific competitors to your product. In some industries, third-party vendors collect such information. Notable examples are IMS in the pharmaceutical industry and Nielsen and IRI in the

fast-moving consumer goods markets. Absent such vendors, companies may not have access to competitive data. In such a case, you could
determine your pricing actions as if you are a monopolist, which is
the subject of Chapter 4. If you are really not a monopolist or a very
dominant player, competitors will most likely react to your pricing
actions. Nevertheless, the monopolist markup formula in Chapter 4
provides an upper bound on the price you can charge and want to
charge.

2. **Develop objectives and strategy.**
   Objectives can be broadly classified as financial objectives, which
   include sales revenue, profit, cash flow, ROI, cost reduction, and the
   like, and marketing objectives, which include unit volume, market
   share, market leadership, brand image, and so forth. *Objectives* are
   targets that you wish to achieve. *Strategy* describes the action plan to
   realize the objectives. Setting a price for the product is part of the action
   plan, the go-to-market strategy. Other elements of the go-to-market
   strategy include channel choice and marketing communication. All
   three influence demand, but price will typically have a more immediate impact on company objectives for the product. An aggressive profit
   objective would typically require raising price, whereas an aggressive
   volume or share objective would require reducing price. If the objective is to recover costs of R&D quickly, as in the case of a patented
   pharmaceutical drug, a high price is warranted. The go-to-market
   elements have both strategic and tactical components. For example,
   to support the objective of a premium brand image, pricing must be
   high and distribution limited. BMW and Mercedes price their cars at
   the high end of the products in their competitive set. This high price
   reflects their pricing strategy. The tactical component is the actual
   MSRP, dealer support and incentives, special financing plans, and so
   on. Satisfying an aggressive volume objective would require targeting a
   large customer base. The pricing strategy consistent with this targeting
   decision could involve versioning, as Dell follows in selling computers through its web site, as well as low-priced computers available
   through select retailers such as Walmart. Consistency in pricing also
   helps communicate the company's view of the value of its products.
   For example, the company Bose, which sells stylishly designed, small
   home theater systems and speakers, radios, and noise-canceling head-
   sets, rarely discounts its products. In addition, the company ensures
   that the price is the same in all the channels. Is the pricing objective to
   be a loss leader? In such a case, the product is priced at or below cost,

with the objective of using the low price on this product to sell other products to the customer.

3. **Know your costs.**

You need to know how much it costs to make and sell your product. Without this information, you will not know whether the product is profitable. This seems simple enough, but there are two types of costs to keep in mind; fixed and variable. Variable costs are those incurred in the actual making and selling of the product. These include cost of raw materials, labor, sales commissions, and so on. Fixed costs are those incurred in running the plant or office. These costs include leases, rents, depreciation of the machinery, salaries, and so forth. The distinction between fixed and variable costs is irrelevant in the preparation of the standard income statement for reporting purposes, but is critical to understand price–volume trade-offs. Before you invest in a product, it is prudent to perform a break-even analysis. You need three things to do a break-even analysis; the fixed costs that must be covered, the unit variable cost, and the price. Start with the price that you believe the market will bear and compute the break-even volume. Is this volume feasible to achieve? If it is too high, the temptation is to increase the price, forgetting there is a negative relationship between price and volume. In reality, there is some inertia in price response, so small increases may not be noticed. What about the fixed and variable costs? Can they be reduced? Next, perform some what-if or sensitivity analysis to understand the price–volume trade-offs. The simple way to do this is to assume that both fixed and variable costs do not change, change the price, and calculate the incremental volume that you must achieve when you experiment with price reductions, and what volume loss you can afford when you experiment with price increases. These calculations are shown in Chapter 4. In these calculations, we did not say anything about what the competition might do. If you cut your price, the competition may do so as well. In such a case, the anticipated volume increase from your price cut may not happen, and you will lose money. If you increase price and the competition does not react, you will make more money if your volume loss is less than computed, and vice versa.

4. **Know your value to the buyer.**

An understanding of the market environment helps in setting product objectives and specifying a product strategy. One could have a product with the desired characteristics available in the right channels, but product success is not assured unless one gets the price right. This is where an understanding of customer value is important. Factors that customers use to evaluate the worth of goods and services include prior experience, word of mouth, comparison shopping, appearance, quality and style of your advertising, and the like. The context of the purchase (is the buyer an agent, is it for a special occasion, a convenience purchase, or an emergency purchase) make a difference as well. Charging a price much less than customer value drives unit volume but hurts profits because money is left on the table. Charging too high a price hurts volume and leads to lost profits from those who cannot afford the price. An obvious question to ask is whether there are different segments of customers with different valuations. What product changes are needed to price differently to these different segments? Which are the key competitive products in these segments? Can we quantify the value of our product in each of these segments? Value is relative and reflects the value of the differentiation, both objective and subjective, to customers in the segments.

Create a checklist of the variety of ways that customers can be segmented on valuation, or, equivalently, on price sensitivity. These include demographics such as age, income, and gender; purchase timing, such as when the product is purchased or consumed; purchase quantity; benefits, such as convenience, speed, peace of mind, and security; purchase location; and purchase history. What must be done to separate the higher-value, less price-sensitive customers from the lower-value, more price-sensitive customers? If this can be done, you should be able to charge the high-value customers a higher price than you charge the low-value customers. Additional costs will most likely be incurred in serving different customers at different prices, because of changes to products, changes in cost to serve, and so forth. If the cost differences are smaller than the price differences, however, greater profit will result because of price segmentation. This is consistent with our statement that charging a single price is never optimal.

In the end, buyers will not purchase the product or service if the price is more than the value they place on the offering. It does not matter how sophisticated our knowledge of costs are, and how wonderful we think our product is. This is why cost-plus pricing, though simple conceptually and practically, is not a good way of pricing. You could be high priced because your costs are high or your margin expectations are high, but it is more likely that you are leaving money on the table because your price is too low. A study by Marn, Roegner, and Zawada (2003) notes that the vast majority of poor pricing decisions involve pricing too low, not too high. This is why understanding the value that customers place on your product or service is vital. This is not easy to do, and we have described several ways to do so in Chapter 3. The fact that it is not easy to do means that the one who does it has an advantage in pricing effectively versus the ones who do not.

5. **Choose a price.**

Setting the price is the hardest thing to do. Fixed costs determine what you have to cover. Variable costs yield a floor price. Identifying the EVC of your product provides a ceiling. But the actual price to charge depends on many more factors. Is there an imbalance between supply and demand? What is the relative size of your strong market? What is the size of the competitors' strong market? What is your company/brand image? Do you have a strong position or weak position in the market? What are the switching costs in the market? The greater they are and the more behavior has to change to adopt your product, the lower the success of your product – in pricing terms, the harder it is to get a price premium.

You have the opportunity to set a price above that of your competitors if your market is insensitive to small shifts in price, consists mainly of growing businesses, your product or service is a vital part of a widely used system, has a high perceived value, or your product or service represents a small fraction of a buyer's total annual expenditures. In general, you would set the price for your product or service at or below that of the competition if your market is sensitive to price changes, you are attempting to enter a market that is new to you, your business is small enough so that lowering prices will not start a price war.

6. **Set transaction-specific price elements.**

Customers – both channel partners and end customers – expect a discount or reduction in price for buying in certain combinations at certain times, or by exceeding certain dollar or unit amounts. These price reductions can take on a variety of flavors, as illustrated in Chapter 4, and include case discounts, cash discounts, co-op advertising, discounts on freight charged, annual volume rebates, and the like. Some of these discount policies may be standard in the industry, and may be accepted as the cost of doing business. However, that does not mean that they cannot be challenged or, more importantly, changed. You need to ask what purpose is served by these discount policies. Do they lead to the desired behavior on the part of the recipient? Is it to encourage quick payment? Exploit economies of scale? Induce trial? Increase loyalty? Can shifting the discounts to the component that matters most to the recipient lead to higher volumes and or greater profits to you? For example, some channel members may value the freight discount more than an early payment discount, and vice versa. Thus, optimizing the transaction specific elements should be an important part of your pricing.

Formulating a pricing strategy is easy. Sticking to it is difficult. The first temptation to deviate from the policy occurs when a customer asks for a price cut. If the customer has a compelling alternative to your offering – that is, you are not differentiated in any important way from your rival – then concede. There is little point in agonizing over something that is as inevitable as gravity. However, if there is a dimension (or two) along which you dominate, there is little reason to concede. If the buyer demurs, one should unbundle one's offering; that is, remove the components of your offering that differentiate you from other sellers and cut the price. The idea is to emphasize the added value that you provide. Remember, the goal is not to keep the business at *any* price, but at the *right* price.

If you cannot keep the customer without a price cut, you have learned something. That customer does not value what you provide. You are either in the wrong business or targeting the wrong customer.

A second temptation occurs when a potential new customer solicits a bid for your business. The important thing is to determine why the customer is considering changing suppliers.

1. Is this a high-maintenance customer – that is, one who is costly to serve? This may explain why the customer is shopping around; its existing supplier wishes to dump this customer.
2. If it is for a feature or function that you offer but the customer's existing supplier does not, then you have identified a point of differentiation. In this case, there is no need to be aggressive on price to get the customer's business.
3. In the absence of differentiation, the only issue in the buyer's mind is price. Recognize that if you agree to make an offer, you may not be selected. You could be used by the buyer to squeeze its existing supplier. If this ploy succeeds, your rival drops its price. In fact, your rival may have to drop its price for other customers as well (because of contracts and arbitrage opportunities), thereby lowering the reference price for the product/service you both provide. This, in turn, puts downward pressure on your price.

Because competition benefits only the buyer, if you decide to bid for this buyer's business, you should ask for some of this benefit back. The trick is to identify an acceptable scheme for doing so. Examples of what some sellers ask for are bid preparation expenses, a last-look provision, or a volume commitment.

In the event your bid is successful, what next? If your rival cannot afford the loss, it may respond by raiding your customers, precipitating a price war.

A third temptation to deviate from strategy occurs when a rival has cut its price. Before responding, verify that the rival has indeed cut its price. Second, determine why. If a response is called for, consider substitutes to a price cut, such as improved quality, speed, or bundling, on which you may have an advantage. Although these are not free, they shift competition from price to a dimension in which you are superior. The problem with a price cut is that a new, lower price changes the reference price for buyers, making it harder to sustain a price increase in the future. That said, the use of substitutes for a price cut for a sustained period become expected by the buyer and thereby blunt their usefulness.

Be selective in your price cuts. You are under no obligation to cut the price to everyone. Focus on the segment targeted by the rival. Estimate the volume at risk and cut price on those units only.

You should also know what the rival has to lose. If the rival's strong market is small relative to the contested portion, then it is in its interest to cut prices and it will probably do so again after you respond. Might it not be a good idea to relinquish some market to this rival to reduce the incentive to cut price further? In other words, think about the total cost associated with an aggressive response, rather than just the first move.

Most important, what next? The "game" does not end after one round of price cutting.

NINE

Appendix on Game Theory

The word *game* in game theory is not limited to parlor games, such as bridge or Scrabble. It applies to all situations in which two or more agents are in competition with one another, such as a negotiation between labor and management or a price war between rival firms.[1]

Let us begin with a simple situation to provide a flavor of what is to come.

John is currently the monopoly supplier of SOMA. Oskar is thinking of entering the SOMA business. What Oskar decides depends on how John will react to his entering the market. Will John lower prices to ruin Oskar, or will he maintain his current prices?

Oskar expects to be $50 million ahead if he enters the market and John accommodates his entry. If John decides to retaliate by lowering prices, Oskar will lose $100 million in total.

Oskar believes that John stands to make $500 million as a monopolist. This amount will be reduced to $400 million if John accommodates Oskar's entry. If John lowers prices in retaliation, he loses $200 million.

John has just announced that should Oskar enter the market, he will start a price war by lowering prices. Assuming that Oskar cannot afford to lose $100 million, should he enter the SOMA industry?

If Oskar believes John's threat, the answer is, of course, no. But why should Oskar believe this? Notice the following: if Oskar enters, which action gives John the higher profit? Accommodating Oskar's entry. He wins $400 million rather than lose $200 million. Assuming that John thinks that more money is better than less, isn't accommodation what he would choose? Put differently, do you think John would hurt himself in order to carry out

---

[1] The reader interested in a more comprehensive treatment should consult Dixit and Skeath (1999) or McCain (2010). A gentler introduction is Rosenthal (2011).

his threat of retaliation? Knowing this, does it not make sense for Oskar to enter?

But wait. If John lets Oskar enter the market, won't that encourage others to do the same, thus hurting John's profits even more? If this is the case, shouldn't John take a drubbing now to deter others who might wish to enter? Following this line of argument, perhaps John has already developed a reputation for retaliation, so his threat is credible. Given this, Oskar should not enter.

The reason that there is no clear answer is that the John/Oskar game has not been completely defined. On the surface, it seems that there are only two players: John and Oskar. However, the presence of others makes a difference to what John might do. Second, there is the issue of John's reputation. What kind is it? This too would make a difference. All this illustrates the first important principle of game theory: define the game completely.

The first step is to identify the **players** in the game and what their **objectives** are. This is not always as easy as it seems, but failing to do so can have profound consequences. A telling example of failing to carry this step out correctly is described in Stanley Karnow's history of the Vietnam war.

The day after the fall of Dien Bien Phu (May 7, 1954), the Geneva conference that resulted in the partition of Vietnam convened. There were nine delegations. Of these, only three concern us: the United States, the Viet Minh, and the People's Republic of China. John Foster Dulles represented the United States in these negotiations. Dulles viewed the Chinese and the Viet Minh as one entity, "hypnotized," in Karnow's words, "by his own vision of monolithic Communism bent on world domination." But this was not the case. Even though much of Viet Minh military support came from China, they did not have the same interests. The Chinese wanted an agreement that would prevent the United States from using Indochina as a pretext to threaten China. The Viet Minh, on the other hand, wanted a political settlement in which the French would withdraw and leave the Vietnamese to settle their own differences. In particular, the Chinese were willing to accept the idea of a divided Vietnam to ensure their goals, something that was anathema to the Viet Minh. Pham Van Dong, leader of the Viet Minh delegation, summarized the behavior of Zhou Enlai, leader of the Chinese delegation, with these words: "He has double-crossed us."

By ignoring the fact that the Viet Minh and the People's Republic of China were two distinct players, Dulles eliminated the possibility of a settlement that would distance the People's Republic from the Viet Minh.

The next step is to identify the **strategies** that players have at their disposal. For example, is it acceptable to threaten others with grievous bodily harm in the game you are playing? When identifying strategies, two items are worth paying special attention to. The first is whether the game is to be played once or many times. The answer to this question influences the kinds of strategies one can employ. Second, is it possible to communicate and contract with other players in the game?

The third step is to figure out, insofar as it is possible, the **outcomes** and their associated **consequences** from players choosing each of their strategies. It is also important to distinguish outcomes that are the results of strategy choices from those that are produced by factors beyond the control of any of the players.

Last is the matter of **information**: who knows what, and when. It is not always the case in a game that all players know the same things. Some may be better informed than others, and information can be revealed as the game progresses. Ignoring this possibility is a recipe for failure.

9.1 Representing the Game

Some games involve a single simultaneous move by all players. An example is the childhood game of rock-paper-scissors. Others involve a sequence of moves unfolding over time. We call the first **simultaneous move** games and the second **sequential** games. How one chooses to represent a game depends on whether it is a simultaneous or sequential game. The representation of simultaneous games is described first. As a simplifying assumption, we will assume (until further notice) that players play for money (and only money) and all prefer more money to less.

9.1.1 Simultaneous-Move Game

Simultaneous move games are represented by a multitude of lists:

1. A list of players
2. For each player, a list of the player's strategies
3. For each strategy, one for each player, a list of (monetary) payoffs that each player receives.

Until further notice, we will assume that these lists are known to all players.

In a game with just two players, these lists can be represented by a table.

Example 20 Two Firms, Two Locations
Two competing fast-food chains, M and W, have each decided to open one restaurant in a small midwestern town. The town has two shopping centers,

Table 9.1. *Two Firms, Two Locations*

M/W	L	S
L	600, 600	1200, 800
S	800, 1200	400, 400

denoted by L and S, constituting the two natural places for such restaurants. It is estimated that the expected daily number of buyers is 1200 at L and 800 at S. It is assumed that if they locate at the different centers, they would each get the local traffic and that if they locate at the same center, they will equally split the number of local customers, and the customers from the other center will be lost.

We can summarize the situation by payoff Table 9.1, which describes two choices, or strategies in the language of game theory, for each of the two players, M and W. The table entry corresponding to every pair of strategies is a pair of numbers, describing the corresponding pair of payoffs that result from the selected pair of strategies. For example, the top left entry is (600, 600) because these are the expected number of customers they each receive if they both choose the location L. But the top right entry, corresponding to M choosing L and W choosing S, has the payoffs (1200, 800). The left-hand entry in each cell is the payoff to M and the right-hand entry the payoff to W. □

It will be useful to mention some terminology and conventions about payoff tables. First, when M chooses the strategy L, M forces the game to be played in the top row (with the final choice being determined by the choice made by W) and when M chooses the strategy S, the game is restricted to the bottom row. For this reason, we often refer to player M in this game as the *row player*. Similarly, every strategy choice of W restricts the game to a certain column and, thus, we refer to W as the *column player*. When the row player chooses a row and the column player chooses a column, the game results in the pair of payoffs corresponding to the selected entry.

Following a convention used by most game theorists, we will, in general, refer to the row player as player 1 and to the column player as player 2. To aid in exposition, it is also convenient to differentiate the gender of the two players. For this reason, we will think of player 1 as a "he" and player two as a "she." With this convention the sentence "he chooses S because he thinks that she chose L" makes good sense, whereas the nondifferentiated sentence, "she chooses S because she thinks that she chose L," can be quite confusing.

Because the payoff tables are matrices with a pair of numbers in every entry, simultaneous move games are sometimes referred to as *matrix games*.

Table 9.2. *Seller/Buyer Game*

s/b	B	N
H	1,1	0,0
M	2,0	0,0
L	3, −1	0,0

In general, the entries in the payoff table do not have to be symmetric and the number of strategies may be greater than two. Our next example illustrates this point.

Example 21   A Seller/Buyer Quality Game
This game describes a single isolated transaction between a buyer (b) and seller (s) of a certain item, say a hot dog at a busy tourist area, at a known fixed price. The seller's strategies involve choosing one of three quality levels for the item, H, M, or L, and the buyer's strategies are to buy, B, or not to buy, N. Assuming that the choices of the two players are executed without knowledge of the strategy choice of the opponent, we view this as a two-person one-shot strategic game with the payoffs displayed in Table 9.2.

When the buyer does not buy, both players break even, as represented by the zero payoffs down the entire second column. But if the buyer plays B, the payoffs depend on the quality offered by the seller in a monotonic fashion, decreasing to the seller (from 3 to 1) and increasing to the buyer (from −1 to 1), as quality is increased.

Games such as this one, in which player 1 has three strategies and player 2 has two, are referred to as 3×2 games.   □

Coordination Game
Try your hand at setting up the payoff table for the coordination game. Two players, each with a penny hidden in their hands, must place their pennies face up on a table at the same time. If both pennies show heads or tails, both players win $1; otherwise, they get nothing. Call the players Row (R) and Column (C).

9.1.2 Sequential Games

When players make moves in rounds with dependencies between the rounds, the different stages of the game are represented by dots, called **nodes**; nodes are linked by arrows, called **directed edges**, that specify the order in which stages occur. A path from one node to another represents a sequence of

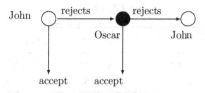

Figure 9.1. Game tree

moves and countermoves by players. This congregation of dots and arrows is called a **game tree**.

In the case of a two-player game, the nodes come in three colors: black, white and red, say. A white node represents a stage in the game at which player 1 must make a move. The edges directed out of the node represent the strategy choices that player 1 has at that stage of the game. A black node represents a stage in the game at which player 2 must make a move. A red node represents a point in the game at which "chance" makes a move, such as a dice throw. Let us illustrate with an example.

A benevolent plutocrat sets up the following three-stage game between John and Oskar:

Stage 1: The plutocrat offers John $1 million. If John accepts, the game ends. If John rejects, the game goes to the next stage.

Stage 2: The plutocrat offers Oskar $2 million. If Oskar accepts, the game ends. If Oskar rejects, the game moves to stage 3.

Stage 3: The plutocrat offers John $3 million. If John accepts, the game ends. If John rejects, the game ends.

The extensive form representation of the game is shown in Figure 9.1.

The white circles represent stages in which John moves and the black circle the stage in which Oskar moves. The arrows that emanate from each circle represent the moves that each player can make at that stage of the game.

A strategy in a sequential game is a complete plan for playing the game, taking all contingencies into account, including what other players will do. In the game tree, a strategy reduces to a set of instructions on which the directed edge is to be chosen at *every* white (black) node.

We discuss sequential games in greater detail later.

9.2 Playing the Game

You want to maximize money, and so does your opponent. What strategy should you choose? Not surprisingly, for many games this will be a hard

Table 9.3. *Price Game*

Firm 1/Firm 2	Price = $2	Price = $1.50
Price = $2	$75, $?	$0, $?
Price = $1.50	$100, $?	$50, $?

question to answer. Instead, let us start with a simpler question. What, if any, strategies should one *not* play?

9.2.1 Dominated Strategies and the Price Game

In the **price game**, two firms choose their prices simultaneously and customers purchase from the firm with the lowest price. In case of ties, the market divides equally between the two firms. The firms cannot collude or communicate with each other. In this game, it is clear that no firm would select a price for its product that is higher than that of its competitor. If it did, it would get no business. Thus, we would expect both firms to try to choose the same price.

To make matters concrete, suppose that you and your opponent supply a market for widgets that consists of 100 individuals, each of whom will buy one widget. Each widget costs you $0.50 to make. You do not know the manufacturing costs of your opponent. For simplicity, you and your opponent are limited to charging one of two prices, $2 a unit and $1.50 a unit. Table 9.3 summarizes the profit consequences of various price choices. The rows correspond to the price/strategy choices of firm 1 (you), and the columns represent the price/strategy choices of firm 2 (opponent). The left-hand entry of each cell is the profit to firm 1, and the right-hand entry is the profit to firm 2, represented by a "?."

Consider firm 1. No matter what firm 2 does, firm 1 is always better off choosing a price of $1.50. If firm 2 chooses a $2 price, firm 1 makes $100, as opposed to $75. If firm 2 chooses a $1.50 price, firm 1 is better off choosing a $1.50 price than a $2 price. The $2 price is an example of a **strictly dominated strategy**. A strategy is strictly dominated if there is some other strategy in the game that does strictly better than this strategy no matter what the opponent does. Applying the dominance idea does not require any information about the payoffs that opponents will receive. No rational person will choose a strictly dominated strategy.

To illustrate the dominance idea, here is a more elaborate payoff matrix (Table 9.4). The strategies of the column (she) player are labeled with

Table 9.4. *A* 3 × 3 *game*

Row/Col	a	b	c
A	4	5	−3
B	−100	−200	0
C	5	7	0

lower-case letters and those of the row player (he) with upper-case letters. Only the payoffs to the row player are shown. Row strategy A does not strictly dominate row strategy B. Strategy A does better than strategy B only if the column player chooses a or b. If the column player chooses c, then the row player is better off choosing his strategy B. Row strategy C strictly dominates row strategy A. No matter which strategy the column player chooses, the row player is always better off choosing C over A. What about C over B? C does not strictly dominate B. It is true that if the column player chooses a or b, the row player is better off choosing C over B. However – and this is crucial – when the column player chooses c, strategy B delivers the same payoff as C to the row player. Strict dominance requires that one strategy beats the other *every* time. It is not enough for C to beat B some times and tie with it the other times. This distinction may seem like hair splitting, but it cannot be ignored. For the moment, let us suspend discussion of this issue.

To give a formal definition of strict dominance, let a_{ij} be the payoff to the row player from playing row i and from the column player choosing column j. Strategy row p **strictly dominates** i if $a_{pj} > a_{ij}$ for all column strategies j. To deal with the situation in which one strategy beats another sometimes and ties with it other times, we have the notion of weak dominance. Formally, strategy row p **weakly dominates** strategy i if $a_{pj} \geq a_{ij}$ for all column strategies j with strict inequality for at least one j. In the previous example, row strategy C weakly dominates B.

The idea that one should not choose a strictly dominated strategy in a game is a compelling one. It should apply with equal force to weakly dominated strategies as well. For the moment suppose that it does, with a caveat to be revealed later.

Example 22 A Seller/Buyer Quality Game
In Table 9.5, notice that for player S, strategy H is weakly dominated by strategy M.

Also, strategy M is weakly dominated by strategy L. □

Table 9.5. *Seller/Buyer Game*

S/B	B	N
H	1,1	0,0
M	2,0	0,0
L	3, −1	0,0

The principle of eliminating dominated strategies from consideration is a simple one but is extremely powerful in some situations.

Example 23 Two-Tiered Bids

On October 15, 1996, executives from CSX (the largest railroad in the eastern United States) and Conrail (the third largest railroad in the eastern United States) announced a $8.3 billion merger. On the day of the announcement, Conrail's stock price rose from $71.00 to $85.13, whereas CSX's dropped from $49.50 to $46.75.

According to the merger agreement, CSX agreed to pay $92.50 per share in cash for the first 40 percent of Conrail shares (the front-end offer) and exchange CSX stock at the ratio of 1.85619:1 (CSX:Conrail) for the remaining 60 percent (the back-end offer).[2] *At the time, CSX's stock price was $46.75. The "blended" price of the offer was $0.4 \times 92.50 + 0.6 \times 1.85619 \times 46.75 = $89.07 per share.*

Such an offer is called two-tiered, and the mechanics are as follows. If CSX acquires strictly less than 40 percent of the shares, those who tendered their shares to CSX get $92.50 per share.[3] *If CSX acquires exactly 40 percent of the shares, those who tendered to CSX get $92.50 a share. The remaining 60 percent of shares are bought out at the back-end offer price. If CSX gets more than 40 percent of the shares, then CSX pays the blended price for every share. The two-tiered offer was set to expire on November 16, 1996.*

Whether you, as a Conrail shareholder, should sell your shares to CSX on these terms depends also on what will happen if CSX fails to acquire Conrail. Conrail's stock price could fall back to its previous price of $71.00 a share. Alternatively, CSX might increase its initial offer. However, Conrail's post announcement share price of $85.13 is well below the back-end offer of $86.78 or the blended price of $89.07 a share. Another possibility is that another bidder, perhaps Norfolk Southern Railroad, might try to acquire Conrail. To

[2] The actual offer was structured differently to comply with the Pennsylvania antitakeover law. However, the difference was cosmetic only.
[3] Actually, CSX reserved the right to withdraw its offer if the acquisition failed. We will assume that CSX will not exercise this right.

Table 9.6. *Two-tiered Offer*

You/Other	Sell to CSX	Keep
Sell to CSX	$89.07, $89.07	$92.50, $86.78
Keep	$86.78, $92.50	$92.25, $92.25

keep things simple, and being optimistic, suppose that in the event that CSX fails to acquire Conrail, Conrail's shares will be worth $92.25. Suppose you are a Conrail shareholder. Would you tender your shares to CSX?[4] To focus your thoughts, suppose there are only two shareholders of Conrail, each owning one share of Conrail. You are one of the two. If both of you tender to CSX, you both get the blended price of $89.07 for your shares. If one of you tenders and the other does not, the one who tenders gets $92.50 and the other gets $86.78, the back-end offer. If neither tenders to CSX, you each get $92.25 per share.

The CSX offer has set up a game between you and the other shareholder. You each have two strategies, tender to CSX or not. In real life, it is difficult to coordinate and collude with other shareholders because of their numbers and their geographical dispersion. However, assume this to be true in our simple setting. In particular, this means that you both must decide what to do in ignorance of the other.

We can represent the possibilities in a payoff table (Table 9.6). Observe that the keep strategy for you is strictly dominated by sell to CSX. The same is true for the other shareholder. Thus, you can guess that the outcome of the game will be that both of you sell and get the blended price. Notice, however, that both of you would have been better off had you kept your shares.

What happened? Eight days after the merger announcement, Norfolk Southern countered with a hostile $9.1 billion offer for Conrail. Norfolk's offer amounted to $100 per share, but it was conditional on a number of things, such as obtaining a majority of the shares, financing, and Conrail terminating its merger agreement with CSX. Given the conditions and the potential delays in completing Norfolk's offer, CSX countered, on the same day, that Norfolk's bid was worth only $90.00 per share in real money. On November 6, CSX amended its tender offer to $100 per share at the front end. The deadline to vote on accepting the two-tiered bid was moved to December 23, 1996. Two days after that, Norfolk raised its bid to $110 per share.

Four days before the vote deadline, CSX sweetened the back end of its two-tiered offer by about $15 per share and postponed the deadline to January 17, 1997. Within hours, Norfolk responded with an offer of $115 cash per share.

---

[4] Ignore the tax aspects of the transactions.

Table 9.7. *Price Game II*

Firm 1/Firm 2	Price = $2	Price = $1.50
Price = $2	$75, $75	$0, $100
Price = $1.50	$100, $0	$50, $50

Four days before the January deadline, Norfolk made an unconditional $115 per share offer for 9.9 percent of Conrail's stock. On January 17, shareholders of Conrail voted 65.1 percent of shares against the two-tiered offer. After the vote, CSX and Norfolk met and decided basically to divide Conrail between them. □

Sequential Elimination

By eliminating strictly dominated strategies in the price game, we can work out what firm 1 (he) should play. This by itself does not determine the outcome of the game. To do that we need to know the payoffs to firm 2 (she). For this example, suppose that firm 2 has exactly the same manufacturing costs as firm 1. Then we can fill in the question marks in Table 9.3 to yield the payoff matrix in Table 9.7. By symmetry, the $2 price strategy is strictly dominated for firm 2 as well. Given this, we can comfortably expect (and recommend) that both players choose the $1.50 price strategy. Notice the use of the word "we" in the previous sentence. As the outside observer of the game, we can tell what the outcome will be. What about the players themselves? Put yourselves in the shoes of firm 1. If all you know are your payoffs, then you can deduce only that you should choose the low price. You cannot predict what your rival will do. If you know your rival's payoffs, can you predict the outcome? Not without knowing your rival's intentions. This is where the rationality assumption comes in. Knowing both your rival's payoffs and that your rival is rational allows you to conclude that the rival will pick the low price.

In this game, each player has only two strategies, so the presence of strictly dominated strategies for each of them is enough to determine the outcome. What is the case in more elaborate games?

Example 24 A Seller/Buyer Quality Game

Recall Table 9.5. Put yourself in the shoes of player s. As noted earlier, for player s, strategies H and M are weakly dominated by strategy L. Thus, as player s, you will choose strategy L. Can you predict what your opponent will do? Not unless you know her payoffs. Suppose you do. Notice that player b has

Table 9.8. *Reduced Seller/Buyer Game*

s/b	B	N
L	3, −1	0,0

no strictly (or even weakly) dominated strategies. Thus, you cannot predict with certainty what this player will do. Suppose now that player b knows your payoffs and knows that you are rational as well.

Player b can deduce that you, player s, will play L. So, b, in choosing a strategy, will ignore your strategies H and M. Thus, as far as b is concerned, the game reduces to row L (after eliminating rows H and M). However, you know that b knows your payoffs and that you are rational, so you can deduce that b will be looking at Table 9.8. At this point, for the buyer strategy, B is strictly dominated by strategy N. You can thus predict that the outcome is (L,N). □

Two things drive the game to a single possible outcome. The first is that both players know the entire game, and they know that they know this, and so on. This is called **common knowledge** of the game. The second is that both players know that each is rational, and they know that they know this, and so on. This is called **common knowledge** of rationality. We assume that both kinds of common knowledge hold.

Example 25 *Consider now a more elaborate example in Table 9.9. In this*

Table 9.9. *A 3 × 2 game*

R/C	1	2
1	3, 6	7, 1
2	5, 1	8, 2
3	6, 0	6, 2

game, C does not have a strictly dominated strategy. R, however, does. Row 1 is strictly dominated by row 2. Thus, R will eliminate row 1. Now we will assume that C knows or expects that R will do this.[5] Thus, C can conclude that row 1 will never be played. Delete row 1 from the matrix. In the 2-by-2 matrix that remains (see Table 9.10), column 1 is strictly dominated by column 2. Therefore, C will eliminate column 1.

R knows this and will eliminate row 3. Thus the outcome will be (row 2, column 2). □

---

[5] This assumption is not as mild as it seems.

Table 9.10. *Reduced game*

R/C	1	2
2	5, 1	8, 2
3	6, 0	6, 2

Does the outcome of the game depend on the order in which dominated strategies are eliminated? No, provided that only strictly dominated strategies are eliminated. However, the order matters when the strategies eliminated are weakly dominated.

9.2.2 Backward Induction and the Centipede Game

The analog of eliminating strictly dominated strategies in extensive form games is called **backward induction**. To illustrate the idea, consider the centipede game.[6] It is an extension of the ultimatum game. In this game, there are two players (Aubrey and Maturin) and an indifferent god. God starts by placing $1 on the table. Aubrey has the choice to take it (the $1) or leave it on the table. If Aubrey takes the money, the game ends there. If not, God puts another dollar down (bringing the pot to two dollars) and gives Maturin the chance to take it or leave it. If Maturin takes the $2, the game ends. Otherwise God puts down another dollar (raising the stakes to $3) and gives Aubrey the chance to take it or leave it. If no one takes the money, the game continues in this fashion until the pot reaches $10. If no one takes the $10, the players know the game ends, with God taking the money. Aubrey and Maturin are not allowed to collude.

Table 9.11. *Further reduced game*

R/C	2
2	8, 2
3	6, 2

If you are Aubrey, what should you do? Most people frame the analysis in terms of how long they are prepared to stay in before they lose their nerve and bolt with the money. They reason *forward* from the first round of play. The reasoning goes something like this. I could take the $1 now or pass; at worst, I don't get $1, which was found money anyway. Now the pot goes to

---

[6] So called because the game tree looks like a centipede.

$2. What is the chance that Maturin will pass? If he does, then I could get $3, and so on.

Assuming Aubrey and Maturin are rational, the correct thing to do is to reason backward. This is because in the last round of the game (if it is ever reached) you can always tell precisely what will happen. In the last round, Maturin has a choice between $10 and nothing. Assuming that Maturin is rational, he will take the money. Thus, on the last round you know Maturin will take the money and you know that he knows and he knows that you know, and so on. Therefore, in the next-to-last round what should you do? If you pass, you know that Maturin will take the money and you get nothing. Thus, in the next-to-last round you should take the money. In the round before that (round 8), Maturin knows that if he passes, you will take the money in round 9. What will he do? He will take the money in round 8. Because you know he will take the money in round 8, in round 7 you should take the money. Working back to round 1, it should now be obvious that you should take the money in round 1. Is this the way you would play? Would scaling the payoffs by 1 million change your answer?

9.2.3 Equilibrium

Some games are not dominance solvable. The matching pennies game is one example. In such cases, it is usual to resort to an equilibrium principle to limit the range of possible outcomes. The most well known of these equilibrium notions is named after John Nash. To motivate its definition consider the PD game introduced in Section 7.1.

In this game, if both firms chose the strategy of pricing at $3, they would be better off. Knowing this, why don't they agree on a $3 price? They could agree to fix the price at $3,[7] but what incentive is there for either to keep the agreement? If firm 1 believes that firm 2 will charge a $3 price, firm 1's best course of action is to renege and lower prices to $2.50. In the language of game theory, the ($3, $3) agreement is not an equilibrium. A pair of strategies, say x for player 1 and y for player 2, is an equilibrium if player 1 cannot do strictly better by playing something other than x if player 2 plays y, and vice versa. An equilibrium is a pair of strategies that form a *self-enforcing agreement*. If I believe that you will play y, my best course of action is to play x; and if you believe that I will play x, your best course of action is to play y.[8] The price pair ($3, $3) is not an equilibrium, because

[7] In violation of American law.
[8] It is self-enforcing in the limited sense that a single player cannot do better by deviating.

Table 9.12. *Rock, Paper, Scissors*

R/C	Rock	Paper	Scissors
Rock	0, 0	−1, 1	1, −1
Paper	1, −1	0, 0	−1, 1
Scissors	−1, 1	1, −1	0, 0

at least one firm could do better by deviating. The price pair ($2.50, $2.50) is an equilibrium. Neither firm is made better off by unilaterally switching to another strategy.[9]

This dilemma in the PD game is that the outcome of the game that is individually rational ($2.50, $2.50) is not *collectively* rational (where both firms choose the $3 price).[10]

Existence
Not every game has an equilibrium as we have defined it. As an example, consider the schoolyard game of rock-paper-scissors. For readers unfamiliar with the game, a payoff matrix that captures the essence of it is displayed here. The reader can verify that the game does not have a equilibrium in the sense defined earlier.

The trick to guaranteeing the existence of an equilibrium in all games[11] is to allow the players to randomize.[12] Thus, a player's strategies are described by a probability vector. In rock-paper-scissors, R's strategies would be the set of vectors (p_1, p_2, p_3) such that

1. $p_1 + p_2 + p_3 = 1$ and
2. $p_1, p_2, p_3 \geq 0$,

where p_i is the probability that R chooses row i.

The original set of strategies (in this case, rock-paper-scissors,) is called **pure strategies**, whereas the strategies obtained by randomizing are called **mixed strategies**. The payoff from a randomized strategy is just the expectation of the utilities of the various pure strategies.

[9] If a game is dominance solvable, the outcome will be an equilibrium.
[10] The PD is, in fact, an instance of the well known Prisoner's Dilemma game.
[11] At least those with a finite number of strategies.
[12] This is not without controversy, but a full discussion of it is outside the scope of this appendix.

References

Anderson, J. C. and J. A. Narus. *Business Market Management*, Prentice Hall, 2004.

Bailyn, B. *The New England Merchants in the 17th Century*, Harvard University Press, 1955.

Baker, W., M. Marn, and C. Zawada. "Price Smarter on the Net," *Harvard Business Review*, Vol. 79, No. 2, February 2001.

Blattberg, R. and S. Neslin. *Sales Promotions*, Prentice Hall, 1990.

Cassady, R. *Auctions and Auctioneering*, University of California Press, 1979.

Dixit, A. and S. Skeath. *Games of Strategy*, W. W. Norton and Company, 1999.

Dupuit, A. "De la mesure de l'utilité des travaux publics," *Annales des ponts et chausses*, Second series, 8, 1844.

Ghemawat, P. "Capacities and Prices: A Model with Applications," working paper, Harvard Business School, 1986.

Gigliano, J., M. Georgiadis, D. Pleasance, and S. Whaley. "The price of loyalty," *McKinsey Quarterly*, No. 4, 68–77, 2000.

Gwartney, J. and R. Stroup. *Economics: Private and Public Choice*, 8th edition, Harcourt College Publishers, 1997.

Harris, F. H. deB. "Large-scale Entry Deterrence of a Low-cost Competitor: an early success of of airline revenue management," *International Journal of Revenue Management*, No. 1, 5–27, 2007.

Henry, B. R. and E. F. Zelek, Jr. "Establishing and Maintaining an Effective Resale Price Policy," *Antitrust*, 8–17, 2003.

Kahng, B. and I. Yang. "Bidding Process in Online Auctions and Winning Strategy: Rate Equation Approach," *Physical Review E*, Vol. 73, p. 067101, 2006.

Karnow, S. *Vietnam*, Penguin Books, 1984.

Krishna, V. *Auction Theory*, Academic Press, 2002.

Lillien, G., A. Rangaswamy, and A. De Bruyn. *Principles of Marketing Engineering*, Trafford Publishing, 2007.

Marn, M., E. Roegner, and C. Zawada. "Pricing new products," *McKinsey Quarterly*, No. 3, 40–49, 2003.

Marn, M., E. Roegner, and C. Zawada. *The Price Advantage*, John Wiley & Sons, 2004.

Mattutes, C. and P. Regibeau. "Mix and Match: Product Compatibility Without Network Externality," *RAND Journal of Economics*, Vol. 19, No. 2, 221–234, 1988.

McAfee, R. P., J. McMillan, and M. D. Whinston. "Multiproduct Monopoly, Commodity Bundling, and Correlation of Values," *Quarterly Journal of Economics*, Vol. 104, 371–383, 1989.

McCain, R. A. *Game Theory*, World Scientific Press, 2010.

Morton, F. S., F. Zettelmeyer, and J. Silva-Risso. "Consumer Information and Discrimination: Does the Internet Affect the Pricing of New Cars to Women and Minorities," *Quantitative Marketing and Economics*, Vol. 1, 65–92, 2003.

Neter, J., M. H. Kutner, C. J. Nachtsheim, and W. Wasserman. *Applied Linear Regression Models*, 3rd edition, Irwin, 1996.

Noble, P. M. and T. S. Gruca. "Industrial Pricing: Theory and Managerial Practice," *Marketing Science*, Vol. 18, No. 3, 435–454, 1999.

Rosenthal, E. C. *The Complete Idiot's Guide to Game Theory*, Alpha Press, 2011.

Taylor, W. "An Interview with Swatch Titan Nicholas Hayek," *Harvard Business Review*, March–April 1993.

Tellis, G. "The Price Elasticity of Selective Demand: A Meta-Analysis of Econometric Models of Sales," *Journal of Marketing Research*, 25 (November), 1988.

Thaler, R. "Mental Accounting and Consumer Choice," *Marketing Science*, Vol. 4, No. 3, 1985.

Tirole, J. *Industrial Organization*, MIT Press, 1988.

Tversky, A. and Kahneman. "The Framing of Decisions and the Psychology of Choice," *Science*, Vol. 211, 453–458, 1981.

Tybout, A. and B. Calder (eds.). *Kellogg on Marketing*, 2nd edition, John Wiley & Sons, 2010.

U.S. General Accounting Office (GAO), *Report to the Chairman, Committee on Commerce, Science, and Transportation, U.S. Senate: Telecommunications, Issues Related to Competition and Subscriber Rates in the Cable Television Industry*, October 2003.

Wilson, R. B. *Nonlinear Pricing*, Oxford University Press, 1993.

Index

Printed in the United States
By Bookmasters